THE WORLD'S GREAT
FIGHTERS
FROM 1914 TO THE PRESENT DAY

THE WORLD'S GREAT
FIGHTERS
FROM 1914 TO THE PRESENT DAY

ROBERT JACKSON

GREENWICH EDITIONS

This Edition published by Greenwich Editions in 2001
Greenwich Editions
10 Blenheim Court
Brewery Road
London N7 9NT

A member of the Chrysalis Group plc

ISBN 0-86288-475-6

Editorial and design by
Amber Books Ltd
Bradley's Close
74-77 White Lion Street,
London N1 9PF

Printed in Italy

CONTENTS

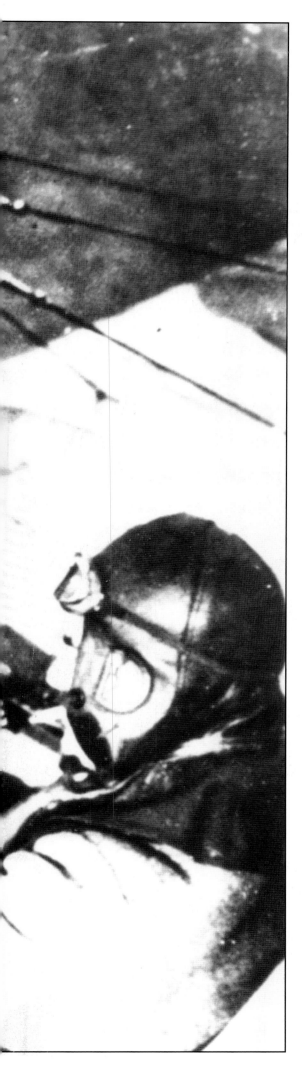

CHAPTER 1
BIRTH OF THE 'FIGHTING AEROPLANE'

The first major conflict of the twentieth century saw the primitive scouts of the early war years move from firing pistols at each other to mounting rapid-firing machine guns that fired through the aircraft's propeller arc.

The first decade of the twentieth century, in the years that followed the Wright Brothers' historic flight in December 1903, saw amazing advances in the development of heavier-than-air flying machines, and some significant steps forward in techniques that would play a major part in the development of air fighting. The aircraft's role as a potential war machine was summarised by an Italian officer, Major Giulio Douhet, in 1909. Douhet wrote: 'At present we are fully conscious of the importance of the sea. In the near future, it will be no less vital to achieve supremacy in the air.' The military potential of the aircraft was demonstrated several times in 1910, the year after Douhet's prophetic words; on 19 January, for example, Lieutenant Paul Beck of the US Army released sandbags, representing bombs, over Los Angeles from an aeroplane flown by pioneer aviator Louis Paulhan, and on 30 June Glenn H. Curtiss dropped dummy bombs from a height of 50ft (15m) in an area representing the shape of a battleship, marked by buoys on Lake Keuka. The feasibility of discharging firearms from an aircraft was also demonstrated on 20 August 1910, when US Army Lieutenant Jacob Earl Fickel fired a 0.30in (7.62mm) rifle at a ground target at Sheepshead Bay, New York. More significantly in terms of future development, a German

named August Euler had filed a patent some weeks earlier for a new device enabling a fixed machine gun to be fired from an aircraft.

FIRST MISSION

Perhaps fittingly, in the light of Douhet's remarks, it was the Italians who were the first to demonstrate the usefulness of the aircraft in war. On 22 October 1911, following Italy's declaration of war on Turkey over a dispute involving the Italian occupation of Cyrenaica and Tripolitania, Capitano Carlo Piazza, commanding the Italian Expeditionary Force's air flotilla, carried out a reconnaissance of Turkish positions between Tripoli and Azizzia in a Blériot XI. It was the first operational mission by a heavier-than-air craft.

The air arms of the world's major powers were also beginning to take shape in 1910. On 10 February the French Army took delivery of its first aircraft, a Wright biplane, at Satory near Versailles, and General Roques, in charge of military aviation, launched a campaign to recruit pilots. The artillery provided three men, the infantry four, and the cavalry rejected the request with disdain! The first French military pilot to receive his brevet was Lieutenant Felix Camerman, who was subsequently promoted to command the aviation school at Chalons. By the end of 1910 the newly formed Aéronautique Militaire had 29 military aircraft (Blériots, Breguets, Farmans, Antoinettes and Voisins) and 39 pilots.

In October 1910 the German Army received the first of seven aircraft on

■LEFT: Roland Garros in the cockpit of his Morane-Saulnier Monoplane. Flying with Escadrille MS.23, Garros destroyed no less than five enemy aircraft in three weeks.

order, all Etrich Taube (Dove) types; a training school had already been set up at Döberitz some weeks earlier. The first German pilot to be awarded his brevet was Lieutenant Richard von Tidemann, a Hussar officer, who flew solo on 23 July 1910.

On 1 April 1911 the Air Battalion of the Royal Engineers, whose origins went back to a School of Ballooning founded at Aldershot in 1892, was formed at Larkhill, Wiltshire, under the command of Major Sir Alexander Bannerman. It consisted of two companies; No 1 (Airship, Balloon and Kite) and No 2 (Aeroplanes). The battalion had three airships and an assortment of aircraft described as 'an antique Wright which had originally belonged to C.S. Rolls; a somewhat antique and very dangerous Blériot; "The Paulhan" (a type no longer sold by Paulhan), a de Havilland, a Henry Farman, four Bristols and a Howard Wright.' In December 1911, a Royal Navy flying school was established at Eastchurch, Kent, with six Short biplanes loaned by Frank McLean, a pioneer of the

■BELOW: The observer/gunner's position in the nacelle of a Maurice Farman MF.7 Longhorn. This Farman type was widely used by the Allies in the early months of the war.

Royal Aero Club; and in May 1913 the Royal Flying Corps came into being, absorbing the Royal Engineers Air Battalion and the Royal Navy's aviation assets. The new Corps included a Military Wing, a Naval Wing, and a Central Flying School, as well as logistical and technical support units.

MILITARY FLYING IN AMERICA

The year 1911, meanwhile, had also witnessed the foundation, in March, of the Belgian Army's first military aviation school, and the beginnings of naval aviation in the United States. Progress with military aviation in the USA, although an Aeronautical Division of the Army Signal Corps had been formed in 1907, had been slow, and it was not until 5 March 1913 that the Aeronautical Division established the First Aero Squadron at Galveston Bay, Texas City, under the command of Captain Charles de Forest Chandler. The Aeronautical Division's sole Wright biplane, on which a nucleus of officers had learned to fly, was joined by a Curtiss D, a Burgess H and a Martin TT seaplane.

It was Captain Chandler who, on 2 June 1912, had taken part in the first US trials of an aircraft armed with a machine gun.

The aircraft was the Signal Corps' Wright biplane, which on this occasion was flown by Lieutenant Thomas de Witt Milling at College Park, Maryland, Chandler manning the Lewis gun. Just a few weeks later, on 3 October, a recoilless aircraft gun designed by Commander Cleland Davis, USN, was given initial tests at the Naval Proving Ground, Indian Head; the weapon was intended to fire a large-calibre shell.

British and French designers were also showing considerable interest in the 'fighting aeroplane' concept at this time. One of the first companies to recognise the potential of the aeroplane for waging, and not merely observing, war was Vickers Ltd of Great Britain. At the 1913 Aero Show at Olympia, London, the firm exhibited its Type 18 'Destroyer', a two-seat biplane with a water-cooled Wolseley pusher engine and a free-firing, belt-fed Maxim gun mounted in the nose. The aircraft was later redesignated EFB.1 (Experimental Fighting Biplane No 1) and was the progenitor of the FB.5 'Gunbus', which was to equip several RFC squadrons in France in 1915. Also in 1913, the pioneer airman Claude Grahame-White demonstrated his Type XV, in which a Lewis machine gunner sat on a special platform below the pilot. Another British design to mount a machine gun experimentally in 1913 was the Royal Aircraft Factory FE.3, designed as a two-seat scouting aircraft and night

■ABOVE: The Vickers FB.5 Gunbus equipped the first-ever specialised fighter unit: No 11 Squadron RFC, which took the aircraft to France in July 1915.

bomber. Like many other designs of the time the aircraft had a pusher layout, so that the observer/gunner in the front cockpit had an unrestricted field of fire. A $1\frac{1}{2}$-pounder Coventry Ordnance Works (COW) gun was installed in the pod-shaped front fuselage, firing through an opening in the nose. The aircraft performed well, but it was structurally weak and gun firing trials were only carried out on the ground.

WEIGHT PENALTY

By the beginning of 1914, there was no longer any doubt that the machine gun provided the obvious solution to the question of armament for the 'fighting aeroplane'. There were several problems to be overcome, however, before the solution became a practical reality. Firstly, machine guns could only be fitted to the sturdier of the types then in service; on other, lower-powered aircraft, the weight penalty was unacceptable. There was also the problem of aiming and firing any sort of gun, as pilot and observer were surrounded by a considerable wing area, with its

Airco D.H.2

Type: single-seat scout
Country of origin: United Kingdom
Powerplant: one 100hp (74.5kW) Gnome Monosoupape piston or 110hp (82kW) Le Rhone rotary

Performance: maximum speed 93mph (150km/h)
Weights: empty 943lb (428kg); maximum take-off 1441lb (645kg)
Dimensions: wing span 28ft 3in

(8.61m); length 25ft 2in (7.68m); height 9ft 6in (2.91m)
Armament: one forward-firing 0.303in (7.7mm) Lewis gun on flexible mounting

attendant struts and bracing wires, and seated either behind or in front of a large and vulnerable wooden propeller.

Nevertheless, the British flying services soon adopted the 27lb (12kg) American-designed Lewis gun as standard armament for its observation aircraft, particularly the 'pusher' types in which the observer, who sat in front of the pilot, had a large cone of fire upwards, downwards and to either side. In the beginning, the gun mounting was usually devised by the observer to suit himself. The French selected the Hotchkiss, which like the Lewis was air-cooled; a belt-fed weapon, it initially proved too inflexible for the observer and so a drum feed was adopted. The Germans chose the lightweight Parabellum MG14, a modification of the water-cooled Maxim; this also had a drum magazine.

Despite the realisation that military aircraft needed an effective armament, almost all the machines that went to war in August 1914 carried no weapons, other than the carbines and sidearms with which pilots and observers were armed. So it was that the German thrust into Belgium on 4 August was supported by a small number of Etrich Taube aircraft, all unarmed and dedicated to reconnaissance, while similar missions were flown by

unidentified and unarmed Belgian aircraft in the Liège area.

AIR ARM STRENGTHS

In August 1914 the heavier-than-air component of the German Imperial Air Service comprised 246 aircraft, 254 pilots and 271 observers. There were 33 Feldflieger Abteilungen (Field Flight Sections), each with six aircraft, and eight Festungflieger Abteilungen (Fortress Flight Sections), each with four aircraft. The former came under direct operational control of the army, one being assigned to each individual army headquarters and one to each army corps, while the latter had the task of protecting fortress towns along the German frontiers. About half the available aircraft were Taube types, which in the years leading up to the war were built in large numbers. The unarmed Taube had a top speed of 60mph (96km/h). Other types in service, all biplanes, were the AEG B.II, Albatros B.II, Aviatik B.I and B.II, and the DFW B.I.

France's Aviation Militaire (as the service was renamed) had at its disposal 132 aircraft, with a further 150 in reserve, the latter mostly assembled at Saint-Cyr. The first-line aircraft were divided between 24 Escadrilles, each having six machines on average, although the number varied somewhat. Five were

equipped with Maurice Farmans, four with Henry Farmans, two with Voisins, one with Caudrons, one with Breguets, seven with Blériots, two with Deperdussins, one with REPs and one with Nieuports. All these units were tasked with reconnaissance and were assigned to the five French field armies engaged on the Western Front.

The other main belligerents on the continent of Europe in August 1914, Russia and Austria, were poorly equipped in terms of aircraft. The Russian Imperial Air Service had 24 machines while the Austrian Air Service had 36, mostly Taube types. The small Austrian aviation industry, in fact, did not really develop until the summer of 1915, when it underwent a rapid expansion following Italy's entry into the war.

On the outbreak of war the Royal Flying Corps possessed about 180 aircraft of all types, but many were elderly training machines and only 84 of them could be classed as fully airworthy. The Royal Naval Air Service had 71 aircraft, of which 31 were seaplanes, based at a series of locations along the east coast of Britain, from the English Channel to Scotland. These stations were within flying distance of one another, enabling the RNAS to mount overlapping coastal patrols.

DEPLOYMENT TO FRANCE

On 13 August 1914 Nos 2, 3, 4 and 5 Squadrons deployed to France with 64 aircraft, 105 officers and 775 other ranks in support of the British Expeditionary Force (BEF), initially assembling in the Amiens area. A temporary RNAS flying base was also set up at Ostend and seaplane patrols initiated between that location and Westgate, Kent, to protect the troopships carrying the BEF to France. On the 19th, the first RFC reconnaissance flight of the war was made from Maubeuge, Belgium, by Captain Philip Joubert de la Fert, (who was to be C-in-C RAF Coastal Command in World War II) of No 3 Squadron in a Blériot, and Lieutenant G. W. Mapplebeck of No 4 Squadron in a BE.2. The RFC suffered its first fatality on 22 August, when an Avro 504 of No 5 Squadron, piloted by Lieutenant V. Waterfall, was shot down by enemy rifle fire over Belgium.

With reconnaissance activity increasing in the days preceding the Battle of the Marne, it was only a matter of time before the first aerial encounters took place. As yet, none of the aircraft of either side was armed, although their crews carried side arms and sometimes carbines. The crews of No 5 Squadron RFC had been experimenting with the mounting of a machine gun in the observers' cockpits of their Henry Farmans, but the extra weight resulted in an unacceptable performance loss. Then, on 25 August, an enemy two-seater was forced to land after being 'buzzed' by three BE.2s of No 2 Squadron RFC. One of the British pilots, Lieutenant H.D. Harvey-Kelly, landed nearby and, with his observer, chased the enemy crew into a wood before setting fire to the German aircraft and taking off again. In a separate incident, Lieutenant de Bernis, the observer of a French aircraft piloted by Roland Garros, fired six or seven shots with a carbine at two German Albatros aircraft, with no visible result. A second German aircraft was captured later that day near Le Quesnoy.

AERIAL COMBAT

It was not until October 1914, however, that the first true aerial combat took place. On the 4th, a Voisin pusher biplane of Escadrille VB24, armed with a Hotchkiss machine gun and flown by Lieutenant Joseph Frantz, with Corporal Quénault as his observer, shot down an Aviatik two-seater near Reims. The crew of the Aviatik, both of whom were killed when their aircraft crashed in flames, were Wilhelm Schlichting (pilot) and Lieutenant Fritz von Zangen. Corporal Quénault fired 47 rounds at the Aviatik, which was the first aircraft in history to be shot down and destroyed by another. Frantz who survived the war, as did Quénault, added two more Aviatiks to his score in May 1915. He died in Paris in September 1979, Quénault in Marseille in April 1958. On 22 November it was the turn of the RFC to score, when an Avro 504 fitted with a Lewis gun encountered an Albatros and the British observer, Lieutenant L.G. Small, emptied two drums of ammunition at it. The damaged Albatros made a forced landing, and its two-man crew was captured.

In February 1915 No 11 Squadron RFC, then based at Netheravon in Wiltshire, took delivery of its first Vickers FB.5, developed from the Type 18 'Destroyer' mentioned earlier. The two-seat FB. (Fighting Biplane) 5 was armed with a drum-fed Lewis gun mounted in the front cockpit and powered by a Gnome Monosoupape 'pusher' engine. Production aircraft at first were allocated to squadrons in small numbers, and No 11 Squadron, the first to be fully armed with the type, became the first specialised fighter squadron ever to form. The squadron deployed to Villers-Brettoneux, France, in July 1915 and for several months carried out offensive patrols and ground attack work. No 18 Squadron, similarly armed with FB.5s, also arrived in France in November 1915. However, the FB.5, good workhorse as it

■BELOW: Designed by Geoffrey de Havilland, the Airco DH.2 single-seat 'pusher' scout arrived at the front with No 24 Squadron in February 1916. The squadron had its first victory on 2 April.

turned out to be, was no match in air combat for the aircraft the Germans now had in the air fighting arena.

MAJOR REVOLUTION

The year 1915 saw a major revolution in air fighting tactics with the development of technology that enabled machine guns to fire forwards through the propeller disc. Hitherto, the only way to arm a tractor biplane (one with its engine fitted in the nose) with a forward-firing machine gun was to mount the weapon on top of the upper wing, so that the bullets passed above the propeller arc, but such an arrangement made aiming and reloading very difficult. Synchronisation was the answer; this meant, quite simply, relating the rate of fire of a machine gun to the rate of revolution of a propeller so that the bullets missed the advancing and retreating blades. Experiments to this end had been carried out before the war in France and Germany by Raymond Saulnier of Morane-Saulnier and Franz Schneider of LVG, and Schneider had in fact patented a primitive synchronisation device in 1913. An updated version was installed in an LVG E.VI monoplane early in 1915, but the aircraft was destroyed in an accident and no further examples were built.

In France, despite encouraging early tests, Raymond Saulnier was unable to raise development funds from the authorities and resorted to the cheaper and more basic method of fitting steel wedge-shaped deflector plates to the propeller blades so that any bullet striking them would be diverted harmlessly. In March 1915 this device was tested operationally by Roland Garros of Escadrille MS.23, a noted pre-war aviator who had been seconded to assist Saulnier with his experiments. In less than three weeks, flying a Morane-Saulnier monoplane, he destroyed five enemy aircraft, but on 19 April 1915 he was forced to land behind enemy lines after his aircraft was hit by ground fire. He failed to set fire to the Morane, which was examined by German technical officers. The Germans copied the idea, but trials proved disappointing. Whereas French bullets had a copper coating, German bullets, which were plated with chrome, shot the propeller blades to pieces. The French device was shown to Anthony Fokker, the Dutch designer who – having been turned down by the British and the French – was building aircraft for Germany. Fokker quickly realised that the deflector-plate idea was too dangerous to be really successful; severe vibrations set up when the bullets struck the plates would, in time, shake the engine loose from its mounting. The Dutchman therefore set about designing a simple engine-driven system of cams and push-rods which operated the mechanism of a Parabellum machine gun once during each revolution of the propeller while the pilot depressed the trigger. In effect, the propeller fired the gun. (Much of the design work on this gear, in fact, was carried out by three members of Fokker's engineering staff, Heber, Leimberger and Lübbe.) The mechanism was successfully demonstrated on a Fokker M5K monoplane; this was given the military designation E.I (the 'E' signifying Eindecker, or monoplane), and so became the first German aircraft dedicated to the pursuit and destruction of enemy aircraft. It was to be February 1916 before RFC aircraft equipped with interrupter gear, designed by Vickers, reached the squadrons in France, and Aviation Militaire units received similar gear at about the same time.

THE 'FOKKER SCOURGE'

In the meantime, British and French aircrews suffered a fearful martyrdom at the hands of the 'Fokker Scourge.' It began on 1 July 1915, when Lieutenant Kurt Wintgens of Feldflieger Abteilung 6b, flying the Fokker M5K, shot down a French Morane monoplane. There was no doubt about this claim, but since the Morane fell inside French lines it was not upheld by the German High Command. Meanwhile, the production Fokker E.I had begun to reach the front-line German units in June, and the small number of machines available, in the hands of pilots whose names would soon become legendary, began to make their presence felt. Foremost among them were Lieutenants Max Immelmann and Oswald Boelcke, both of Feldflieger Abteilung 62. Immelmann's chance to

Fokker E.III

Type: single-seat scout
Country of origin: Germany
Powerplant: one 100hp (74.5kW) Oberursel U.1 9-cylinder rotary engine

Performance: maximum speed 83mph (134km/h)
Weights: empty 1100lb (500kg); maximum take-off 1400lb (635kg)
Dimensions: wing span 31ft 3in

(9.52m); length 23ft 11in (7.3m); height 9ft 6in (3.12m)
Armament: one fixed forward-firing 3.1in (7.92mm) LMG 08/15 machine gun

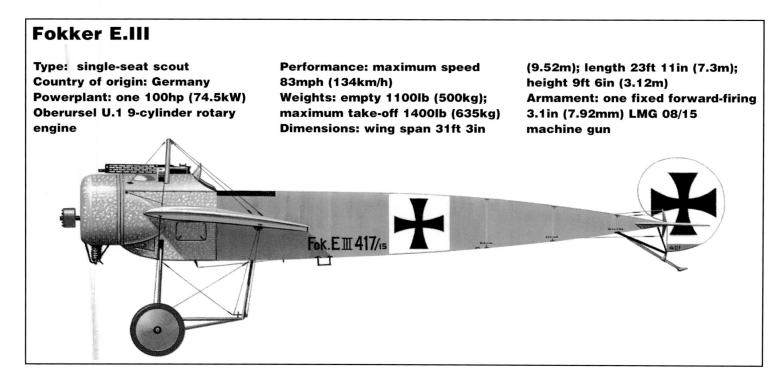

RIGHT: The Albatros Dr.I was that company's submission for a new triplane scout for the German Air Service. Some 14 German and Austrian firms submitted designs.

test the Fokker in action came on 1 August 1915, when he took off with Boelcke to attack some British aircraft which were bombing the German airfield at Douai. The subsequent combat report tells the story:

'At 6am on 1 August Lieutenant Immelmann took off in a Fokker fighting monoplane in order to drive away the numerous (about 10 or 12) enemy machines which were bombing Douai aerodrome. He succeeded in engaging three machines showing French markings in the area betwen Arras and Vitry. Heedless of the odds against him, he made an energetic and dashing attack on one of them at close quarters. Although this opponent strove to evade his onslaught by glides and turns and the other two enemy aircraft tried to assist the attacked airman by machine gun fire, Lieutenant Immelmann forced him to land westward of and close to Berbières after scoring several hits on vital parts of the machine.'

The wounded British pilot was taken prisoner. Although there were several more skirmishes in the days that followed, it was the end of August before Immelmann gained his second victory. He described what happened in a letter to his mother:

'Suddenly I saw an enemy biplane attack Boelcke from behind. Boelcke did not seem to have seen him. As if by agreement, we both turned round. First he came into Boelcke's sights, then into mine, and finally we both went for him and closed up on him to within 50 to 80 metres. Boelcke's gun appeared to have jammed, but I fired 300 rounds. Then I could hardly believe my eyes when I saw the enemy airman throw up both his arms. His crash helmet fell out and went down in wide circles, and a second later the machine plunged headlong into the depths from 2200 metres. A pillar of dust showed where he hit the ground.'

NEW TACTICS

By the end of October 1915 Immelmann had increased his score to five. Whereas most of his colleagues regarded air combat as something of a sport, Immelmann approached it from a scientific standpoint, evolving new tactics

and improving his efficiency as his experience grew. He developed a new combat manoeuvre which was to remain standard in the air fighting textbooks for many years: the Immelmann turn. This involved building up speed in a dive towards the enemy, then pulling up into a climb and opening fire from below in order to achieve surprise. After firing, the Fokker pilot continued to climb until he was in the near-vertical position, at which point he applied hard rudder, stall-turned and dived on his adversary from the opposite direction. These tactics worked well as long as the Fokker was superior to all other aircraft at the front; they later became dangerous when more powerful engines enabled Allied aircraft to climb hard after the attacking fighters and open fire when the latter were at the critical stall turn position.

The definitive version of the Fokker Monoplane was the E.III, armed with twin Spandau machine guns, and Abteilung 62 re-armed with the new type at the end of 1915. On 13 January, Immelmann and Boelcke each destroyed a British aircraft while flying E.IIIs; both were awarded Germany's highest decoration, the Ordre Pour le Mérite. The German tactics of the time involved individual Fokker pilots quartering sectors of the sky over the front, a procedure that was outlined by Immelmann in another letter home.

'Lieutenant Leffers is further southward [of Douai]. Bapaume, where I have been busy so often, belongs to his sector. Since there is nothing more to be

found in our area, one has to poach on the hunting grounds of others. Baron von Althaus is still further southward, and Parscau another bit further on [Verdun]. Berthold is further away to the north. So far each of these has shot down four opponents. Our territories are marked off exactly by the trenches. Naturally the artillery shells us if we come within its range...'

BLIND SPOT

The Fokker Monoplane was the first dedicated fighter aircraft to see operational service, and for months it made Allied reconnaissance flights into German territory virtual suicide missions. The RFC's BE.2s suffered particularly heavy losses at the hands of the Fokkers; apart from being inherently stable and consequently not very manoeuvrable, the BE.2 had a vulnerable blind spot under its belly which the German pilots exploited to the full, zooming up under their victims and firing as they went. The denial of vital air reconnaissance to the Allies was a serious matter, and steps were quickly taken to combat the Fokker menace. First to react was the French Aviation Militaire, which in the summer of 1915 introduced the single-seat Nieuport 11 biplane, nicknamed 'Baby' because of its diminutive size. With a machine gun mounted on its upper wing, the Nieuport 11 also served with the RFC and RNAS and was built under licence in Italy, where it remained the standard fighter type until 1917.

The Nieuport 11 virtually held the line until the introduction of two British fighter types, the FE.2b and DH.2. Designed and built by the Royal Aircraft Factory, the original FE.2a had been completed in August 1913, but it was a year before the first 12 aircraft were ordered, the first of these flying in January 1915. Had matters moved more quickly, and production of the FE.2 been given priority, it is possible that the Fokker Monoplane would never have achieved the supremacy that it did. The first FE.2b flew in March 1915, and in May a few production examples arrived in France for service with No 6 Squadron RFC at Abeele, Belgium, but it was not until January 1916 that the first squadron to be fully equipped with the FE, No 20, deployed to France. A two-seat 'pusher' type powered by a 120hp (89.4kW) Beardmore engine and armed with one Lewis gun in the front cockpit and a second on a telescopic mounting firing upwards over the wing centre-section, the FE.2b was slightly slower than the Fokker E.III but a match for it in manoeuvrability.

ENTER THE DH.2

No 20 Squadron was followed, on 8 February 1916, by No 24, equipped with Airco (Aircraft Manufacturing Company) DH.2s. The DH.2 was a single-seat 'pusher' type whose prototype had been sent to France in July 1915 for operational trials; unfortunately, it was brought down in enemy territory on 9 August. The DH.2 was powered by a 100hp (74.5kW) Monosoupape engine and was armed with a single Lewis gun mounted on a pivot in the prow, enabling

■BELOW: Major W.G. 'Bill' Barker demonstrating a Bristol F.2B Fighter of No 139 Squadron to HRH the Prince of Wales, sitting in the rear cockpit, at Villaverla, Italy, in 1918.

it to be traversed from left to right or elevated upward and downward. In practice, pilots found this arrangement too wobbly and secured the gun in a fixed forward-firing position, using the whole aircraft as an aiming platform. Rugged and highly manoeuvrable, the DH.2 was to achieve more success in action against the Fokkers than any other Allied fighter type. No 24 Squadron was commanded by Major L.G. Hawker, who on 25 July 1915, while flying a Bristol Scout of No 5 Squadron, had been awarded the Victoria Cross for engaging three enemy aircraft in quick succession and shooting one down. It soon became one of the best-known Allied air units. It gained its first victory on 2 April 1916 and claimed its first Fokker on the 25th of that month, and from then on its tally rose steadily. In June 1916 its pilots destroyed 17 enemy aircraft, followed by 23 in July, 15 in August, 15 in September and 10 in

November. On 23 November, however, Major Hawker was shot down by an up-and-coming German pilot named Manfred von Richthofen after a bitter, 35-minute combat over Bapaume. A lucky shot apparently creased Hawker's head, knocking him unconscious, and he crashed out of control. Richthofen later admitted that Hawker gave him the hardest fight of his career. Had it not been for that single bullet, Hawker might have gained the upper hand and the legend of the 'Red Baron' might never have been born.

ALBERT BALL

Meanwhile, in March 1916, Nos 1 and 11 Squadrons of the RFC had re-armed with the Nieuport 11 (known simply as the Nieuport Scout in British service). The aircraft had an excellent rate of climb, although its top speed of 96mph (154km/h) left something to be desired

and it was prone to suffer structural damage during violent manoeuvres. It took a very sure touch to get the best out of the Nieuport; one pilot who had it was a 19-year-old second lieutenant, formerly of the Sherwood Foresters, named Albert Ball. Ball's first posting to France was to No 13 Squadron, flying BE.2cs, but at every opportunity he would visit No 11 Squadron, which shared the same airfield, and borrow one of their Nieuports. At this time – summer 1916 – No 11 was engaged in attacks on enemy observation balloons, a highly dangerous undertaking, and Ball destroyed one of these in July. It was the first of 43 victories that were to be gained by the young officer before his death in action in 1917.

By the summer of 1916 the Allied fighter squadrons were beginning to hold their own against the Fokkers. In the middle of the year two new Fokker types,

■ABOVE: An SE.5a in Palestine. The SE's fin and rudder were originally designed for a rival scout, the FE.10, which was not adopted. Some SE.5s were fitted with bomb racks.

the D.I and D.IV, began to appear over the front; they were designed to replace the E.III, but in fact fell far short of expectations. The Fokker D.I was no match in either climb or manoeuvrability for the Nieuport Scout, and by the end of the year most of those supplied to units on the Western Front had been transferred to the less-dangerous skies of the Eastern Front. Germany's real hopes for regaining air superiority lay with the Albatros D.I which, armed with twin 0.30in (7.92mm) calibre Spandau guns and powered by a 160hp (119.3kW) Mercedes engine, made its appearance in September 1916. It was the first German fighter to carry a two-gun armament

Albatros D.V

Type: single-seat scout
Country of origin: Germany
Powerplant: one 180/200hp
(134.2kW/149.1kW) Mercedes D.II
in-line engine

Performance: maximum speed
116mph (186km/h)
Weights: empty 1515lb (687kg);
maximum take-off 2066lb (937kg)
Dimensions: wing span 29ft 7in

(9.05m); length 24ft (7.33m);
height 8ft 10in (2.70m)
Armament: two fixed forward-firing
3.1in (7.92mm) LMG 08/15
machine guns

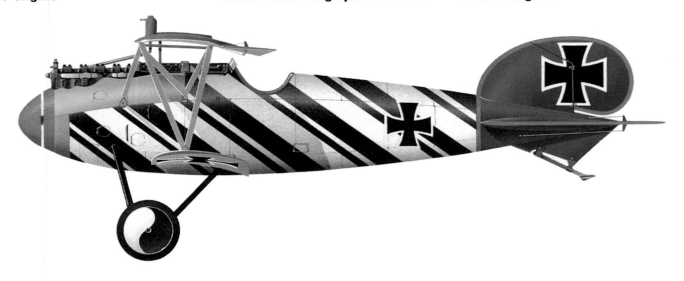

without suffering a loss of performance, and although it was less manoeuvrable than the Fokker types, it had better speed, climb and firepower. In October 1916 an improved version, the Albatros D.II, also reached the front-line units, and by the end of the year over 200 were in service.

Another German fighter type that entered service in the summer of 1916 was the Halberstadt D.II, mounting a single Spandau and powered by a 120hp (89.4kW) Mercedes. Although highly manoeuvrable and capable of holding a long, sustained power dive without its wings breaking off (a problem with some German types), the Halberstadt was not a favourite among German pilots, most of whom seemed incapable of using it to its fullest advantage. The notable exception was Oswald Boelcke, who flew both the Halberstadt and the Albatros and gained several victories with the former type. About 100 Halberstadt D.IIs were in service by the end of 1916, but in the early part of 1917 they began to give way to the later Albatros variants.

THE 'EAGLE OF LILLE'
In June 1916, while the battle of the Somme raged, the wind of change began to sweep through the German Air Service. The old Feldflieger Abteilungen were now disbanded and replaced by

Jagdstaffeln (Fighter Squadrons) in which Germany's best and most experienced fighter pilots were to be concentrated. On 13 June, Max Immelmann bade farewell to his comrades of the old Section 62, most of whom were leaving for the Eastern Front; he, together with Oswald Boelcke and several other notable pilots, was to stay behind and form the first of the new squadrons, Jagdstaffel 2 (Jagdstaffel 1 existing only on paper). The new unit was to be equipped with Halberstadts.

On 18 June, Jagdstaffel 2 engaged in a dogfight with several FE.2bs between Loos and Douai. Immelmann, who was flying one of the older Fokker E.IIs, as his own machine was unserviceable, drove one of the FEs down to a forced landing, then climbed to search for another victim. At that moment, eye-witnesses saw Immelmann's machine appear to stagger in mid-air, oscillate violently and literally fall apart. The wings collapsed and tore away, while the fuselage broke in two. The front part, including cockpit and pilot, fell like a stone, and Immelmann was killed instantly. Later, the British claimed that Immelmann had been shot down by 2nd Lieutenant G.S. McCubbin and Corporal J.H. Waller of No 25 Squadron, flying one of the FEs, but German experts who examined the wreck attributed the ace's death to failure of the

interrupter gear, followed by the destruction of the propeller and subsequent break-up of the airframe. Whatever the reason, the man who had become known as the 'Eagle of Lille' would claim no more victims. His final score was 17.

BOELCKE'S JAGDSTAFFEL
Jagdstaffel (abbreviated to Jasta) 2 was to have a complement of 14 fighters, not Halberstadts in the first instance – these would arrive later – but Albatros D.IIs. (The 'D' prefix signified 'Doppeldecker', or biplane.) In the first instance, Jasta 2 was to be based at Lagnicourt in the Somme sector, from where it would be able to challenge some of the RFC's most effective units. Delivery of the Albatros fighters was slow, and it was not until 17 September 1916 that Boelcke was able to lead the Jasta into action as a team for the first time. On that day, accompanied by five other pilots, he encountered eight BE.2cs of No 12 Squadron RFC, escorted by six FE.2bs, on their way to attack the railway station at Marcoing. Boelcke attacked just as the BEs were releasing their bombs, after positioning his fighters across the British machines' avenue of escape. In the ensuing battle, two BEs and four of their escorts were shot down. This success provided tremendous encouragement not only for the pilots of

Jasta 2, but also for other German units which were going into action. During the weeks that followed, air superiority took a marked swing back in the Germans' favour. Throughout these weeks, Boelcke's staffel remained in the thick of the fighting, its pilots scoring a combined total of 27 victories in the last fortnight of September alone. The cost to themselves was three aircraft.

Oswald Boelcke was killed on 28 October 1916, not as a result of enemy action, but in a collision with another aircraft. His personal score was 40 enemy aircraft destroyed. More importantly, Boelcke had laid the foundations of air fighting tactics, beginning with the concept of the 'pair', the basic air fighting formation that is still in use today. The lessons he passed on to the pilots under his command were hammered home relentlessly. It was not sufficient just to be a good pilot. They had to know everything about their aircraft: its combat radius, its maximum and cruising speeds at various altitudes, what stresses it could sustain in violent manoeuvres, and so on. He made them strip engines and put them together again, so that they could carry out

makeshift repairs if engine trouble compelled them to make a forced landing. He also instructed them on the finer points of marksmanship, stressing that it was always better to get in close and fire in short bursts, aiming for the cockpit. He taught them how to maintain their machine guns, and how to clear stoppages quickly while still exercising full control over their aircraft. He taught them the value of teamwork and of keeping a good lookout at all times. The day of the lone hunter, he pointed out, was over. He allocated formation positions to his pilots so that they would get used to having the same wingmen alongside, and painted the nose and tail of his own aircraft red so that it would be easily recognizable in the mêlée of a dogfight, or when his pilots were forming up over a rendezvous point. If the Jasta became dislocated in the course of a fight, the pilots were to make for a rendezvous point previously selected by Boelcke. If no one else turned up, individual pilots were to go home, keeping just below cloud cover if possible to reduce the risk of being attacked from above. Such was the legacy of expertise that Oswald Boelcke left behind him.

THE ZEPPELIN THREAT

Meanwhile, as the Germans and the Allies struggled to establish air superiority over the Western Front, one of the British types that had suffered so badly at the hands of the Fokkers – the BE.2 observation aircraft – had itself been pressed into service in the fighter role, in the air defence of the United Kingdom against attacks by enemy airships. In the beginning, the Royal Naval Air Service had been made wholly responsible for the air defence of the British Isles, but during 1915 it had become increasingly apparent that the RNAS was ill equipped to deal with the Zeppelin threat. It was clear that if matters were to improve, the Royal Flying Corps, which had assisted the RNAS to a limited extent in the course of the year, would have to become much more involved, even to the extent of assuming the air defence commitment in full. The Admiralty and the War Office, however, found it hard to agree on anything, beyond the fundamental facts that Zeppelins were difficult to find in the dark and that night flying was fraught with peril, so while very brave young men in wholly inadequate aircraft

Fokker Dr.I

Type: single-seat scout
Country of origin: Germany
Powerplant: one 110hp (82kW)
Oberursel Ur.II 9-cylinder rotary
engine

Performance: maximum speed
115mph (185km/h)
Weights: empty 894lb (406kg);
maximum take-off 1291lb (586kg)
Dimensions: wing span 23ft 7in

(7.19m); length 18ft 11in (5.77m);
height 9ft 8in (2.95m)
Armament: two fixed forward-
firing 3.1in (7.92mm) LMG 08/15
machine guns

were striving to confront the enemy, another war was being waged in Whitehall – a prolonged and unseemly wrangle over the responsibility for Britain's air defence.

In June 1915, the Director of Home Defence, General Launcelot Kigell, had proposed that the Navy deal with enemy aircraft approaching the coast and that the Army take over once the enemy had come inland; this was firmed up by the Army Council in November, but it was not until 10 February 1916 that a formal agreement to this effect was endorsed by the War Committee. With effect from 12 noon on 16 February 1916 the Commander-in-Chief Home Forces was to assume responsibility for the defence of London, and for the rest of the country on the 22nd.

Meanwhile, by prior agreement with the RNAS, the RFC had positioned three BE.2cs at Cramlington on 1 December 1915 for the defence of Tyneside, and on 18 March 1916 these formed the nucleus of the newly formed No 36 Squadron, the first RFC squadron formed for the specific task of home defence. Flights

■BELOW: A Fokker Dr.I triplane and ground crew. The Dr.I's design was greatly influenced by the Sopwith Triplane, whose handling qualities greatly impressed the Germans.

were quickly established at Ashington, Hylton and Seaton Carew. Later in March, for the air defence of the southern part of the region, No 33 Squadron was transferred from Filton to Beverley in Yorkshire, with a detached flight at Bramham Moor, Tadcaster. In September 1916 No 76 Squadron formed at Ripon, with detached flights at Copmanthorpe, Helperby and Catterick, and in the following month No 77 Squadron became established at Edinburgh, with flights at Whiteburn, New Hagerston and Penston. By the end of the year, therefore, the north was defended by four front-line squadrons, all equipped with BE.2 and, later, BE.12 aircraft, the BE.12 being a single-seat version of the BE.2 with a different engine. Between them they had at their disposal no less than 34 landing grounds between Humber and Tyne and 35 between Tyne and Forth. Despite these deployments, no raider was destroyed by the northern air defences in the course of seven attacks that were made on targets from the Forth to the Humber between the beginning of March and the end of September 1916.

LONDON AIR DEFENCE

Meanwhile, on 1 February 1916, the various air defence detachments in the London area had been brought together under No 19 Reserve Aeroplane

Squadron, a newly formed unit with its HQ at Hounslow. On 25 March the London defences were again reorganised and placed under the new No 18 Wing, and on 15 April No 19 RAS became No 39 (Home Defence) Squadron. At the beginning of June 1916 eight RFC squadrons were dedicated to home defence. These were No 28 at Gosport and Newhaven; No 33 at Bramham Moor, Coal Aston, Beverley and Doncaster; No 36 at Cramlington, Turnhouse and Seaton Carew; No 39 at Hounslow, Hainault Farm, Suttons Farm and North Weald; No 50 at Dover and Wye; No 51 at Thetford, Norwich and Narborough; No 52 at Hounslow, Goldhanger and Rochford; and No 54 at Castle Bromwich, Lilbourne, Papplewick and Waddington. Between them, they had an established aircraft strength of 134; their actual strength was 60, mostly various types of BE.2. While the RFC strove to achieve some form of effective night defence organisation, a warning system was established and observer posts set up all over the country. These were connected with warning control centres and gradually began to prove their worth. Girls' names were used to identify individual Zeppelins, which were listed in alphabetical order as they crossed the coast. One of the first lines of defence against the incoming Zeppelins was the

ABOVE: The first of the Albatros 'V-strutters', the D.III was the most effective of all the Albatros fighters produced during World War I. The pilot here is Lt von Budde of Jasta 29.

interception of their wireless traffic by direction-finding stations, and by the end of 1916 a network of huge sound locator mirrors, some built into cliffs, had also been set up.

ANTI-AIRSHIP WEAPONS

By August 1916 the squadrons of the Home Defence Wing had adopted a system whereby aircraft operating from the landing grounds around the country were assigned individual patrol areas which overlapped, so that if a Zeppelin was sighted mutual support was readily available – at least in theory. Although aircrews had now amassed a considerable amount of experience in night operations, and were aware that night flying held no special complications, the Zeppelins remained notoriously hard to locate without searchlight assistance, anti-aircraft shellbursts or marker rockets, the latter fired by the coastal observers.

Then there were the allied problems of armament and interception techniques. Because the Zeppelin presented so vast a target, the favoured method of attack was from above, using small bombs, either the

20lb (9kg) Hale or the 60lb (27.2kg) incendiary designed at the Royal Laboratory, Woolwich, but there were alternative weapons. One was the Ranken Dart, devised by Engineer Lieutenant Francis Ranken, RN. Originally used by the RNAS, and also adopted by the RFC, the dart weighed about one pound and consisted of an iron-pointed metal tube containing high explosive and black powder. The tail unit embodied spring-loaded vanes which opened and locked into position when they touched the Zeppelin's envelope after the head had penetrated inside, and at the same time activated a detonator rod. The dart, held fast to the envelope, would then burst into flames, igniting the gas from the airship's ruptured cells. The darts were carried in batches of 24, which could be released all at once or in small groups.

Another anti-Zeppelin weapon was the Fiery Grapnel, which was carried in pairs attached to a BE2c. The idea was to approach the Zeppelin from right angles with the grapnel trailing behind, then to leap over the intended victim and allow the weapon to engage its envelope, whereupon an explosive charge would ignite leaking hydrogen.

The problem with these devices was that, because of the Zeppelin's superior rate of climb, it was usually difficult, if not impossible, for an attacking aircraft

to get above it. The answer, clearly, was to be able to attack from any position, including below, using incendiary bullets. Such bullets had existed for some years. One had been invented by a New Zealander, John Pomeroy, in 1908 and had been offered without success to the British Government in 1914; it was only in 1916, after Pomeroy had written to David Lloyd George, that the Munitions Inventions Department agreed to sponsor development. In August that year, an order for half a million rounds was placed on behalf of the RFC.

SUCCESSFUL NIGHT FIGHTER

The Admiralty had shown more interest in an explosive bullet designed by Flight Lieutenant F.A. Brock, and this was also ordered for both the RNAS and RFC, as was a phosphorus incendiary bullet designed by a Coventry engineer, J.F. Buckingham. This mixture of bullets was on issue to the home defence squadrons by the end of August 1916. The result was immediate, and dramatic. On the night of 2 September, the German Army's Schütte-Lanz airship SL11 (Captain Wilhelm Schramm) was shot down in flames at Cuffley by Lieutenant William Leefe Robinson of No 39 Squadron. On 22 September L32 (Lieutenant Werner Peterson) fell in flames over Essex after being attacked by 2nd Lieutenant

special arrangement with the United States, had done most of their flying training in Texas and, unlike many of their British contemporaries, already possessed a considerable degree of skill.

The flow of fresh personnel into the RFC during the early months of 1917 did much to raise morale as the Corps prepared to support the planned spring offensives. The primary tasks of the RFC were, as always, reconnaissance and artillery observation, but the observation aircraft had to be protected from the attentions of enemy scouts, and this requirement had in turn given rise to the rapid development of fighter tactics that

Frederick Sowrey, while Alois Böcker's L33 crash-landed near Little Wigborough, having suffered severe damage from anti-aircraft fire and the efforts of Lieutenant Alfred Brandon of 39 Squadron. Finally, on 1 October, one of a force of eleven Zeppelins that set out to raid England was shot down over Potters Bar by 2nd Lt W.J. Tempest. She was the L31, commanded by Lieutenant-Commander Heinrich Mathy.

All these successes had been in the south. But on the night of 28/29 November the northern air defences at last had their chance. Zeppelin L34, Lieutenant-Commander Max Dietrich, was shot down off the coast by 2nd Lieutenant Ian Pyott of No 36 Squadron, flying a BE.2c from Seaton Carew, soon after bombing targets in south-east Durham. All 20 crew perished. Another airship, the L21, was also destroyed that night by naval pilots from Great Yarmouth. All the German airships destroyed during the closing weeks of 1916 were the victims of BE.2Cs. The irony is that the sedate BE.2c, remembered as the 'Fokker Fodder' of the Western Front, never gained the recognition it deserved as the world"s first successful night fighter.

As 1916 drew to a close, new fighter equipment that would alter the course of

■ABOVE: A Nieuport 11 making a low run across its airfield. The aircraft was originally designed to compete in the 1914 Gordon Bennett air race, which was cancelled due to the war.

the air war over the Western Front was gradually becoming available to the Allies, and skills and tactics learned at terrible cost were being passed on to a younger generation of pilots by those who had survived the battles of 1915–16. The losses sustained by the RFC by the end of 1916 were, in fact, so severe that they brought about a manpower crisis, so that early in 1917 the War Office found it necessary to order regimental commanders to appeal for volunteers for transfer to the flying service to train as pilots and observers. Hundreds came forward, many for no reason other than that they preferred to face death in the air rather than in the mud and slime of the trenches, and at the same time the first Commonwealth and Dominion volunteers also began to arrive. They were led by the Canadians, who, by

■RIGHT: The Spad XIII, a development of the earlier Spad VII, entered service at the end of May 1917 and subsequently equipped over 80 French escadrilles, 8472 examples being built.

were designed to secure air superiority over an area of considerable depth behind the enemy lines while the observation machines went about their business.

BRISTOL FIGHTER

The first Allied offensive of 1917 involved a major French attack on the Aisne while the British pinned down a large part of the enemy forces in the north, the main objective in their sector being the capture of Vimy Ridge. The offensive began on 17 March and ended on 4 April. The First and Third British Armies were supported by 25 RFC squadrons, about half of them equipped with single-seat fighters. It was

during this battle that a new British combat aircraft, the Bristol F.2A Fighter, made its operational debut. Fifty F.2As were built; powered by a 190hp (141.6kW) Rolls-Royce Falcon engine giving it a top speed of around 115mph (185km/h) and armed with a centrally mounted forward-firing Vickers gun and a single Lewis mounted in the rear cockpit, the first examples arrived in France with No 48 Squadron towards the end of March.

The squadron had only six Bristols in operation at the time of its arrival at its new base, Bellevue, and they were rushed into action before their pilots had time to

get used to them or to develop proper tactics with them. At first they were flown like earlier two-seaters, orientated around the observer's gun as the primary weapon, and losses were heavy. During their first patrol on 5 April 1917, six Bristols led by No 48 Squadron's CO, Major W. Leefe Robinson VC (who had earlier distinguished himself by shooting down the German Schütte-Lanz airship SL11 at Cuffley on 2 September 1916) encountered five Albatros D.IIs led by Manfred von Richthofen. The British pilots adopted the standard two-seater tactic of turning their backs on the enemy to allow their observers to bring

their guns to bear. It was a serious mistake, and four of the six – including Leefe Robinson, who spent the rest of the war in a prison camp – were shot down.

Later, in an interview with a Berlin newspaper, Richthofen was openly contemptuous of the British machine, with the result that many German pilots came to regard the Bristol Fighter as easy game – with fatal consequences to themselves. When flown offensively, in the same way as a single-seat fighter, it

proved to be a superb weapon and went on to log a formidable record of success in action. Several hundred Bristol Fighters were ordered in 1917, these being the F.2B version with a 220hp (164kW) Falcon II or 275hp (205kW) Falcon III engine, wide-span tailplanes, modified lower wing centre sections and an improved view from the front cockpit. The F.2B eventually served with six RFC squadrons – Nos 11, 20, 22, 48, 62 and 88 – on the Western Front, as well as with

■ABOVE: A Sopwith Pup flown by Squadron Commander E. H. Dunning touching down on 2 August 1917 on aircraft carrier HMS *Furious*, the first successful landing on a moving ship.

No 67 (Australian) Squadron in Palestine, No 139 Squadron in Italy, and with Nos 33, 36, 76 and 141 on home defence duties in the United Kingdom. The pilot who perhaps did most to vindicate the Bristol Fighter was a

Canadian, Lt Andrew McKeever, who destroyed 30 enemy aircraft while flying F.2Bs, his various observers shooting down 11 more.

THE SUPERLATIVE SE.5

Another new type to enter RFC service in the spring of 1917 was the SE.5 single-seat scout, which was delivered to No 56 Squadron in March. Powered by a 150hp (112kW) Hispano-Suiza engine, the aircraft had a maximum speed of 120mph (193km/h). Armament comprised a synchronised Vickers gun firing through the propeller and a drum-fed Lewis mounted over the wing centre section. Although less manoeuvrable than either the French-built Nieuports and Spads, the SE.5 was faster and had an excellent rate of climb, enabling it to hold its own in combat with the latest German fighter types. The SE.5s of No 56 Squadron flew their first operational patrol on 22 April 1917. A subsequent one, in May, was graphically described in the book *Sagittarius Rising* by Cecil Lewis, who was then one of the squadron's pilots.

'The May evening is heavy with threatening masses of cumulus cloud, majestic skyscapes, solid-looking as snow mountains, fraught with caves and valleys, rifts and ravines...Steadily the body of scouts rises higher and higher, threading its way between the cloud precipices. Sometimes, below, the streets of a village, the corner of a wood, a few dark figures moving, glides into view like a slide into a lantern and is then hidden again...

'A red light curls up from the leader's cockpit and falls away. Action! He alters direction slightly, and the patrol, shifting throttle and rudder, keep close like a pack of hounds on the scent. He has seen, and they see soon, six scouts three thousand feet below. Black crosses! It seems interminable till the eleven come within diving distance. The pilots nurse their engines, hard-minded and set, test their guns and watch their indicators. At last the leader sways sideways, as a signal that each should take his man, and suddenly drops...'

One of No 56 Squadron's flight commanders was Captain Albert Ball, who was then the RFC's leading ace, the holder of the DSO and two bars, plus the MC. On that evening of 7 May 1917, Ball had taken off a while earlier from Vert Galand to carry out an offensive patrol in the direction of Douai aerodrome, the base of Jagdstaffel 11, which was commanded by a German officer who was already legendary: Manfred von Richthofen.

■ **BELOW: The Sopwith Camel F.1, evolved to succeed the Pup and Triplane, lacked their docile handling characteristics, but destroyed more enemy aircraft than other Allied types.**

Royal Aircraft Factory S.E.5a

Type: single-seat scout
Country of origin: United Kingdom
Powerplant: one 200hp (149kW)
Wolseley 8-cylinder Vee engine
Performance: maximum speed

138mph (222km/h)
Weights: empty 1410lb (639kg);
maximum take-off 1988lb (902kg)
Dimensions: wing span 26ft 7in
(8.11m); length 20ft 11in (6.38m);

height 9ft 6in (2.89m)
Armament: one 0.303in (7.7mm)
Vickers and one 0.303in (7.7mm)
Lewis machine gun

BALL'S LAST BATTLE

As the fight was joined it began to rain, cutting down the visibility. The section leaders of No 56 Squadron tried hard to hold their men together, but in the confusion of the dogfight the squadron became split up. Some of the pilots broke away and made for home; others, including Ball, headed for a pre-arranged rendezvous over Arras. There, Ball joined up with another flight commander named Crowe and the two continued their patrol, joined by a lone Spad. Near Loos, Ball suddenly fired off a couple of signal flares and dived on a red-and-yellow Fokker Triplane, following it into a cloud. It was the last time that he was seen alive. Of the 11 S.E.5s that had set out, only five returned to base. The credit for Albert Ball's death was claimed by Lothar von Richthofen, Manfred's brother. The claim was false, and to this day mystery surrounds the RFC pilot's demise. He was either shot down by a machine gun mounted on a church steeple, or became disorientated in low cloud and went out of control. The Germans buried him near Lille, and dropped a message to that effect over No 56 Squadron's aerodrome. A month later, it was announced that Ball had been posthumously awarded the Vicotria Cross. His score of enemy aircraft destroyed at the time of death was 47; he was 22 years old.

'SPITFIRE' OF WORLD WAR I

The original SE.5 was followed into service, in June 1917, by the SE.5a, with a 200hp (149kW) Hispano-Suiza engine. The type was first issued to Nos 56, 40 and 60 Squadrons, in that order, and by the end of the year had been delivered to Nos 24, 41, 68 and 84. Deliveries were slowed by an acute shortage of engines, but the pilots of the units that did receive the SE.5a were full of praise for the aircraft's fine flying qualities, physical strength and performance. It is probably no exaggeration to say that, in most respects, the S.E.5a was the Spitfire of World War I.

It certainly had none of the vicious tendencies of the Sopwith Camel – although in fairness, once the Camel had been thoroughly mastered it was a superb fighting machine, and in fact it was to be credited with the destruction of more enemy aircraft than any other Allied type before the conflict ended. Early production Camels were powered either by the 130hp (97kW) Clerget 9B or the 150hp (111.8kW) Bentley BR.1 rotary engine, but subsequent aircraft were fitted with either the Clerget or the 110hp (82kW) Le Rhone 9J. Armament comprised twin Vickers guns mounted in front of the cockpit, and four 20lb (9kg) Cooper bombs could be carried under the fuselage for ground attack. The first unit to receive Camels was No 4 Squadron

Royal Naval Air Service, followed by No 70 Squadron RFC, both in July 1917.

Delivery of the SE.5 and the Camel came too late to prevent heavy RFC losses, which continued to mount steadily during the spring of 1917. There were three main reasons for the growing casualty rate. First, the RFC was still critically deficient in adequate combat aircraft; secondly, the prevailing westerly wind – which tended to carry the mêlée of air combat deep into enemy territory – was in the Germans' favour; and thirdly, the RFC insisted on maintaining an offensive policy throughout, no matter what the cost. Faced with superior enemy aircraft, it inevitably suffered an increase in losses because of this. By April 1917 new pilots were being sent to the front with as little as seventeen and a half hours' flying experience, which precipitated a vicious circle; the more inexperienced the British pilots, the higher the success rate of the German fighter squadrons. By the middle of 'Bloody April' in 1917, the average life expectancy of an RFC pilot in France had dropped to two months. During the first week of April 1917 the RFC lost 75 aircraft in action, mostly victims of an emerging band of tough, resolute air fighters nurtured in the traditions of Germany's first air aces and fighter tacticians, Oswald Boelcke and Max Immelmann.

RICHTHOFEN'S 'CIRCUS'

At their head was Rittmeister Freiherr Manfred von Richthofen. In accordance with the German policy of concentrating their best pilots into single crack units, most of their leading aces served with Richthofen's Jagdstaffel 11. In June 1917 Jastas 4, 6, 10 and 11 were merged into a single Jagdgeschwader (Fighter Wing) under Richthofen's command. Although patrols were still flown at Jasta strength, Richthofen could, in response to an increase in Allied air activity, concentrate a large number of fighter aircraft in any particular sector of the front. Moreover, the Jagdgeschwader was highly mobile and could be switched quickly from one part of the front to another in support of ground operations.

The principal German fighter aircraft in the spring of 1917 was the Albatros D.III, which had first been issued to Jasta 11 in January that year. Powered by a Mercedes D.III engine, it had a maximum speed of 108mph (173km/h) and carried an armament of twin synchronised 0.30in (7.92mm) Spandau machine guns. By April 1917 all 37 Jastas at the front were equipped with either the D.III or the earlier Albatros D.II. However, the most widely used of all the Albatros fighters was the D.V, which made its appearance in mid-1917. It was not a great improvement over the excellent D.III, but it was produced in large numbers, over 1500 serving with the Jastas on the Western Front alone. Later in the year, starting in August, some Jastas also began to receive the Pfalz D.III, which like the Albatros was powered by a Mercedes engine and featured twin Spandau machine guns. However, even at its peak the Pfalz fully equipped only half a dozen units, and for some reason German pilots seem to have been prejudiced against it; this attitude is hard to understand, because the Pfalz was a sturdy machine, capable of absorbing a great deal of battle damage, and it could be dived harder and faster than the Albatros.

TRIPLANE TYPES

The other new German fighter type introduced in 1917 was the Fokker Dr.I Triplane. Its design was inspired by the

■RIGHT: Rittmeister Freiherr Manfred von Richthofen (right), the famous 'Red Baron', destroyed 80 Allied aircraft to become the top-scoring ace of World War I before his death in April 1918.

Sopwith Triplane, an excellent and highly manoeuvrable fighter which served with Nos 1, 8, 9, 10, 11 and 12 Squadrons of the Royal Naval Air Service on the Western Front during most of 1917. The Fokker Triplane was never used in large numbers, but it registered astonishing successes in the hands of leading German aces such as Von Richthofen and Voss.

To counter the threat posed by the Jagdgeschwader in the summer of 1917, the RFC was forced to adopt a similar policy of concentrating its best fighter pilots and squadrons in opposition to Von Richthofen wherever his squadrons appeared. These elite RFC units were the cradle of the leading British fighter aces. No 56 Squadron, for example, in addition to Albert Ball, numbered among its ranks

such famous fighter pilots as Captain James McCudden, Lt Rhys-Davids, Capt Brunwin-Hales with 27 victories and Capt Henry Burden with 22; then there was Capt W.A. (Billy) Bishop of No 60 Squadron (and later of No 85), a Canadian who was to survive the war as the second-ranking RFC fighter ace with 72 victories, being narrowly beaten to the top by Major Mick Mannock, who had a score of at least 74. Mannock flew with No 40 Squadron, as did two other leading fighter aces: Captain G.E.H. McElroy, a Canadian with a score of 46, and Major Roderic Dallas, a New Zealander, with 39.

FRENCH PIONEERS

In fact, the formation of large, concentrated fighter groups had been

pioneered by the French during the Battle of the Somme in the summer of 1916, when the Cachy Group (so called after its operational base near Amiens) came into existence under Captain Brocard of N.3 Cigognes. (To avoid confusion, it should be pointed out that the French squadrons bore the initial letter of the aircraft type they were flying; the Cigognes were using Nieuports at the time, and later, when they converted to Spads, their designation was changed to Spa.3.) The Cachy Group comprised N.3, with Lieutenant Georges Guynemer as its leading pilot, and Captain Féquant's N.65, which included another ace, Lieutenant Charles Nungesser. At the end of 1916 the French Aéronautique Militaire possessed three Groupes de Combat: GC 11 under Commandant Le Révérend, GC 12 under Commandant Brocard, and GC 13 under Commandant Féquant. Eleven more would be formed before the end of hostilities. Each Groupe comprised four Escadrilles, each with 15 aircraft and 15 pilots. The Groupes de Combat came under the orders of the French Army commanders and, like their Royal Flying Corps counterparts, had the task of establishing air superiority and protecting observation aircraft. In 1917, mixed units of fighters and bombers were employed in carrying out offensive operations.

The aircraft on which most of the French aces cut their teeth was the Nieuport 11C-1 Bébé, which entered service in the summer of 1915 and which was also used in some numbers by the RFC and RNAS. It was this little aircraft which helped to redress the balance of power following the appearance over the Western Front of the Fokker E.III Monoplane, with its synchronised machine gun firing through the propeller. The Bébé was followed into service, in May 1916, by the Nieuport 17C-1, which equipped Escadrilles N.3, N.38, N.55, N.57, N.65 and N.103. It also served with eight RNAS and five RFC squadrons.

STABLE GUN PLATFORM

In the autumn of 1916 many Escadrilles began to equip with a new fighter type, the Spad (Societé Pour Aviation et ses Derivées) VII. Although less manoeuvrable than the Nieuport types, the Spad VII was a strong, stable gun platform with a top speed of 119mph (191km/h) and an excellent rate of climb. The Spad VII was also used by the RFC and RNAS, and filled a crucial gap at a time when many units were still equipped with ageing and vulnerable aircraft. In May 1917, however, the French Escadrilles de Chasse began to standardise on a new type, the Spad XIII. Like its predecessor, it was an excellent

gun platform and was extremely strong, although it was tricky to fly at low speeds. Powered by a Hispano-Suiza 8Ba engine and armed with two forward-firing Vickers guns, it had a maximum speed of nearly 140mph (225km/h) – quite exceptional for that time – and could climb to 22,000ft (6710m). The Spad XIII subsequently equipped more than 80 Escadrilles.

Such, in broad outline, was the state of air power on both sides of the front – discounting bomber and observation types for the moment – when the British opened a new offensive in Flanders in June 1917, the main effort taking place in the Messines sector. The attack was supported by 18 RFC squadrons with a total of 300 aircraft, about one-third of them single-seat fighters. On the first day of the offensive, 7 June, Captain W.A. Bishop of No 60 Squadron was awarded the Victoria Cross for destroying four out of seven enemy aircraft in a daring single-handed attack on an airfield near Cambrai. He was flying a Nieuport 17.

By the end of the month the RFC's reserves were sadly depleted. The situation was further aggravated by the withdrawal on 21 June of two of its best fighter squadrons, Nos 56 and 66, for home defence. This also helped to delay the re-equipment of the RFC units in France with new aircraft, notably the Sopwith Camel.

Fokker D.VII

Type: single-seat scout
Country of origin: Germany
Powerplant: one 160hp (119.3kW) Mercedes D.III water-cooled in-line engine

Performance: maximum speed 117mph (189km/h)
Weights: empty 1620lb (735kg); maximum take-off 1940lb (880kg)
Dimensions: wing span 29ft 2in

(8.90m); length 22ft 8in (6.95m); height 9ft (2.75m)
Armament: two fixed forward-firing 3.1in (7.92mm) LMG 08/15 machine guns

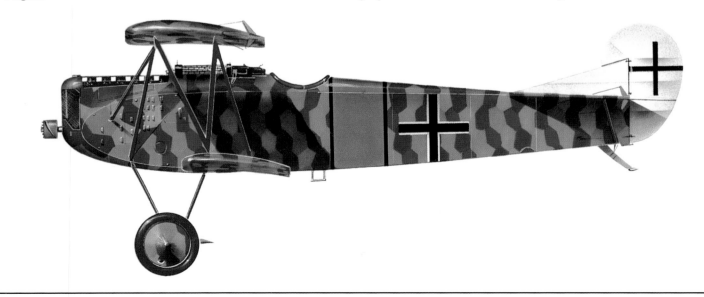

Fokker D.VIII

Type: single-seat scout
Country of origin: Germany
Powerplant: one 110hp (82kW)
Oberursel UR.II rotary engine
Performance: maximum speed

115mph (185km/h)
Weights: empty 1238lb (562kg);
maximum take-off not known
Dimensions: wing span 27ft 7in
(8.40m); length 19ft 3in (5.86m);

height 9ft 3in (2.82m)
Armament: two fixed forward-firing
3.1in (7.92mm) LMG 08/15
machine guns

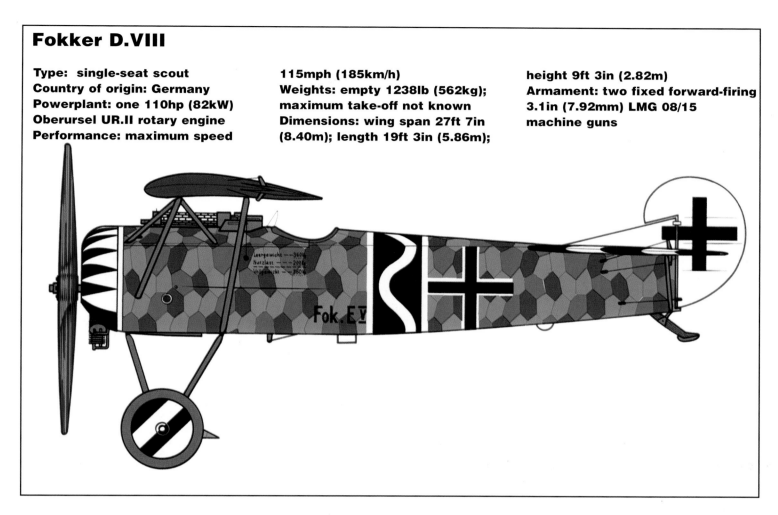

For the RFC crews, stretched to their utmost during July, it was some consolation to know that Von Richthofen was out of action for a time. On 6 July, 40 fighters of the Richthofen Geschwader had attacked six F.E.2ds of No 20 Squadron, escorted by four Sopwith Triplanes of No 10 Squadron RNAS; two FEs were shot down, but an observer in another – 2nd Lt E.A. Woodbridge – got in a good burst at Richthofen's red Albatros and sent it down to make a forced landing. Richthofen was wounded on the head.

NAVAL FIGHTERS

The spring and summer battles of 1917 saw Royal Naval Air Service fighters employed in growing numbers on the Western Front. The first really effective combat aircraft to serve with the RNAS was the Sopwith 1½-Strutter, so called because of its unusual wing bracing. Originally designed as a high-performance two-seat fighter, with a 110hp (82kW) Clerget 9Z engine, this aircraft went into production for the RNAS at the beginning of 1916 and was the first British aircraft to feature an efficient synchronised forward-firing

armament. Early aircraft were armed with a forward-firing Vickers machine gun and a Lewis gun in the rear cockpit, later aircraft having a Scarff ring for the observer's gun in place of the original Nieuport mounting. The 1½-Strutter was first deployed to France with No 5 Wing RNAS in April 1916, being used initially for bomber escort, but it later switched to the bombing role, as did aircraft issued to Nos 43, 45 and 70 Squadrons RFC. It is worth noting that some 4500 1½-Strutters were completed by French manufacturers, some being supplied to Belgium and Russia. Many, after being replaced by Sopwith Camels on the Western Front, served in the UK's home defence squadrons, while others went to sea aboard the Royal Navy's early aircraft carriers and other major warships, flying from specially constructed platforms in the latter case.

One fighter type which served with both RNAS and RFC throughout 1917 was the Sopwith Pup, the first examples being issued to Nos 2 and 8 (Naval) Squadrons in the autumn of 1916. The Pup was armed with a single synchronised Vickers gun mounted centrally in front of the cockpit and had a

top speed of 110mph (177km/h). Although by far the greater number of Pups served with the RFC, the aircraft was always associated with the RNAS, and particularly with the many operational trials it carried out on the Royal Navy's aircraft carriers and cruisers. It was also a very capable fighter aircraft; in the last two months of 1917, Pups of No 8 (Naval) Squadron accounted for 20 enemy aircraft.

OUTSTANDING FIGHTER

The most outstanding fighter aircraft to serve with the RNAS in 1917, however, was without doubt the Sopwith Triplane, a successful attempt by Sopwith's talented designer, Herbert Smith, to produce yet more manoeuvrability from the basic design which had produced the Pup. Powered by a 130hp (96.9kW) Clerget 9B engine and armed with a single synchronised Vickers gun (although a few examples were fitted with twin Vickers) the Triplane had a maximum speed of 113mph (182km/h) and had superlative agility and rate of climb, so much so that it had still not been outclassed when the Sopwith Camel began to replace it in the summer of

1917. So impressed were the enemy that no fewer than 14 German and Austrian manufacturers, including Anthony Fokker, produced triplane designs of their own, but never quite succeeded in matching the Sopwith aircraft. The Triplane equipped six RNAS squadrons on the Western Front and one of its leading exponents was Major Raymond Collishaw, a Canadian from British Columbia who had been a member of the support team which had accompanied Captain R.F. Scott's ill-fated Antarctic expedition of 1912. On the outbreak of war two years later, at the age of twenty-one, he had abandoned his career as a seaman and volunteered for flying duties with the RNAS. Collishaw first went to France flying a Sopwith Pup on escort missions. Changing to Sopwith 1½-Strutters, he scored his first victory on 12 October 1916, shooting down a Fokker Monoplane near Oberndorf. Two weeks later he destroyed two more enemy aircraft in a single sortie, an exploit that earned him the French Croix de Guerre. Because of the promise he showed as a pilot and fighter leader, he was allowed to form a Canadian flight of No 10 RNAS Squadron, now equipped with Sopwith Triplanes. He had always been impressed by the distinctive markings adopted by many German fighter pilots, so he had the flight's Triplanes doped black all over and bestowed names on them: Black Death, Black Roger, Black Sheep, Black Prince and Black Maria, the latter his personal aircraft.

RENOWNED

The 'Black Flight' quickly became renowned along the front, its five pilots achieving respectable scores, often in combat with the Richthofen Geschwader. In June 1917 one of them, Lt J.E. Nash from Hamilton, Ontario, was shot down and killed by the German ace Karl Allmenröder, who in turn was shot down and killed by Collishaw on the 25th of that month. By the time Collishaw was sent home to Canada for a rest in July, his personal score stood at 37 enemy aircraft destroyed.

The days before the third battle of Ypres, which opened on 31 July, were marked by intense air activity on both sides. At this time the combined strength of the RFC, RNAS, Aéronautique Militaire and the small Belgian Air Corps on the Western Front was 852 aircraft, of which 360 were fighters; the German strength was 600 machines, of which 200 were fighters.

To bolster the Allied fighter strength in Flanders, two French Escadrilles – including the Cigognes – were sent to Dunkirk from the Lorraine sector. Charles Nungesser, having experienced engine trouble, was flying alone a few hours behind the rest when he was suddenly attacked by a British aircraft near Arras and took 15 bullets through

■BELOW: Arguably the best fighter aircraft produced in World War I, the Fockker D.VII was much prized as war booty after the Armistice. This particular example was Albatros-built.

ABOVE: Originally designated E.V, the Fokker D.VIII's early service career was delayed when faulty workmanship caused wing failure. It did not reach the front in quantity until October 1918.

his Nieuport. Convinced that the attacking aircraft was a captured one, flown by a German pilot, he engaged it and shot it down, landing nearby to inspect the wreck. The pilot was dead, and Nungesser, finding some identity documents on the body, discovered to his dismay that the man who had tried to kill him was in fact an RFC pilot; a very inexperienced one, as a subsequent enquiry established.

The air offensive that preceeded the battle opened on 11 July, and on that first day 14 German aircraft were destroyed for the loss of nine British. A few days later Von Richthofen was back in action, his head still in bandages, and a series of massive dog fights took place between his Jagdgeschwader and Allied fighter formations. On the 26th, no fewer than 94 single-seat fighters fought one another at altitudes varying between 5000ft and 7000ft (1524m and 2134m) over Polygon Wood, and the following evening 30 Albatros fighters attacked eight FE.2ds over the same area. It was a trap; no sooner had the German fighters come down to intercept than they were attacked by 59 S.E.5s and Sopwith Triplanes. Nine enemy aircraft were destroyed for the loss of one SE.5.

TOUGH BATTLEGROUND

The Cigognes had seldom encountered pilots of the calibre of those who made up the Richthofen Jagdgeschwader in the skies of Lorraine, where they had helped to defend the embattled fortress of Verdun, and they found Flanders a tough battleground. Georges Madon had an incredible escape when, flying a new Spad XIII with which the Escadrille was equipping, he collided with an enemy two-seater. With his upper wing completely torn away, he spun out of control through a terrifying 10,000ft (3050m). Literally at the last moment his aircraft miraculously righted itself before crash-landing in the Allied lines. His only injury was a broken finger. Another ace, Lieutenant Albert Deullin, was not so lucky. During a fight with an enemy monoplane, he took two bullets in the region of his kidneys and crash-landed, gravely wounded. He survived to fly and fight again in 1918. Alfred Heurtaux, attacking a two-seater near Ypres, was hit in the thigh. Fainting through loss of blood, he went into a spin and recovered just in time to right his aircraft. He spotted a field dead ahead and went down to land on it; it turned out to be an RFC aerodrome, and the British whisked

him off to hospital. Among the other French pilots, Lieutenant Chaput crashed and was injured, while the ace of aces, Guynemer, was wounded and hospitalised. Nungesser and Jean Navarre fought on, but it was an increasingly grim business.

One day in July, Nungesser made a lone diving attack on six German scouts over Houthulst Forest. He made a single pass, shooting down two of them and then using his superior speed to get away. The others made off eastwards under the command of a young pilot who, after flying two-seater reconnaissance missions with a unit known as Abteilung 5, had recently transferred to single-seaters with Jasta 27. His name was Hermann Göring.

DEATH OF A LEGEND

On 6 September 1917 Georges Guynemer, now a captain, shot down his 54th victim. Five days later, accompanied by Lt Bozon-Verduraz, he took off on his last

Halberstadt D.IV

Type: single-seat scout
Country of origin: Germany
Powerplant: one 120hp (89.4kW)
Mercedes D.II in-line engine
Performance: maximum speed

93mph (150km/h)
Weights: empty 1146lb (520kg);
maximum take-off 1610lb (730kg)
Dimensions: wing span 29ft 10in
(8.6m); length 23ft 11in (7.3m);

height 8ft 9in (2.67m)
Armament: one fixed forward-firing
3.1in (7.92mm) LMG 08/15
machine gun

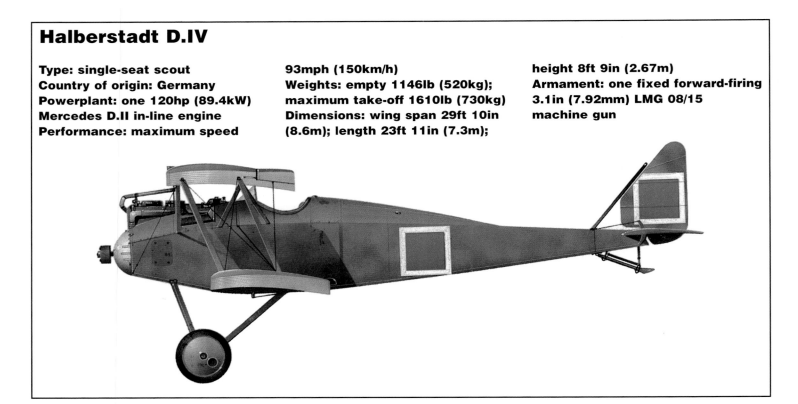

patrol. Bozon-Verduraz' combat report tells the terse story:

'At 09.25, together with Captain Guynemer, attacked an enemy two-seater over the lines at Poelcapelle. Made one pass and fired thirty rounds. Captain Guynemer continued to pursue the enemy as I was obliged to break off to avoid eight single seaters, which were preparing to attack me. I did not see Captain Guynemer again. At 10.20, attacked a two-seater at 5,900 metres over Poperinghe. Fired ten rounds at point-blank range, then gun jammed. Pursued the enemy, but was unable to clear the stoppage and returned to base.'

It was three days before the French authorities had an inkling of what had happened to Guynemer; a German newspaper carried a report stating that the French ace had been shot down by a Captain Wissemann, but it was to be another month before the news was officially confirmed. In response to a note sent via the Spanish Embassy, the Department of Foreign Affairs in Berlin issued the following statement:

'Captain Guynemer fell in the course of an air fight at 10.00 am on 11 September last, close to Cemetery of Honour No 11 to the south of Poelcapelle. A medical examination revealed that the index finger of the left hand had been shot away, and that the cause of death was a bullet in the head.'

After a brief examination by a German patrol, Guynemer's body was left in the wreckage until it could be recovered safely. Before this could be done, however, the British artillery laid down a heavy barrage on the area where Guynemer's aircraft had come down, completely obliterating all trace of the machine and its pilot.

FRENCH ACES

About a week after Guynemer's death, the man who claimed to have shot him down wrote home to his family, telling them not to worry about him, and that never again was he likely to meet an adversary who was half as dangerous as Guynemer. Only nineteen days later, Wissemann was himself shot down and killed by a man who was destined to emerge from the holocaust of the 1914–18 War as the top-scoring Allied fighter pilot. His name was René Fonck. This pilot, who had scored his first victories over the Somme battleground in 1916, and who had joined the Cigognes in April of the following year, soon began to consolidate his position as one of France's best fighter pilots. In October 1917, in the course of a total sortie time of thirteen and a half hours, he destroyed ten enemy aircraft. His tactics were simple. He would cruise at high altitude, so that he was almost always above his opponents; then, choosing his moment carefully, he would use his height and speed

advantage to gain surprise. His aim was excellent, and a single firing pass on the dive was usually enough to send down his enemy. By the end of 1917 Fonck's score stood at 19 enemy aircraft destroyed, placing him equal third with two other talented pilots, Captains Albert Deullin and Georges Madon. In second place was Captain Alfred Heurtaux, with 21, and leading the field was Lieutenant Charles Nungesser, the senior surviving French pilot, with 30 victories.

On the German side, the second top-scoring ace after Manfred von Richthofen was Lieutenant Werner Voss of Jagdstaffel 10, who had destroyed 47 Allied aircraft by the beginning of September 1917. Voss was due to go on leave with his two brothers, and on 23 September they arrived at his aerodrome, intending to travel back to Germany together. Before departing, Voss decided to go out on an offensive patrol, flying a Fokker Triplane. This type had first made its appearance on the Western Front early in September and, in the hands of an experienced pilot, was a formidable fighting machine. But even experienced pilots were not invincible; Lieutenant Kurt Wolff, the commander of Jagdstaffel 11 and an ace with 33 victories, had been shot down and killed in a Triplane on 5 September by Flight Sub-Lt N. MacGregor of No 10 (Naval) Squadron, flying a Sopwith Camel.

THE 'HUSSAR OF KREFELD'

Soon after starting his patrol, Werner Voss shot down a de Havilland DH.4, heading back towards the front line after a sortie, but then he developed engine trouble and returned to base, exchanging his Triplane for another. At 6.00 pm, in poor visibility, he took off again accompanied by two Albatros Scouts, which still formed the main equipment of Jasta 11. Approaching the front line, they saw an air battle in progress between a variety of British and German aircraft, including the SE.5s of No 60 Squadron. Voss immediately manoeuvred into position to attack one of these, which was flown by Lt H.A. Hamersley and which had become separated from the rest.

Twenty minutes earlier, six SE.5s of 'B' Flight, No 56 Squadron, had taken off from their airfield at Estrée Blanche. The flight was led by Captain James B. McCudden, who was accompanied by Lts Gerald Bowman, Arthur Rhys-Davids, Keith Muspratt, Richard Maybery and R.T.C. Hoidge. The flight attacked an enemy two-seater, which was shot down by McCudden, and then reformed and climbed to attack a formation of six Albatros Scouts, flying just below the cloud base. At that moment, McCudden spotted Hamersley's lone SE.5, pursued by Voss, somewhat lower down.

Abandoning the Albatros formation, he went after the Triplane in a diving turn, followed by Arthur Rhys-Davids. The pair closed in rapidly on the German, one on either side, taking it in turns to fire in short bursts. Voss, with four more SE.5s coming down hard and already effectively boxed in, took the only course of action open to him. Using the Fokker's remarkable manoeuvrability to the fullest advantage, he decided to fight his attackers by turning to face them, doubtless hoping that he could hold them at bay until reinforcements arrived. The manoeuvre took McCudden completely by surprise, as he wrote later: 'To my amazement he kicked on full rudder without bank, pulled his nose up slightly, gave me a burst while he was skidding sideways, and then kicked on opposite rudder before the results of this amazing stunt appeared to have any effect on the controllability of his machine.' With a burst of gunfire through his wing, the startled McCudden broke away sharply. At that moment, a red-nosed Albatros D.V joined the battle. Its pilot, almost as skilful as Voss himself, took on the task of protecting Voss's tail, and with his assistance the German ace abandoned his purely defensive tactics and got in some damaging shots at the SE.5s that were trying to out-turn him. The battle went

on for a full 10 minutes, but the help the German pilots were counting on never arrived, and the outcome was inevitable. The combat report of Lieutenant Rhys-Davids describes the last frantic minutes of the fight:

'The red-nosed Albatros and the triplane fought magificently. I got in several bursts at the triplane without apparent effect, and twice placed a new drum on my Lewis gun. Eventually I got east of and slightly above the triplane and made for it, getting in a whole Lewis drum and a corresponding number of rounds from my Vickers. He made an attempt to turn in and we were so close that I was certain that we would collide. He passed my starboard wing by inches and went down. I zoomed, and saw him next with his engine apparently out, gliding east. I dived again and got one shot out of my Vickers. I reloaded, keeping in the dive, and got in another good burst, the triplane effecting a slight starboard turn, still going down. I had now overshot him, but never saw him again.'

■ BELOW: The Avro 504K was one of the stalwarts of World War I, being used in many different roles, including that of night fighter. It equipped six home defence squadrons in 1918.

McCudden, who had temporarily broken off the fight to change an ammunition drum, witnessed the Triplane's last moments. He noted that it seemed to stagger and then fly erratically for a short time before going into a steep dive, streaming smoke, and exploding on impact with the ground. A few moments later the red-nosed Albatros also went down in flames.

Later, James McCudden wrote of Voss: 'His flying was wonderful, his courage magnificent, and in my opinion he was the bravest German airman whom it has been my privilege to see fight.' But perhaps the feelings of the British pilots were best summed up by young Rhys-Davids himself, the man who had ended the career of the 'Hussar of Krefeld', as Voss was nicknamed. As his colleagues gathered around to congratulate him, he shook his head and murmured, as he set his glass aside: 'Oh, if only I could have brought him down alive!'

By September 1917, the Allied fighter squadrons in Flanders had succeeded, for

■**BELOW: Based on the D.I landplane, the Albatros W.4 seaplane fighter was developed quickly to defend German bases on the coast of Flanders. First production W.4s arrived early in 1917.**

the time being, in establishing a measure of air superiority. On 25 September, the RFC's fighters claimed 19 victories for the loss of only one British aircraft. No 56 Squadron, which had returned to France in July after a brief period on air defence duty in England, continued to be in the forefront of the battle; by the end of September its score of enemy aircraft destroyed had risen to 200. This figure was matched, on 9 October, by No 1 Squadron, now equipped with Sopwith Camels. As the winter closed in, however, aerial activity was curtailed, and a curious lull fell over the Western Front; although offensive patrols were flown by both sides, there were few serious clashes. Then, on 12 March, air activity, particularly opposite the sectors held by the British, increased dramatically. By the third week of March the Germans had air superiority on the Somme, with 730 aircraft, including 326 fighters, opposing 579 RFC machines, of which 261 were fighters. Opposite the French sectors the Germans had a further 367 aircraft of all types. By 16 March, there were clear indications that the Germans were concentrating their best geschwader to the south of Lille, the normal operating area of Von Richthofen's Jagdgeschwader 1 (JG1). In the evening of 20 March, RFC

observation aircraft returned with the intelligence that enemy troops in the front line opposite the British Third and Fifth Armies were being relieved by fresh units, a sure sign that a major attack was about to develop. Many of the new units had been reassigned from the Eastern Front, where hostilities between Russia and the Central Powers had ceased following the Treaty of Brest-Litovsk, concluded on 2 March 1918.

FURIOUS BARRAGE

At 4.45 am on 21 March 1918, the German artillery opened up with a furious barrage of high explosive and gas shells that pounded the whole length of the British-held front. More than 50 miles of the front, from Monchy to Tergnier, was flooded with poison gas. Long-range artillery was also brought into action, shelling supply dumps and communications centres up to 28 miles to the rear. The German observation aircraft had done their work well; all known or suspected British gun positions had been meticulously plotted and were now attacked with the aim of weakening the defensive shell curtain and counter-battery fire, and all ground likely to be sheltering reserves was heavily shelled. Then, out of the dense mist, advancing

Sopwith Camel F.1

Type: single-seat scout
Country of origin: United Kingdom
Powerplant: one 130hp (96.9kW)
Clerget rotary engine
Performance: maximum speed

115mph (185km/h)
Weights: empty 929lb (421kg);
maximum take-off 1453lb (659kg)
Dimensions: wing span 28ft
(8.53m); length 18ft 9in (5.72m);

height 8ft 6in (2.59m)
Armament: two fixed forward-firing
0.303in (7.7mm) Vickers machine
guns; up to four 25lb (11.3kg)
bombs

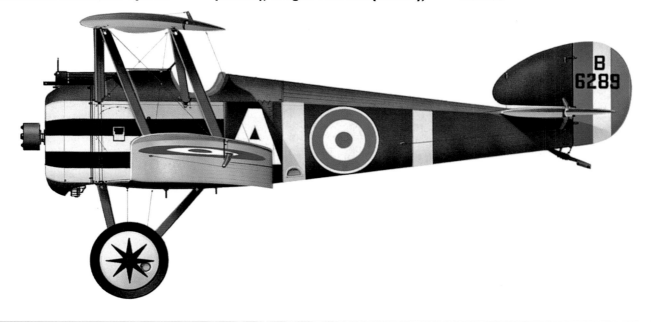

before a creeping barrage of high explosive, 56 German divisions hurled themselves forward to the attack. General Gough's Fifth Army, outnumbered by four to one, was soon reduced to isolated units, pockets of resistance making gallant last stands far behind the forward German echelons, their surviving artillery fighting close-range actions over open sights. For several vital hours neither the men in the forward positions, nor the staff officers at Brigade, Division, Corps and even Army Headquarters had any real idea what was happening. Communications had been severed by the preliminary artillery onslaught; frantic light signals went unobserved in the fog, which also rendered air reconnaissance impossible on Fifth Army's disintegrating front. On the left, General Byng, commanding the Third Army, had slightly better intelligence thanks to the crew of a solitary RE.8 of No 59 Squadron, which took off into the murk as the sun was rising and, flying at almost ground level, was able to monitor the German advance for more than an hour before it was hit and put out of action by a shell.

About mid-morning, the mist thinned sufficiently to allow more reconnaissance sorties to be flown. There followed a

stream of signals from excited RFC crews, indicating a profusion of targets ranging from sunken roads clogged with masses of German infantry to gun batteries being brought into action or moving forward. For the first time, air observation revealed the extent of the disaster that had befallen the two British armies. Every available RFC aircraft that was capable of attacking targets on the ground was thrown into the fray, but operations were hampered throughout 21 March by continual adverse weather, which was worst in the Fifth Army's area. All day long, the aircrews flew though shifting veils of fog and mist that would part briefly for a few seconds to reveal enemy forces pushing relentlessly across country from St Quentin. The squadrons cooperating with the Fifth Army attacked wherever and whenever they were able, while the Corps squadrons did their best to provide the British artillery with worthwhile targets. During the days and weeks that followed, the Allied airmen continued to attack the advancing enemy at every opportunity, and in so doing contributed in no small measure to the eventual halting of the German offensive. And in the midst of it all, there occurred an event that passed virtually unnoticed: on 1 April 1918, the RFC and RNAS

merged to form a single service, the Royal Air Force.

RED BARON

Shortly after ten o'clock in the morning of 21 April, three weeks after the RAF came into being, Rittmeister Freiherr Manfred von Richthofen walked across the grass of Cappy aerodrome, the base of his Jagdgeschwader 1, towards his scarlet-painted Fokker Dr.I Triplane. He had scored his 80th victory the day before. Today, Von Richthofen would be leading two Staffeln of fighters on an offensive patrol over the front line. At 10.30 he was airborne, flying westwards over the valley of the Somme at the head of 15 triplanes. It was not long before they sighted a likely prey in the form of two RE.8 observation aircraft of No 3 Squadron Australian Flying Corps, engaged in counter-battery work. Four triplanes broke away and dived down to attack them through a barrage of fire put up by British anti-aircraft guns.

A couple of miles away, at the head of eight Sopwith Camels of No 209 Squadron RAF, based at Bertangles, a 24-year-old Canadian named Roy Brown, already a veteran with a Distinguished Service Cross and 12 combat victories, saw the white puffs of the shell bursts and turned to investigate. A few moments later he picked out the two RE.s, being severely harassed by the triplanes, and led his fighters at full throttle to their rescue. Overhead, the remaining triplane pilots waited for an opportune moment to dive down and join the fray as soon as the Camels had committed themselves to engaging their four colleagues.

FIRST ACTION

One of the Camel pilots was going into action for the first time. An old school friend of Brown's, his name was Lieutenant Wilfred R. May. Brown had told him not to get mixed up in a general dogfight, if one chanced to develop, but to stay on the fringes and get in a shot if the opportunity presented itself. Now, as he watched the other Camels start their attack, May picked out a Fokker that

■BELOW: Albatros D.Va of Jasta V, Imperial German Military Aviation Service, pictured early in 1918. The D.V/Va suffered from structural weakness of the lower wing spar.

looked like a sitting target and dived after it. He closed on it and opened fire, missing his target by a hopeless margin in his excitement and inexperience. As he tried to correct his aim, his guns jammed; in his enthusiasm he had kept the triggers depressed for too long and the weapons had overheated. He had no alternative but to break off the pursuit and dive away towards the sanctuary of the British lines, again obeying Brown's earlier instructions. From his vantage point above the mêlée, Richthofen had seen the lone Camel break away. It was just the moment he had been waiting for, the kind of situation that had brought him so many victims. Putting his triplane into a shallow dive, he positioned himself on May's tail and gradually overhauled the British aircraft. Up above, Lieutenant Hans Wolff, whose task it was to guard Richthofen's tail at all times, was alarmed on seeing his leader diving towards the British lines and prepared to go after him. At that moment, however, he was attacked by a Camel and had to take evasive action. By the time he had

shaken off his opponent he had lost sight of the scarlet triplane.

The first hint that May had of the doom descending on him was the rattle of Richthofen's machine guns. Later, he confessed to a feeling of sick horror as he twisted in his seat and saw the scarlet triplane only yards behind, the black-helmeted head of its pilot clearly visible behind the gun sight. He flung the Camel into a steep turn but failed to shake off his pursuer; Richthofen was too wily a hand to be thrown off by basic manoeuvres of that sort. High above, Roy Brown, who had been involved in a dogfight with several enemy fighters, suddenly found himself alone. Looking down, he saw May's Camel and the scarlet triplane twisting and weaving along the Somme valley. Without hesitation, he dived down to the aid of his friend. By this time, May was virtually exhausted. Richthofen continued to fire in economical short bursts, his bullets ripping through the fabric of the Camel's wings and sending up flurries of spray from the river below. The speeding

aircraft were now down to less than 200ft (60m) as they flew along the course of the Somme.

STARTLED FEAR

Brown arrived just in time, pulling out of his dive above and slightly to the right of the Fokker. Correcting with rudder, he got the triplane squarely in his sights and opened fire with his twin Vickers. Bullets stitched a trail of holes along the triplane's fuselage. Richthofen looked around, and Brown clearly saw what he took to be an expression of startled fear on the face behind the goggles. A moment later, the German pilot slumped sideways in the cockpit. The Fokker swerved violently, then righted itself and nosed over into a glide. It hit the ground and bounced, shedding a wheel, then slid to a halt the right way up two miles inside the British lines, close to some Australian trenches. Not only Brown had fired at Von Richthofen. Near Corbie, two Australians of the 24th Machine Gun Company – Sergeant C.B. Popkin and Gunner R.F. Weston – had loosed off a

long burst at the triplane as it flew low past them in pursuit of May. A few seconds later, two anti-aircraft Lewis guns of the 53rd Battery, 14th Australian Field Artillery Brigade, manned by Gunners W.J. Evans and R. Buie, had also fired on it. Later, all these men were to claim the credit for shooting down Von Richthofen. The triplane's heavy landing was witnessed by Sergeant-Major J.H. Sheridan of the 3rd Battery, Royal Artillery, who had been watching the chase. Sheridan waited for the German pilot to climb out, but when there was no movement the soldier ran forward and peered into the cockpit. The pilot was slumped forward, his head resting against the breech of one of the Spandau machine guns. One hand still gripped the stick. Blood oozed from his mouth and from a hole in his chest where a bullet had made its exit, having traversed his body after entering the right side. There was no doubt that he was dead.

The next day, a British aircraft flew over the German airfield at Cappy and dropped a message. It read: 'To the German Flying Corps. Rittmeister Baron von Richthofen was killed in aerial combat on 21 April 1918. He was buried with full military honours. From the British Royal Air Force.'

Manfred von Richthofen's body was later removed to a German war cemetery, and in 1925 it was finally laid to rest in Berlin. Roy Brown flew several more missions before being sent to England, where he was admitted to hospital suffering from severe stomach trouble and nervous strain. After the war he went back to Canada and became a businessman. He died in 1944 at the age of 50, having never fully recovered his health. Lieutenant W.R. May went on to score 13 victories and win a Distinguished Flying Cross; he too went back to Canada, where he took up a career in civil aviation. He died in 1952.

Although Roy Brown was officially credited with the killing of Von Richthofen, no one knows to this day whose bullet sent him down; but the identity of whoever killed him is unimportant. What was important was the profound effect that the death of the seemingly invincible Von Richthofen had on millions of Germans, soldiers and civilians alike. According to the German C-in-C, General Ludendorff, the psychological impact of his death was equivalent to the loss of 30 divisions. The Richthofen Geschwader continued to fight

hard under new commanders, but the loss of Von Richthofen's personal leadership was noticeable. For the German Flying Corps, it was as though that day in April 1918 marked the start of the slide into final defeat.

NEW FIGHTERS

Although the morale of the German Flying Corps suffered badly as a result of Von Richthofen's death, the pilots who fought on into the last months of the war had the advantage of new fighter types which, had there been time to produce them in sufficient quantity, would have seen German air power reign supreme.

On 6 May 1918, 16 Spads of Spa.57, led by Lieutenant Jean Chaput, were patrolling in support of the French Eighth Army on the Oise when the Frenchmen encountered a formation of German aircraft of a type they had not seen before. Chaput, who had gained his 16th combat victory on 21 April, the day Von Richthofen was killed, led his pilots into the attack. They claimed five enemy aircraft destroyed, but the encounter left them completely exhausted and they knew that the German type was likely to prove a formidable opponent. One by one the Spad pilots straggled back to base, discovering to their dismay that Jean Chaput was missing. Troops in the French front line reported that they had seen a Spad spiralling down from the combat to make a heavy landing in no-man's land; it was Chaput's machine and the pilot was dead, with three bullets in his body.

The enemy biplane, it turned out, was the Fokker D.VII, the first of a series of new German fighter types. It had its origins late in 1917, at a time when the German Flying Corps was beginning to lose the ascendency and technical superiority it had enjoyed for nearly three years. The German High Command considerd the situation to be so serious that it ordered German aircraft manufacturers to give top priority to the development of new fighters; the prototypes of the various designs would take part in a competitive fly-off at Johannisthal, and the winning firm would receive large production contracts for its aircraft. Anthony Fokker's contender, the D.VII fighter biplane, was completed in November 1917 with rather more haste than its designer would have wished, and a lot of last-minute work had to be done before the aircraft performed to Fokker's satisfaction. It was worth the effort; by the fourth day of the fly-off there was no longer any doubt that the Fokker was by far the best all-round design, superior to the other competitors on every count except, perhaps, rate of climb. The Rumpler D.I tended to lose height in turns at high altitude while the Fokker stayed firmly under control; the Albatros D.VI was almost a duplicate of the earlier D.V and showed no improvement, the Pfalz D.XII showed dangerous structural weaknesses, the Roland-designed LFG D.VI had very poor visibility from the cockpit, and the AEG contender was a hopeless failure all round.

MAJOR ORDERS

Although the fly-off ended with Fokker confident that his D.VII had beaten the other designs hands down, he was astonished when Captain Falkenhayn, adjutant to the German Flying Corps Cin-C General von Höppner, asked him to quote a price for the production of 400 aircraft. Up to that time, the largest order Fokker had received for any of his fighter designs had been for 60 Dr.I triplanes. Recovering himself quickly and doing some fast mental arithmetic, he told the adjutant that the total cost would be ten million marks. Falkenhayn

agreed without hestitation, and told Fokker that the Albatros factory was to build the new aircraft on a royalty basis. Despite all the priority given to the production of the D.VII, however, it took time to set up the necessary machinery, and it was not until the last days of April 1918 that the first examples were delivered to Jagdgeschwader 1, which was now commanded by Captain Wilhelm Reinhard. The new aircraft cost Reinhard his life, for he was accidentally killed while flying one a few days later. So JG.1 received its third and last commanding officer, a leader of proven worth who now had 20 victories to his credit and who wore the Pour le Mérite: Hermann Göring.

For the other contenders in the fighter competition, there was a small consolation; pre-production orders were awarded to the respective companies for 50 examples each of the Rumpler D.I and the Roland D.VI, while Pfalz received an order for the construction of 200 D.XIIs.

BEST FIGHTER

Another firm that received a small order was the Siemens-Schuckert Werke (SSW), who were contracted to build 60 examples of their D.III scout. Believed by some German pilots to be the best fighter at

Siemens-Schukert D.III

Type: single-seat fighting scout
Country of origin: Germany
Powerplant: one 200hp (150kW) SuH Sh.IIIa rotary piston engine
Performance: maximum speed
112mph (180km/h)
Weights: empty 1177lb (534kg); maximum take-off 1598lb (725kg)
Dimensions: wing span 27ft 8in (8.43m); length 18ft 8in (6.7m);
height 9ft 2in (2.8m)
Armament: two 7.92mm (0.31in) LMG 08/15 machine guns

the front in the summer of 1918, the SSW D.III was a stubby, compact little biplane of wooden construction powered by a 160hp (119.3kW) Siemens-Halske rotary engine. During flight trials in October 1917, the prototype D.III had reached a level speed of 112mph (180km/h) and climbed to 19,600ft (5974m) in less than 20 minutes, a performance which justified its being ordered into immediate production. At the same time, the IDFLIEG – Inspektion der Fliegertruppen – placed small orders for two further developments, the D.IV and D.V.

The first batch of 30 SSW D.III scouts was delivered for operational trials in January 1918, and in February the IDFLIEG ordered 30 more aircraft. Beginning in late April, 41 examples were allocated to operational units on the Western Front; most of these went to JG.2, which equipped its Jasta 15 with the type. The pilots were delighted with the new aircraft, and a typical verdict on the SSW D.III was that it was highly sensitive on the controls, possessed excellent flying qualities and climbed like a rocket.

One German ace who was a firm advocate of the SSW D.III was Captain Rudolf Berthold, a talented pilot who had begun his combat career with Fliegerabteilung 23 in 1916, scoring his first victories while flying a Fokker Monoplane. He survived a series of close shaves – including a tricky forced landing after a fight with three B.E.2cs and a crash while testing a Pfalz Scout – and in October 1916, while commanding Jasta 14, he gained his 10th victory and was awarded the Pour le Mérite. In August 1917 he assumed command of Jasta 18, and in one month he destroyed 14 RFC aircraft before being shot down himself and severely wounded in the right arm. Returning to action in the spring of 1918, he took command of JG.2, which comprised Jastas 12, 13, 15 and 19. When JG.2 received the Fokker D.VII, he had his aircraft specially modified so that he could fly and fight with his one good hand and the limited use of the other. He was in constant pain from his injury and his determination was greatly admired by his fellow pilots, who nicknamed him the 'Iron Knight'. His

■ABOVE: A Spad XIII C1 of the Escadrille Lafayette (SPA 124), the American volunteer unit operating with the French Aviation Militaire. They were also supplied to the Italian Air Arm.

SSW D.III, which he tested in action during the first weeks of May 1918, was distinctively painted with a red and blue engine cowling and a flaming sword insignia.

MODIFICATIONS
On 23 May 1918, Berthold submitted a report on the aircraft's engine performance to the IDFLIEG, as a result of which the SSW D.IIIs then serving with the Jastas were withdrawn from front-line service at the end of May and returned to the Siemens-Schuckert factory for airframe and engine modifications. It was to be two months before they were returned to operational service, and then they were used mainly for home defence duties. Jasta 15 reverted to the Fokker D.VII, and it was while flying one of these, on 10 August 1918, that Rudolf Berthold scored his last two victories, bringing his total to 44.

Soon afterwards, in a fight with Sopwith Camels, he was shot down and sustained more injuries; he survived them only to be murdered by German communists in Harburg on 15 December 1919.

Another Fokker design of 1918 that at first appeared to show much promise was the E.V. A very simple design, it had a one-piece cantilever parasol wing and twin Spandau machine guns mounted immediately in front of the cockpit. Production E.Vs were delivered to the German Flying Corps from July 1918, but in August Jasta 6, one of the first units to receive the type, experienced three serious crashes due to wing structural failure. Imperfect timber and faulty manufacturing methods were found to have been the cause, but 60 aircraft were immobilised in the factory while investigations were carried out and it was not until September that production was started again, the type now bearing the designation Fokker D.VIII. It was more manoeuvrable than the D.VII biplane and had a better operational ceiling, although it was slightly slower. Only about 90 had been delivered by the end of the war and, although its pilots reported that it handled well, it had little chance to prove itself in action.

POTENT WEAPON

On 12 August, No 43 Squadron at Fienvillers became the first RAF unit in France to receive a fighter that was at last capable of meeting the German Flying Corps' Fokker D.VIIs and Siemens-Schuckert D.IIIs on more than equal terms – the Sopwith Snipe. Conceived in 1917 as a replacement for the Camel, six prototypes of the Snipe had been ordered in the autumn of that year, but a number of modifications had proven necessary and it was not until the spring of 1918 that the Snipe entered production. With 230hp (171.5kW) available from its very reliable Bentley BR2 rotary engine the Snipe was a potent weapon for its day, although, like the Camel, it was by no means easy to handle. Standard armament comprised two synchronised Vickers guns mounted in front of the cockpit. With a top speed of over 120mph (193km/h), an operational ceiling of more than 19,500ft (5944m) and an endurance of three hours, it showed a marked improvement in performance over the Camel. Visibility from the cockpit was better, too, a vital asset from the pilot's point of view. Number 43 Squadron was eventually to receive 24 aircraft, but it would be the middle of September before the last one was

■ABOVE: A sound and strong design, the Pfalz D.XII entered service in September 1918, but its exploits were eclipsed by those of the more numerous Fokker D.VII.

delivered and so, as the new aircraft were initially permitted to fly only defensive patrols on the British side of the lines, the Camels and the SE.5s continued to bear the brunt of fighter operations. This period saw the loss of the RAF's leading air ace, Major Edward 'Mick' Mannock, and of his former rival Major James McCudden. Mannock, who had 73 victories and who would probably have gone on to surpass Von Richthofen's total, was shot down and killed on 26 July 1918 by ground fire, while McCudden was killed in an accident a couple of weeks earlier, on 8 July. In the Aviation Militaire, Rene Fonck had surpassed all others to become France's 'Ace of Aces'; he would end the war with 75 kills to his credit.

AMERICAN ENTRY

In the summer of 1918 the British and French squadrons were joined by a powerful new ally. Although American volunteer airmen – the most famous of whom was Raoul Lufbery, with 17 victories when he was killed in May 1918

– had been fighting alongside the French since 1916, with the Escadrille Lafayette, and two other all-American squadrons were formed within the RFC/RAF, it was not until the summer of 1918 that the American 1st Pursuit Group in France reached its full operational level of five squadrons.

Equipped initially with Nieuport 28s and later with Spads, the Americans came into their own in support of a massive Anglo-French offensive east of Amiens that began on 8 August, a date later described by General Ludendorff as 'the black day of the German Army'. The German Flying Corps suffered appalling losses during those crucial days of August 1918. Among the pilots killed was Erich Löwenhardt, commanding Jasta 10 of JG.1, who by the beginning of August had 53 victories, making him the third-ranking German ace. He was shot down on the morning of 10 August by Captain

■BELOW: Mute testimony to the ravages of war and the high casualty rate of fighter pilots, the remains of a French aircraft lie amid the shattered trees of Houthulst Forest.

Henry Burden of No 56 Squadron during a fight between that unit's SE.5s and JG.1's D.VIIs. Burden shot down two more enemy aircraft that morning, and two more later in the day. RAF pilots reported that the elite German fighter units appeared to have thrown caution to the winds in their attempts to establish air superiority over the battlefront; this was later confirmed by the biographer of Hermann Göring, who wrote that 'with a real contempt for death, the Geschwader suffered terrible losses owing to its reckless behaviour'. By 11 August the Allied offensive had begun to falter as German resistance stiffened, but it had already cost the enemy 22,000 prisoners and 400 artillery pieces. In the air fighting, the recently blooded United States Army Air Service combat squadrons were increasingly active, and their leading fighter pilots were fast emerging. Foremost among them was Lieutenant Edward V. Rickenbacker, who had several victories to his credit by the time the First Pursuit Group rearmed with Spads in August, and who would end the war with a confirmed score of 26. One of the most creditable achievements

by an American pilot during the month, however, was on the first day, when Lt Donald Hudson of the 27th Aero Squadron destroyed three enemy aircraft.

BITTER FIGHTING

For the German Flying Corps, the introduction of new types in the early summer of 1918 came too late. The will to fight was still there, but the economic resources to sustain it were not.

But any illusion the Allies might have harboured about the war coming to a rapid end was soon to be dispelled, for the late summer and early autumn months of 1918 witnessed some of the most bitter and bloody fighting in the history or air warfare. With the failure of their spring offensives, the Germans could no longer hope for an overhelming victory. Their fight now was to preserve the integrity of the German Empire, to beat the Allied armies to a standstill, and to secure an honourable peace. They achieved none of these aims; and when the Armistice was concluded in November, the crushing terms it imposed upon defeated Germany served only to sow the seeds of another war.

CHAPTER 2
FROM BIPLANE TO JET: 1919–39

The end of World War I did little to slacken the pace of aircraft development, and the interwar years saw fighter aircraft built out of stronger materials, powered by more powerful engines, and carrying heavier armament.

The four years of World War I marked history's greatest technological leap forward in terms of military hardware. Yet, almost before the guns had ceased firing, the victorious Allies began dismantling their respective military assets without much thought for the needs of tomorrow. In Britain's case, powerful lobbies in the Admiralty and the War Office almost succeeded in engineering the demise of the Royal Air Force as an independent organisation and in subordinating British air power to the Army and Navy; that they failed to do so was mainly due to the determination of the Chief of the Air Staff, Sir Hugh Trenchard. By 1921 the strength of the RAF was at a very low ebb, with only 24 squadrons of all types at home and abroad (including a solitary fighter squadron in the United Kingdom), but in April 1922 a defence sub-committee recommended the force's expansion to 52 squadrons, totalling some 500 aircraft – later increased to 600 – for home defence. The re-equipment programme had to start from scratch, and to fulfil the air defence role it was decided to standardise on the Sopwith Snipe, the fighter designed during the closing months of World War I to replace the Camel.

FIRST SQUADRON

The first squadron to equip fully with Snipes was No 29, which re-formed at Duxford on 1 April 1923. By the end of the year the fighter strength available for the air defence of Great Britain stood

■ **LEFT: Heinkel He 51 fighters lined up at Dortmund in May 1936. The He 51 performed well initially with the Kondor Legion in Spain, but was outclassed by the Russian I-15.**

at 11 squadrons, equipped predominantly with Snipes. It was still a long way from the planned total of 52 squadrons. It was also clear that the Snipe, although invaluable as an interim aircraft, was quickly approaching obsolescence, and steps were taken to rearm the fighter squadrons with post-war designs at an early date. The first such design was the Gloster Grebe, a product of the Gloucestershire Aircraft Company, whose chief designer was H.P. Folland. Folland had previously worked for the Nieuport and General Aircraft Co, which had been set up in Britain late in 1916 to license-build the fighter designs of the French company. In 1917 the British-based firm began to design its own fighters, the first of which was the Nighthawk. Although it never went into service with the RAF, the Nighthawk deserves its place in history as the first British fighter to be powered by a stationary radial engine instead of the more common rotary type. The Grebe prototype was originally ordered as a Nighthawk; it made its first public appearance at the RAF Air Pageant, Hendon, in June 1923 and entered RAF service with No 111 Squadron in October that year, subsequently equipping five more RAF fighter squadrons. One of them, No 25 Squadron, subsequently became famous for its spectacular aerobatic displays in the mid-1920s. Despite early problems with wing flutter, the Grebe was a highly manoeuvrable and robust little aircraft, and was the first British machine to survive a terminal velocity dive, reaching 240mph (386km/h). Grebes also took part in some interesting experiments; one involved the release of a pair of aircraft from beneath the airship R.33 in October 1926.

Sopwith 7F1 Snipe

Type: single-seat scout
Country of origin: United Kingdom
Powerplant: one 230hp (171.5kW)
Bentley BR.2 nine-cylinder rotary
engine

Performance: maximum speed
119mph (192km/h)
Weights: empty 1312lb (595kg);
maximum take-off 2020lb (916kg)
Dimensions: wing span 30ft 1in

(9.17m) length 19ft 9in (6.02m);
height 8ft 9in (2.67m)
Armament: two fixed forward-firing
0.303in (7.7mm) Vickers machine
guns

FIRST HAWKER FIGHTERS

Although the Grebe replaced the Sopwith Snipe in some first-line RAF squadrons, the true successor to the Snipe was the Hawker Woodcock, the H.G.Hawker Engineering Company having re-established Sopwith's former aviation enterprises. The Hawker Company's early activities involved refurbishing Snipes and Camels for sale overseas. The first of its own designs, the Duiker parasol monoplane, was unsuccessful, but the Woodcock single-seat fighter was accepted after lengthy trials and was delivered to No 3 Squadron in May 1925, becoming the first new British fighter to enter production after the end of World War I. The Woodcock only equipped one other RAF squadron, No 17, but a version of it known as the Danecock (or Dankok) served with the Danish Army and Naval Air Services until 1937. It was at this juncture that the Hawker design office accepted the services of Sydney Camm, who had previously worked for Martinsyde Aircraft Ltd. Later, Camm was to be responsible for one of the most famous fighters of all time, the Hawker Hurricane. In common with other aircraft manufacturers of the 1920s, Hawker produced a series of aircraft prototypes

that covered the whole spectrum of military and naval requirements at that time. Among them were the Hornbill fighter, which had mixed wood and metal construction and which reached a speed of 200mph (322km/h) in 1926 with a 690hp (514.5kW) Rolls-Royce Condor engine, the Hawker Hawfinch, which set trends for several other biplane fighter designs; and the Heron, the first fighter to use the patent all-metal construction evolved by Sydney Camm and works director Fred Sigrist.

From the Gloster stable, the Grebe was followed by the Gamecock, which first flew in February 1925 and equipped five RAF fighter squadrons, beginning with No 23 in May 1925. The Gamecock's service life was relatively short-lived. This was partly because of an abnormally high accident rate; of 90 Gamecock Is that were built, 22 were lost in spinning or landing accidents. The Snipe, Grebe, Woodcock and Gamecock were for the most part replaced in service by the Armstrong Whitworth Siskin IIIA. The first Siskin IIIs, in fact, were delivered to No 41 Squadron at Northolt in May 1924, and a month later to No 111 Squadron at Duxford. These were the only two units to use the early mark, but the Siskin IIIA,

with a more powerful engine and a number of aerodynamic refinements, began to replace the Snipes of No 1 Squadron and the Grebes of No 56 from mid-1927. The type subsequently equipped nine RAF fighter squadrons, all in the United Kingdom.

FRENCH THREAT

The expansion of the Royal Air Force towards the planned target of 52 squadrons was dictated, apart from economic considerations, by the activities of the French. In the late 1920s, an emasculated Germany was not regarded as a serious threat, but the idea of France, a mere 21 miles (34km) away across the English Channel, possessing a larger and more effective air force than Britain's was unthinkable. The speed of formation of new RAF squadrons was therefore dictated by the need to match the French in air matters, and when the expansion of the French Air Force slowed down, so did that of the RAF. The original target date for the 52-squadron force was 1930, but by 1927 this had been put back to 1936, and in 1929 it was again postponed to 1938. As far as the home defence fighter squadrons were concerned, the principal fighter type during the first three years of the 1930s was the Bristol Bulldog, which equipped ten squadrons and, with a top speed of 180mph (289km/h) was much faster than the fighters it replaced. Its contemporary was the Hawker Fury, the epitome of British fighter biplane design and one of the most beautiful aircraft ever built. The first of 118 Fury Mk Is entered service with No 43 Squadron at Tangmere in May 1931, and the type also served with Nos 1 and 25 Squadrons. Further development of a version known as the High Speed Fury led to a production order for 23 Fury Mk IIs, followed by another 75, and the first of these entered service with No 25 Squadron in December 1936, also serving with four more squadrons of what was, by then, RAF Fighter Command.

Other fighter units in the early 1930s were equipped with the Hawker Demon, a fighter variant of the Hart light bomber; 244 Demons were built for the RAF in the United Kingdom, serving with six Regular and five Auxiliary Air Force squadrons.

LAST BIPLANES
The Bulldog was replaced in RAF service by the Gloster Gauntlet, the last of the RAF's open-cockpit fighter biplanes. It was an ironic state of affairs, because the prototype Gauntlet, which had first flown in 1928, had shown an inferior performance to the Bulldog and another contender, the Hawker Hawfinch, and the Bulldog had been chosen in preference. Glosters, however, had proceeded with the development of the Gauntlet as a private venture, refitting it with a 640hp (477.2kW) Bristol Mercury engine, and this gave it a top speed of 230mph (370km/h), well in excess of the Bulldog's. Production orders were placed, and the Gauntlet Mk I entered service with No 19 Squadron in May 1935. The Gauntlet Mk II, with an uprated Mercury engine, began to enter service a year later, and at the peak of its service in the spring of 1937 it equipped 14 home-based fighter squadrons. Meanwhile, Glosters had been pursuing the development of a refined private successor to the Gauntlet, developed to Air Ministry Specification F7/30. Designated SS.37, the prototype was flown in September 1934 and evaluated by the Air Ministry in the following year, the trials resulting in a production order for 23 machines. These were powered by 840hp (626.3kW) Mercury IXS engines and were armed with four Vickers machine guns; they were given the RAF name Gladiator.

First deliveries were made to No 27 Squadron at Tangmere in February 1937, and the type went on to equip eight squadrons of Fighter Command. The Gladiator, the last of the RAF's biplane fighters, although outclassed by German and Italian monoplane fighters, was to render gallant service during the early months of the war in both Europe and the Middle East.

NAVAL FIGHTERS
While the RAF struggled to hold its own in the early 1920s, the Royal Navy had also been striving to keep alive the Fleet Air Arm (which until 1924 was the shipborne component of the RAF). The RN's first post-World-War-I fighter was the Gloster Nightjar, one of a series of aircraft derived from the Nighthawk. Twenty-two were built, and were replaced in 1923 by the Fairey Flycatcher, a highly popular little aircraft that was to remain in service for 11 years. Although the initial production order was for only nine aircraft, subsequent contracts brought the final number produced to 193 aircraft. Flycatchers were delivered to eight fighter flights, serving aboard the aircraft carriers *Argus*, *Courageous*, *Eagle*, *Furious* and *Hermes* in many parts of the world, as well as on shore stations.

Armstrong Whitworth Siskin IIIA

Type: single-seat fighter biplane
Country of origin: United Kingdom
Powerplant: one 420hp (313kW) Armstrong Siddeley Jaguar IV
Performance: maximum level
speed 156mph (251km/h)
Weights: empty 2061lb (935kg); maximum take-off 3012lb (1366kg)
Dimensions: wing span 33ft 2in (10.11m); length 25ft 4in (7.72m);
height 10ft 2in (3.1m)
Armament: two fixed .0303in (7.62mm) machine guns

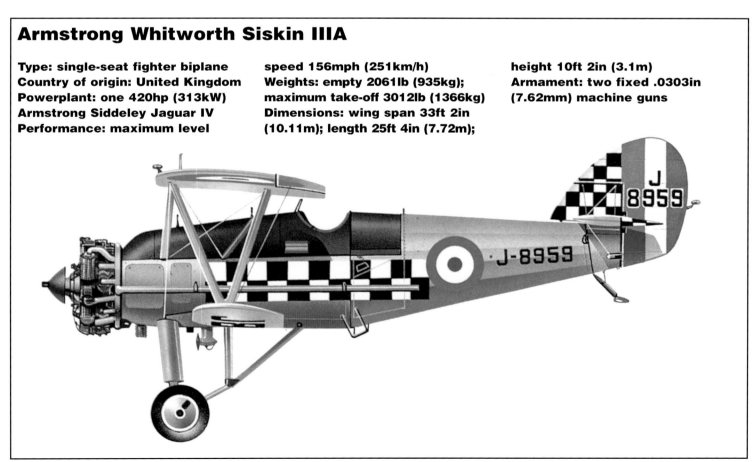

The Flycatcher was selected in preference to a rival, the Parnell Plover, even though the latter was in many ways the better aircraft, with much cleaner lines and a higher maximum speed. Ten Plovers were built in 1923 and served with the Fleet Air Arm for a short period. In 1932, as a replacement for the Flycatcher, the FAA received its first batch of Hawker Nimrod fighters, the Nimrod being the naval version of the RAF's Fury. The first FAA Fighter Flight to be armed with the Nimrod was No 408, operating from the carrier HMS *Glorious* in the Mediterranean. Nimrods equipped four Fighter Flights in all, each flight having six aircraft. Production totalled 54 Nimrod Mk Is and 31 Mk IIs. A contemporary aircraft with the Nimrod was the Hawker Osprey, the naval

equivalent of the Hart, which was used in the fighter-reconnaissance role. The Fleet Air Arm received 37 Osprey Mk Is, 14 Mk IIs, 52 Mk IIIs which had metal propellers, and 26 Mk IVs with uprated engines. From April 1933, when the Fighter Flights were amalgamated to form four squadrons, each squadron operated a mix of Nimrods and Ospreys; for example, No 800 Squadron, formed by the amalgamation of Nos 402 and 404 Flights, operated nine Nimrods and three Ospreys.

FRENCH EXPANSION
Like the RAF, France's Aviation Militaire had been subjected to severe post-war cuts. In November 1918, the service possessed 3222 first-line aircraft in 247 escadrilles, but by 1 January 1920 the

number of escadrilles had been reduced to 135, grouped into regiments. The emphasis was on army cooperation regiments, of which there were nine; there were three fighter regiments, each with nine escadrilles. In 1923, following some reorganisation, the number of fighter regiments was cut to two, equipped with Nieuport-Delage NiD-29s and Spad 81s. One of the most widely used fighters of the post-World-War-I era, the NiD-29 had its origin in a requirement of September 1918, and was the first of Gustave Delage's designs for

■BELOW: Line-up of Gloster Gauntlets, the last of the RAF's open-cockpit fighter biplanes. At the peak of its service the Gauntlet equipped 14 RAF home-based fighter squadrons.

Fiat CR.20bis

Type: single-seat fighter biplane
Country of origin: Italy
Powerplant: one 410hp (305.7kW) Fiat A.20 12-cylinder V-type engine

Performance: maximum speed 161mph (260km/h)
Weights: empty 2138lb (970kg); maximum take-off 3064lb (1390kg)
Dimensions: wing span 32ft 1in

(9.80m); length 22ft (6.71m); height 9ft 1in (2.79m)
Armament: two fixed forward-firing 0.303in (7.7mm) Vickers machine guns

the Nieuport company to dispense with a rotary engine. Instead of opting for an air-cooled radial engine, as did most designers of the time, Delage designed his fighter round the V-type Hispano-Suiza motor, which had proved very successful in the wartime Spad fighters. In its original form, the Nieuport 29 was capable of a maximum speed of 146mph (235km/h). The aircraft did not begin its acceptance trials until the end of 1918, and was therefore too late to see service in World War I; moreover, the original aircraft failed to meet the altitude requirement of 29,930ft (9122m), which was only achieved by a second prototype in June 1919. This aircraft was ordered into production as the NiD-29C1. Over 250 examples were built for the Aviation Militaire, equipping 25 escadrilles at their peak. The type also formed the main fighter element of the Belgian and Italian air arms in the 1920s; it was also produced under licence by Nakajima under the designation Ko-4 for the Imperial Japanese Army Air Force, 602 being built. The NiD-29 was gradually replaced by the NiD-62C1, which began to enter squadron service in 1927 and which by 1932 equipped about two-thirds of the French fighter escadrilles.

The other French fighter type of the early 1920s, the Spad 81, served in much smaller numbers than the NiD-29C1, only 90 being issued to the Aviation Militaire. It was, in fact, a lower-powered version of the Spad 61, which flew for the first time in November 1923. The Spad 61 never served with the Aviation Militaire, but 250 were produced for Poland and 100 for Romania.

In 1923 the French designer Michel Wibault, whose first fighter aircraft had been a 1917 prototype biplane, produced the Wibault 7, a strut-braced parasol-wing monoplane with a radial engine. Designed for high altitude interception, it was a metal-framed aircraft with fabric-covered surfaces. The Wibault 7 had an excellent rate of climb, being able to reach 13,123ft (4000m) in just under 11 minutes. Sixty production Wibault 72s were ordered by the Aviation Militaire, the first entering service in 1926. The Wibault 74 and 75 were naval versions of the 72, being fitted with deck arrester gear for service aboard the aircraft carrier Bearn. Eighteen of each version were completed, and served until 1934. The final French fighter type of the 1920s was the Loire-Gourdou-Lesseure LGL-32C1, 320 of which were built for the Aviation Militaire. The first production examples began to enter service late in 1927, equipping 12 escadrilles, and for the next seven years the LGL-32,

Polikarpov I-15

Type: single-seat biplane fighter
Country of origin: USSR
Powerplant: one 750hp (559.2kW)
M-25B 9-cylinder radial engine
Performance: maximum speed
230mph (370km/h)
Weights: empty 2888lb (1310kg);
maximum take-off 3814lb (1730kg)
Dimensions: wing span 33ft 5in
(10.20m); length 20ft 9in (6.33m);
height 7ft 2in (2.19m)
Armament: four fixed forward-
firing 7.62mm (0.3in) machine
guns, plus 220lb (100kg) of
external ordnance

together with the NiD-62 and the
Wibault 72, formed the entire first-line
fighter strength in metropolitan France.

ITALIAN FIGHTERS

During World War I, Italy's Corpo
Aeronautica Militare had relied heavily
on French-designed combat aircraft, with
the exception of bombers and naval types.
The first Italian-designed fighter, the
Ansaldo A1 Balilla (Hunter), did not
enter service until 1918, and only a small
number of the 108 aircraft built reached
the front-line squadrons. At the time of
the Armistice, 1683 aircraft of all types
were in first-line Italian service.
Afterwards, there was a period of decline
that lasted until 1923, when the Regia
Aeronautica came into being and the
aircraft industry became geared up to
meet the demands of Benito Mussolini's
new fascist government. Inspired by
dreams of creating a new Roman Empire,
one of Mussolini's foremost aims was to
build up Italy's military forces to
formidable strength. Italy was, in fact,
the first of the European powers to
launch a determined policy of
rearmament and, the aviation industry,
building on the lessons of World War I,
produced a number of practical combat

aircraft designs which were to give
excellent service throughout the 1920s.
The first standard fighter of Italian
design to enter service after World War I
was the Fiat CR.1 (the initials being
those of its designer, Celestino Rosatelli),
the development of which began in 1923.
About 100 CR.1s were built, and these
began to enter service in 1924–25 with
units of the 1st Fighter Group, based in
Italy. In all, 240 CR.1s were ordered, and
by 1926 12 fighter squadrons were armed
with the type. Rosatelli followed up the
CR.1 with the CR.20, which flew in June
1926 and had improved reliability,
manoeuvrability and structural strength.
It had a lengthy career, more than 670
aircraft being produced over a seven-year
period. The CR.20 was Fiat's first all-
metal fighter; in the tactical role it saw
action against dissident tribesmen in
Libya and, towards the end of its career,
it was used in support of Italy's invasion
of Abyssinia (Ethiopia) in 1935–36. Its
successor was the Fiat CR.30, which first
flew on 5 March 1932 and which was
designed in response to a requirement
issued by the Italian Air Minister, Italo
Balbo, for a 'super fighter'. The first of
121 CR.30s was delivered in the spring of
1934, but the type was soon superseded

by the more refined CR.32, which made
its appearance in 1933. It was
considerably faster than the CR.30 and
more manoeuvrable. Total production of
the CR.32 amounted to 1212 aircraft.

THE RED AIR FLEET

The expansion of the Soviet Union's
military aviation resources began in
1922, with clandestine German help.
Under the terms of an agreement
negotiated between Leon Trotsky, the
Soviet Commissar for War, and General
von Seeckt, Commander of the German
Reichswehr, hundreds of German
personnel were secretly sent to the Soviet
Union to build aircraft production
facilities and to train Soviet personnel.
Several joint German–Soviet military
exercises were held, involving the
widespread use of aircraft; the lessons
that emerged enabled the Red Air Fleet's
planners to draw up a manual of air
fighting, based largely on the tactics
evolved by the Germans in World War I.
At Fili, near Moscow, an aircraft factory
was established under the direction of
Hugo Junkers, and Andrei N. Tupolev
was appointed as chief designer. In 1927,
after designing a number of general-
purpose types, Tupolev produced the

ANT-4, a twin-engined bomber and reconnaissance aircraft known as the TB-1 in Red Air Fleet service; it was the progenitor of an unbroken line of Tupolev bombers that continues into the 21st century. Next came the ANT-5, an all-metal sesquiplane fighter conceived by Tupolev, Pavel O. Sukhoi and Vladimir Petlyakov. By this time, Tupolev had established a firm reputation as a pioneer in all-metal construction, and the ANT-5, known as the I-4 in Air Fleet service, was the first Russian fighter built in this way. A single-seater with a fixed undercarriage, the I-4 was built of Kolchugalumin, a type of duralumin produced by the Kolchuga factories. With a maximum speed of 170mph (273km/h) the I-4 was superior to all other contemporary Russian fighter designs, and quantity production continued for several years after 1928, the total number built being around 370. Several different versions of the I-4 were produced, including a twin-cannon

■BELOW: The high performance of the Curtiss Hawk racing aircraft led to orders for an armed version, the P-6. Final variant for the US Army Air Corps was the P-6E, seen here.

variant, a seaplane variant and a version fitted with six solid fuel rockets for short take-off.

SUCCESSFUL DESIGNER

The other very successful Soviet aircraft designer of this period, Nikolai N. Polikarpov, produced a single-seat fighter, the I-3, in 1927. In 1929 he modified the basic design and produced the DI-2 two-seat fighter, which had an armament of three machine guns, one in the nose and two on a movable mount in the rear cockpit. In the spring of 1930 Polikarpov, in collaboration with Dmitri Grigorovitch, produced the I-5, a single-seat biplane fighter with exceptional manoeuvrability and an armament of four PV-1 machine guns with a rate of fire of 800–900 rounds per minute. Polikarpov conceived this aircraft in prison, where he and Grigorovitch found themselves for a short time after being charged with sabotage during the first of Stalin's infamous purges. The prototype flew in April 1930, and about 800 I-5s were subsequently built. In 1932 Grigorovitch produced a design of his own, the I-6 single-seat biplane, a very light and manoeuvrable fighter with a maximum speed of 200mph (322km/h). He then produced a two-seat

biplane fighter, the DI-3, characterised by its twin fins and rudders; it was fitted with a 600hp (447.4kW) M-17 engine and three 0.30in (7.62mm) machine guns. The I-7, which appeared shortly afterwards, was a landplane version of a proposed floatplane fighter for the Soviet Naval Aviation, which in fact was not built. Speed of the I-7 was 210mph (338km/h), and the aircraft was armed with four 7.62mm (0.30in) machine guns. The years (1930–33) saw the appearance of three more fighter designs which never left the drawing board. These were the twin-engined I-9, which was to have been fitted with two 480hp (358kW) M-22 engines, giving it an estimated maximum speed of 215mph (346km/h); the I-10 single-seat gull-wing monoplane with a 625hp (466kW) M-25 radial engine and an estimated top speed of 220mph (354km/h); and the I-11, a Polikarpov biplane with an 820hp (611.5kW) AM-34A in-line engine, also with an estimated top speed of 220mph.

POLIKARPOV'S LAST BIPLANES

In 1933 Polikarpov designed the I-13 biplane, forerunner of the famous I-15, which made its first flight in October of that year. The I-15 was a biplane with a

Boeing PW-9C

Type: single-seat biplane fighter
Country of origin: USA
Powerplant: one 435hp (324.3kW) Curtiss D-12D 12-cylinder V-type engine

Performance: maximum speed 158mph (254km/h)
Weights: empty 2400lb (1082kg); maximum take-off 3170lb (1438kg)
Dimensions: wing span 32ft 0in

(9.75m); length 23ft 1in (7.04m); height 8ft 8in (2.64m)
Armament: one 0.50in (12.7mm) and one 0.30in (7.62mm) machine gun in upper front fuselage

fixed undercarriage; the upper wing was gull-shaped, giving an excellent view forwards and upwards. It was fitted with a 750hp (559.2kW) M-25 engine (the licence-built version of the American Wright Cyclone), which gave it a top speed of 220mph (354km/h). It was armed with four 0.30in (7.62mm) machine guns and there was provision for light bombs in racks under the wings. In 1934, the I-15 was followed by the I-15bis, with an improved M-25V engine that raised its top speed to 230mph (370km/h). In a bid to raise the speed still further, Polikarpov then produced the I-153, which featured a retractable undercarriage, but the maximum speed of the early I-153s (240mph/386km/h) was still insufficient when compared with that of the new fighter aircraft which were beginning to enter service with the principal European air forces. The M-25V engine was consequently replaced by an M-62R developing 1000hp (745.7kW), and then by a 1000hp M-63, which raised the I-153's speed to its ultimate of 265mph (426km/h). The I-153, dubbed Chaika (Seagull) because of its distinctive wing shape, was a first-rate combat aircraft and was subsequently to prove its worth in air fighting, being able to out-turn almost every aircraft that opposed it in action. It was armed with four ShKAS 7.62mm (0.30in) synchronised machine

guns, and could carry a light bomb load or six RS-82 air-to-ground rockets. It was the last single-seat fighter biplane to be series-produced in the Soviet Union.

US ARMY AIR SERVICE

The US Army Air Service (USAAS), under the command of General William Mitchell, had ended the war with 45 squadrons, 740 aircraft, 800 pilots and 500 observers. From May 1918 it had enjoyed a brief period of autonomy as a separate Service, following the RAF's example, but in June 1920 it came back under direct command of the US Army. In that year, Congress cut defence spending and reduced the USAAS to 27 squadrons, instead of the 87 which had been planned. In December 1925 a special board convened by President Calvin Coolidge rejected the idea of a separate air force, but recommended that the Air Service be upgraded to Corps status, with the appointment of an Assistant Secretary of War for Air. On 2 July 1926 Congress passed the Air Corps Act, creating the US Army Air Corps, with an increased budget designed to bring USAAC strength to 1800 aircraft within five years. In fact, 12 years were to pass before that target was reached. In 1926, out of a total of 1400 aircraft available on paper, only 78 were pursuit (fighter) types and 59 were bombers; the

remainder were training, observation and general purpose aircraft. In the fighter category, one of the first aircraft to enter service was the Boeing PW-9 (the designation signifying Pursuit, Water-cooled engine), a small and manoeuvrable machine powered by a 435hp (324.4kW) Curtiss V-12 engine. Developed as a private venture under the designation Boeing Model 15, the prototype flew for the first time on 29 April 1923 and was evaluated by the USAAC, which placed its first production orders, totalling 30 aircraft, in 1924. Deliveries of these aircraft to USAAC units in Hawaii and the Philippines began in October 1925. Twenty-five more fighters, incorporating minor modifications, were ordered as PW-9As; these were followed by 15 PW-9Bs (which were actually completed as part of a batch of 40 PW-9Cs and 16

■BELOW: One of the most beautiful fighter aircraft ever, the Hawker Fury entered service with No 43 Squadron at Tangmere in May 1931. The major production version was the Fury II.

PW-9Ds), which featured refinements such as wheel brakes and an increased rudder area.

TRANS-AMERICA FLIGHT
Contemporary with the PW-9 was the Curtiss P-1, which stemmed from the PW-8, 25 of which were built for the USAAS. On 23 June 1924, Lt Russell Maughan of the USAAS made a dawn-to-dusk transcontinental flight across the USA in one of these machines. Fifteen P-1s were ordered initially, their design being based on the XPW-8B, which had tapered upper and lower wings. The P-1 was the first of the famous Curtiss Hawk series of fighters, the USAAC acquiring 25 P-1As, 25 P-1Bs and 33 P-1Cs from 1924. In 1928, two aircraft were modified and, designated XP-6 and XP-6A, took part in the National Air Races, the winner registering 201mph (323km/h). This achievement led the US Army to order 18 fighter variants (nine YP-6s and nine P-6As).

Successive modifications produced the P-6D and the final Hawk variant, the P-6E,

46 of which were delivered in 1932. Boeing, meanwhile, had offered the USAAC a military version of its F4B biplane fighter, developed for the US Navy; this was at first rejected, but the Navy's reports on the performance of the F4B were so glowing that the Army ordered nine examples under the designation P-12, plus a tenth aircraft, the XP-12A, which had a modified undercarriage and ailerons. In all, the USAAC took delivery of 90 P-12Bs, 96 P-12Cs, 110 P-12Es, which entered service in 1931 with more powerful engines and a metal fuselage; and 25 P-12Fs, which again had uprated engines. But for the Army Air Corps, the day of the biplane fighter was fast approaching its end.

FIGHTERS FOR THE FLEET
In early 1925, the US Navy placed an order for 16 examples of the Boeing PW-9, which were delivered later that year under the designation FB-1. These aircraft were not adapted for carrier use and were deployed to US Marine Corps units operating in China. With the

installation of arrester gear on two more aircraft, for carrier trials on the USS *Langley*, the designation was changed to FB-2; the FB-3 and FB-4 were modifications leading to the major production version, the FB-5. This variant flew for the first time in October 1926 and 27 examples were built, all being delivered in January 1927 for service with two US Navy squadrons, two on the USS *Langley* and two aboard the USS *Lexington*. The next variant, the FB-6, was based on the FB-4 prototype and was fitted with a Pratt & Whitney Wasp radial engine. The Wasp installation was retained almost unchanged in Boeing's later XF2B-1 design, which flew on 3 November 1926; 32 production F2B-1 fighter-bombers were delivered to the US Navy from January 1928 for service on board the aircraft carrier USS *Saratoga*. A month later, the prototype of a new fighter, developed jointly by the USN and Boeing in the course of the preceding year, made its appearance. This was the F3B-1, 74 of which were delivered from 1929 for service on board the USS *Langley*, *Lexington* and *Saratoga*. It was followed by the F4B (the fighter that was ordered by the USAAC as the P-12); the Navy ordered an initial batch of 27 F4B-1s for service on board the USS *Langley* and *Lexington*, with a follow-up order for 41 F4B-2s in June 1930 to equip the

fighter element of the air groups on *Lexington* and *Yorktown*. In April 1931 a further order was placed for 21 F4B-3s, with metal fuselages, and this was followed in January 1932 by an order for 92 F4B-2s, which had modified tailplanes. This final version of the Boeing fighter remained in first-line service until 1937, when it was replaced by more modern types.

LAST NAVAL BIPLANES

In 1931 a new name burst onto the scene of US naval aviation. On 2 April that year, the US Navy signed its first contract with Grumman Aircraft, a company whose association with naval fighter aircraft would extend in an unbroken line into the 21st century. The contract involved the building of 27 fighter and 33 reconnaissance versions of the Grumman FF-1, the first military aircraft to be fitted with a retractable undercarriage, all for service on the USS *Lexington*. The prototype XFF-1 flew towards the end of 1931 and entered service in June 1933, followed by the SF-1 in March 1934. The success of the FF-1, which was a two-seater, encouraged the US Navy to order a more compact single-seat version; this was the XF2F-1, which first flew on 18 October 1933. The order involved 54 production F2F1s, deliveries beginning in 1935. In that year an

improved model, the XF3F-1, made its appearance, and deliveries of 54 production F3F1s began in 1936. The model built in the greatest numbers was the F3F-2, the first of 81 production aircraft going into service in 1938. The final variant was the F3F-3, 27 of which were produced. The F3F-3 had an uprated engine and was the last biplane fighter produced by Grumman; it was also the last biplane fighter to serve with the United States Navy.

RED SUN RISING

On the other side of the Pacific, the early 1920s saw the establishment of Kawasaki, Mitsubishi and Nakajima as the 'big three' of Japan's embryonic aircraft industry, whose early development work relied heavily on aid from Britain, the USA, France and Germany, concentrating mainly in the licence-production of foreign designs and on the overhaul of types purchased directly from abroad, such as the Gloster Sparrowhawk (a development of the Nieuport Nighthawk). In 1923, the German Dr Richard Vogt (later of Blohm und Voss) became chief designer for Kawasaki, and he was responsible for designing a two-seat general-purpose biplane, the KDA-2, which entered service with the Imperial Japanese Army as the Type 88. The Mitsubishi design

Arado Ar 68F

Type: single-seat biplane fighter
Country of origin: Germany
Powerplant: one 750hp (559.2kW) BMW VI 12-cylinder V-type engine
Performance: maximum speed

190mph (305km/h)
Weights: empty 4057lb (1840kg); maximum take-off 5457lb (2475kg)
Dimensions: wing span 36ft 1in (11m); length 31ft 2in (9.5m);

height 10ft 9in (3.28m)
Armament: two fixed forward-firing 7.92mm (0.31in) MG 17 machine guns

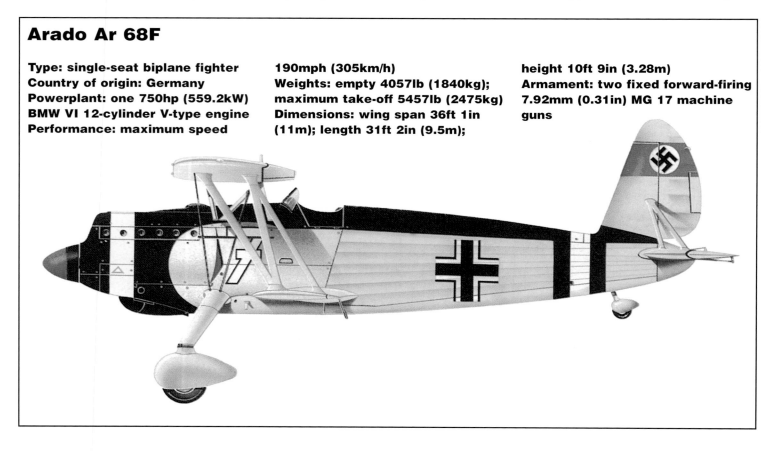

Grumman F2F-1

Type: single-seat biplane fighter
Country of origin: USA
Powerplant: one 650hp (522kW)
Pratt & Whitney R-1535-72 Twin
Wasp Junior radial piston engine

Performance: maximum speed
238mph (383km/h)
Weights: empty 2691lb (1221kg);
maximum take-off 3847lb (1745kg)
Dimensions: wing span 28ft 6in

(8.69m); length 21ft 5in (6.53m);
height 9ft 1in (2.77m)
Armament: two fixed forward-firing
0.3in (7.62mm) machine guns

team was led by Herbert Smith, formerly of the Sopwith company, and in 1922 developed the Mitsubishi B1M, the first Japanese aircraft designed for the torpedo attack role. It remained in production until 1933, by which time 442 had been produced for the Imperial Japanese Navy and 48 for the Army. Its replacement was the Mitsubishi B2M1, a metal structure torpedo-bomber-reconnaissance aircraft which was actually designed by Blackburn Aircraft Ltd as the Navy Type 89. (The 'type numbers' of Japanese aircraft indicated the year in which the aircraft was manufactured according to the Japanese calendar, showing the last two digits. 'Type 89' meant that the B2M1 entered production in 1929, the Japanese year 2589). Herbert Smith's team also designed the Mitsubishi 1MF, carrier-borne biplane fighter, which in February 1923 made the first successful take-off by a Japanese-built aircraft from Japan's first aircraft carrier, the *Hosho*. Production of the 1MF ended in 1929, with the 138th machine. In 1927, the three leading Japanese aircraft manufacturers subitted prototypes in response to a Japanese Army requirement for a new single-seat fighter. All were parasol-wing machines, designed in Japan by teams led wholly or partly by European engineers. The winner was the Nakajima Type 91. (The Curtiss P-1C was also evaluated, but did not measure up to exacting Japanese performance requirements). Deliveries of the Type 91 began in 1931, replacing the

French-designed Nieuport-Delage NiD-29C, which was licence-built by Nakajima, in Army service. The Type 91 first saw action with the 11th Air Battalion, operating with the Army Kanto Command in Manchuria in 1933. By then the Type 91 had become the standard Japanese Army fighter with the newly formed Air Wings (Hiko Rentai).

BRITISH DESIGN

In 1931 Nakajima produced the A2N carrier-borne fighter, which was developed from the Navy Type 3 carrier fighter (this was a version of the British-designed Gloster Gambet, produced as a replacement for the Imperial Japanese Navy's ageing Sparrowhawks). An extremely agile biplane with stylishly tapered, staggered wings, the A2N was very popular with its pilots. It entered service in 1930 as the Navy Type 90 carrier fighter and production ended in 1936 with the 106th aircraft. Nakajima AN2s were used operationally in the Sino-Japanese war, operating from the carrier *Kaga* in the Shanghai area. The A2N's replacement was the Nakajima A4N1, which entered service as the Type 95 carrier fighter. It evolved in response to a Japanese Navy requirement for an interim fighter, 221 being produced between 1935 and 1938. It, too, participated in the Sino-Japanese conflict, carrying out ground attack operations in addition to establishing air superiority. Meanwhile,

Kawasaki had produced the Ki-10 (Type 95) fighter biplane, developed by designer Takeo Doi in response to a Japanese Army requirement of September 1934. The Ki-10 was of all-metal construction, with alloy and fabric covering, and was an unequal-span biplane with N-form bracing struts. Production Ki-10s were operating with six Army squadrons in China shortly after hostilities again broke out with that country in July 1937, and they saw action against Polikarpov I-15bis fighters supplied by the Soviet Union. By the summer of 1939 the Ki-10 was obsolescent, and shortly afterwards the last of Japan's fighter biplanes was withdrawn from first-line service.

PERFORMANCE

The key to the whole question of producing a successful fighter aircraft was the high-performance aero-engine, and in this respect it seemed that the Americans and French had established a commanding lead in the years immediately after World War I. In 1920–23, racing variants of the Nieuport-Delage 29 fighter, fitted with a 320hp (238.6kW) Hispano-Suiza engine, improved on the world absolute air speed record seven times, as well as capturing numerous trophies, while the 1923 Curtiss CR-3 biplanes, powered by 400hp (298kW) Curtiss D.12 engines, achieved first and second places in the Schneider Trophy contest. These foreign successes spurred the leading British aero-engine manufacturers into re-examining their engine design philosophy. From the

Morane-Saulnier MS.225C

Type: single-seat fighter
Country of origin: France
Powerplant: one 500hp (372.8kW)
Gnome-Rhone 9 Kbrs nine-cylinder
radial

Performance: maximum speed
207mph (333km/h)
Weights: empty 2700lb (1223kg);
maximum take-off 3461lb (1570kg)
Dimensions: wing span 34ft 7in

(10.55m); length 23ft 9´in (7.25m);
height 10ft 10in (3.30m)
Armament: two 0.303in (7.7mm)
Vickers machine guns in upper
front fuselage

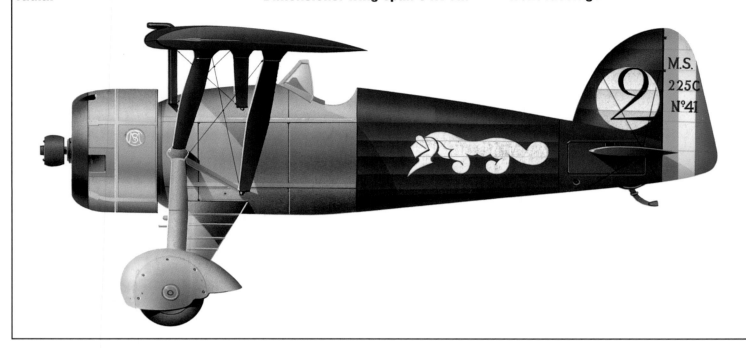

Rolls-Royce stable came the Kestrel,
which represented a considerable
advance over the Curtiss D.12 and was
selected to power the Hawker Hart light
bomber and Hawker Fury fighter. The
Kestrel in its ultimate form – the Kestrel
V – was later developed into the PV.12,
the prototype of the engine that was to
play such an enormous part in World War
II, the Rolls-Royce Merlin. Ironically, it
was an imported Rolls-Royce Kestrel that
powered the prototype of Germany's most
famous fighter, the Messerschmitt Bf 109.
As far as radial engines were concerned,
British efforts in the immediate post-war
years had not been particularly
successful. The first generation of post-
war British fighters – types such as the
Siskin, Grebe and Flycatcher – were
powered by the Armstrong Siddeley
Jaguar, a heavy, complex cumbersome
two-row radial that suffered from a short
running life and lubrication problems.
The situation improved in 1925, with the
Bristol Jupiter; this powered the nimble
Gloster Gamecock, the first viable British
fighter of post-war design, and the later
Bristol Bulldog. Its successor, the
Mercury, was installed in the Gloster
Gauntlet and Gladiator, the last of the
RAF biplane fighters.

RACERS
In 1929 the Schneider Trophy was won
outright for Britain by a Supermarine S.6
racing floatplane, powered by a Rolls-
Royce 'R' engine of 1900hp (1416.8kW).
The success of this engine was a powerful
factor in persuading the Directorate of
Technical Development that Rolls-Royce
had established a firm lead in the design
of high-performance liquid-cooled
powerplants, and in 1934 their PV.12 was
approved for installation in a new
monoplane fighter then being developed
by the Hawker Aircraft Company, the
Fury Monoplane – later to be called the
Hurricane. Similarly, it was the PV.12
that was chosen to power Supermarine's
monoplane fighter design, based on the
S.6 racer – the aircraft that was to
become the incomparable Spitfire. In the
United States, despite the success of the
liquid-cooled Curtiss D.12, aero-engine
manufacturers – notably Wright and
Pratt & Whitney – concentrated on the
development of radial engines for the
future generation of combat aircraft. Both
firms were to make outstanding
contributions to military aviation in
World War II, producing engines that
achieved a remarkable reputation for
reliability – a vital factor in the Pacific

Theatre, where operations involved long
hours of over-water flying. On the other
hand, the US in-line engine that was in
production at the end of 1939 – the
Allison V-1710, which powered the
Curtiss P-40 and early variants of the
North American P-51 Mustang, was
unreliable. In fact, it was replaced in
later versions of the Mustang by the
Packard-built Rolls-Royce Merlin, and the
result was an exceptional combination of
engine and airframe.

In Germany, aero-engine development
progressed rapidly during the early
1930s, with four main companies
involved: DaimlerBenz, Junkers, BMW
and Siemens-Halske. The first two built
inverted 12-cylinder liquid-cooled engines
and the other two, air-cooled radials. The
Daimler-Benz engine was also designed
to take a 20mm (0.78in) gun fitted in the
V formed by the cylinder blocks and
firing through the hollow shaft of the
propeller reduction gear. This
arrangement produced an unexpected
spin-off in that the supercharger had to
be repositioned and it proved
impracticable to fit the carburettor to it
in the normal way. The designers tried
several variations, but in the end they
dispensed with the carburettor altogether

■RIGHT: The Hawker Hurricane I was originally known as the Fury Monoplane Fighter. By the outbreak of World War II, 500 Hurricanes of the 3500 ordered had been completed.

and instead used a multi-point fuel injection system spraying directly on to the cylinders. The result was that the Daimler engine continued to perform well during all combat manoeuvres – unlike the Rolls-Royce Merlin, which tended to cut out because of a negative 'g' effect on the carburettor when the aircraft was inverted or when the pilot put the nose down to dive on an enemy.

ARMAMENT

As well as high power coupled with refined aerodynamics, the other key factor was armament. The fighter aircraft, after all, was designed to be an effective gun platform. For 15 or more of the 20 years that separated the two world wars, the concept of the traditional fighter layout died hard. In the early 1930s the world's leading air arms were still equipped with open-cockpit biplane or parasol-wing fighters, armed with two rifle-calibre machine guns mounted to fire through the propeller disc. The only large-calibre machine gun in general use in the later 1930s was the 0.50in gun mounted in some American fighters and its 12.7mm or 13mm equivalent fitted in a few Continental designs such as the Italian Fiat CR.32. The problem of air armament was well summarised by Squadron Leader Ralph Sorley of Flying Operations 1 (FO1) in the British Air Ministry, who led a vigorous campaign that led to the RAF's new monoplane fighters, the Spitfire and Hurricane, being fitted with eight 0.303in (7.7mm) machine guns. 'The choice' (Sorley wrote): 'lay between the 0.303 gun, the 0.50 gun and a new 20mm Hispano gun which was attracting the attention of the French, and in fact of other countries in Europe who could obtain knowledge of it from them. During 1934 this gun was experimental and details of its performance and characteristics were hard to establish. On the other hand, designs of better 0.303 guns than the Vickers had been tested over the preceding years with the result that the American Browning from the Colt Automatic Weapon Corporation appeared to offer the best possibilities from the point of view of rate of fire. Our own development of guns of this calibre had

been thorough but slow, since we were in the throes of economizing, and considerable stocks of old Vickers guns still remained from the First War. The acceptance of a new gun in the numbers likely to be required was a heavy financial and manufacturing commitment. The 0.50 inch on the other hand had developed little, and although it possessed a better hitting power the rate of fire was slow and it was a heavy item, together with its ammunition, in respect of installed weight...the controversy was something of a nightmare during 1933–34. It was a choice on which the whole concept of the fighter would depend, but a trial staged

on the ground with eight 0.303s was sufficiently convincing and satisfying to enable them to carry the day.'

While the RAF opted for an armament of eight 0.303in (7.7mm) guns – which would be replaced by four 20mm (0.78in) Hispano cannon from 1941 – the Americans decided to standardise on new armament of up to six 0.50in (12.7mm) guns in their new generation of monoplane fighters. The Germans, Italians, Russians, French and Japanese all settled for a mixed armament of cannon and machine guns, a combination that would be retained throughout much of World War II. Although each variation had its commendable points, it was the all-cannon armament, with its greater range and hitting power, that would emerge as the best option.

SECRET TRAINING

In October 1922, under conditions of strict secrecy, 350 German aircraft engineers and fitters arrived in the Soviet Union. Within days of their arrival, they had begun work at a modern aircraft factory at Fili, near Moscow – a factory created by Professor Hugo Junkers, whose advanced D.1, CL.1 and J.1 combat aircraft had made their appearance on the Western Front during the closing stages of World War I. The clandestine movement of German personnel and equipment to the Soviet Union was the first fruit of an agreement on military collaboration drawn up in April 1922 between the Soviet Politburo and the Reichswehr, the post-war German Army. The Russians realised

that the Germans had a great deal to offer not only technically, but also in training and organising elements of the Soviet armed forces; the Germans saw Russia as a base for the secret expansion of their own military power, crippled by the Treaty of Versailles. Early in the following year, a steady flow of German officer cadets entered various military training establishments in the Soviet Union; many went to a flying school which had been set up at Lipetsk and was entirely under German control. One immediate beneficiary of this arrangement was Anthony Fokker, who had succeeded in smuggling 400 aero-engines and enough components to build 120 aircraft, mostly Fokker D.VIIs, out of Germany into neutral Holland before the Allied arms commissioners descended on his German factories in the wake of the Armistice. The D.VII continued in production and was followed by a series of new designs developed from it, the first

of which was the Fokker D.IX. Somewhat larger than than the D.VII, this fighter was powered by a 300hp (223.7kW) Hispano-Suiza engine. Only one prototype was built, and was evaluated by the US Army Air Service as the PW-6. The D.IX was used as the design basis for the more successful D.XI (the D.X was a parasol monoplane, of which ten were built for Spain). The D.XI flew for the first time in May 1923 and 125 were shipped to the Soviet Union, many of them finding their way to the German training establishment at Lipetsk. So did the next variant, the Fokker D.XIII, which flew in September 1924 and set up four speed-with-payload records in the following year. Production of the D.XIII totalled 50 aircraft, all of which were purchased by the USSR on behalf of Germany.

SWASTIKA RISING

When Adolf Hitler and the Nazi Party rose to power in Germany in 1933, and

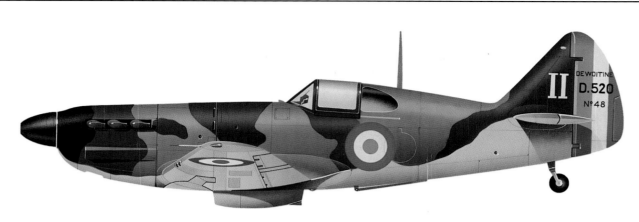

Dewoitine D.520

Type: single-seat fighter
Country of origin: France
Powerplant: one 930hp (693.5kW)
Hispano-Suiza 12Y-4S 12-cylinder
V-type engine
Performance: maximum speed

336mph (540km/h)
Weights: empty 4685lb (2125kg);
maximum take-off 6151lb (2790kg)
Dimensions: wing span 33ft 5´in
(10.20m); length 28ft 9in (8.76m);
height 8ft 5in (2.57m)

Armament: one 20mm (0.78in)
cannon in nose, four wing-
mounted 7.5mm (0.29in) machine
guns

embarked on an open programme of rearmament, the first problem they had to consider – insofar as the creation of a modern air arm was concerned – was that Germany was still disarmed and vulnerable and therefore faced with the prospect of a preventive war, waged by her neighbours to stop her resurrection as a military power. France was Hitler's greatest fear, and France had a large army. The Germans, therefore, had no real choice in deciding whether their air force was to be built around a nucleus of strategic bomber aircraft, as was Britain's, or a nucleus of tactical ground support aircraft protected by an umbrella of fighters, as was France's. Attractive though the strategic option might seem in terms of political advantage, what the Germans needed, if they were to resist any possible military action by the French, was a strong tactical air force that could be assembled quickly and equipped with the most modern combat aircraft Germany's industry could produce. The whole machinery of the new air arm had to be built from scratch. Given the facts that no German air force survived from World War I, except as a secret planning staff within the army, and that the aviation industry was

■ **LEFT: Developed from the Dewoitine D.501, the D.510 was the first French fighter capable of exceeding 250mph (400km/h) in level flight. Some were still in second-line service in May 1940.**

geared entirely for civil aircraft production, the development of the Luftwaffe was an enormously complex task. That it succeeded was hardly due to Hermann Göring, the Reich Air Minister who became Commander-in-Chief of the Luftwaffe in March 1935. A fine pilot who had commanded the Richthofen Geschwader in its latter days, Göring nevertheless remained almost entirely ignorant of the leading principles of air power application throughout his career. The real driving force was Erhard Milch, State Secretary in the new Air Ministry, who possessed a thorough knowledge of the capabilities of the German aircraft industry and who had excellent political connections within the Reich. Milch had left the military after the war and become the head of Luft Hansa, the German airline; this fact, together with his arrogance, later brought him into conflict with Luftwaffe officers who had remained professional soldiers during the difficult years of the Weimar Republic.

PRIORITIES

One of the leading priorities of the new regime was airfield construction. New airfields sprang up all over Germany, often with scant regard to the nature of the foundations on which they were built or the surrounding terrain. Many were little more than grass strips that turned to mud during periods of heavy rain. Those that did have concrete runways later proved inadequate to accommodate

Curtiss P-36 (Hawk 75, Mohawk)

Type: single-seat fighter
Country of origin: USA
Powerplant: one 1200hp (894.8kW)
P&W R-1830-17 14-cylinder radial
Performance: maximum speed

311mph (500km/h)
Weights: empty 4620lb (2096kg);
maximum take-off 6010lb (2726kg)
Dimensions: wing span 37ft 3in
(11.37m); length 28ft 10in (8.79m);

height 9ft 3in (2.82m)
Armament: one 0.5in (12.7mm)
and one 0.3in (7.62mm) machine
gun in upper forward fuselage;
two wing-mounted 0.3in MGs

future generations of advanced combat aircraft, and it was often impossible to extend the runways because of the local topography. Such shortcomings were to hamper the air defence of Germany at its most crucial period. As far as military aircraft construction was concerned, the designer Ernst Heinkel rapidly moved into a leading position, thanks to his willingness to design and build every type of aircraft required by the crash re-equipment programme. In 1933 he produced the He 51 fighter, which evolved through a series of small, streamlined biplane fighter prototypes (the He 37, He 38, He 49 and He 49a). The fourth He 49a, with modifications, became the protoype He 51a, which first flew in mid-1933. First production deliveries of the He 51A-1 were made to JG 132 in April 1935, and the type was later allocated to JG 131 and JG 134. In all, 700 He 51 production aircraft were built. It was succeeded in Luftwaffe service by the Arado Ar 68 biplane fighter, which appeared in prototype form in summer 1934. Development was delayed while a suitable engine was chosen, and first deliveries to operational units were not made until the end of 1936. These were Ar 68Fs, with BMW VI engines; deliveries of the Ar 68E, with the Junkers Jumo 210A, began the following spring. The Ar 68 was the Luftwaffe's last fighter biplane.

THE MONOPLANE ERA

The first of Britain's new monoplane fighters, powered by the Rolls-Royce

Merlin engine and given an armament of eight 0.303in (7.7mm) machine guns, was the Hawker Hurricane, evolved under the design leadership of Sydney Camm to meet Air Ministry Specification F.36/34. The prototype flew on 6 November 1935, powered by a Merlin 'C' engine of 990hp (738.2kW), and began Service trials at Martlesham Heath in March 1936. Hawkers, confident of the success of their design, began preparations for the production of 1000 examples before the first Air Ministry order was forthcoming. An order for 600 machines eventually materialised in June 1936, and the first of these – after some delay caused by the decision to install the Merlin II engine – flew on 12 October 1937, an initial batch being delivered to No 111 Squadron at Northolt in November. The other eight-gun monoplane type, the Supermarine Spitfire, was designed by a team under the direction of Reginald Mitchell, and traced its ancestry to Supermarine's racing floatplanes developed for the Schneider Trophy contest. The prototype made its first flight on 5 March 1936 and, like the Hurricane, was powered by a Rolls-Royce Merlin 'C' engine. A contract for the production of 310 Spitfires was issued by the Air Ministry in June 1936, at the same time as the Hurricane contract, and the first examples were delivered to No 19 Squadron at Duxford in August 1938. Eight other squadrons had equipped with Spitfires by September 1939, and two Auxiliary Air Force units, Nos 603 and 609, were

undergoing operational training. The RAF's third fighter monoplane, the Boulton Paul Defiant, was very different in concept. It was designed to Air Ministry Specification F.9/35, calling for a two-seat fighter in which the entire armament was concentrated in a power-operated, centrally mounted turret permitting a 360-degree radius of fire in the hemisphere above the aircraft. The prototype Defiant flew on 11 August 1937, and some 400 had been ordered by the outbreak of World War II, although a protracted trials programme meant that only three had been delivered. The Fleet Air Arm – now firmly under the control of the Royal Navy – had also received the first of its monoplanes, the Blackburn Skua, which entered service in 1938. Designed specifically as a dive-bomber, the Skua, which had a four-gun wing armament as well as a single rearward-firing gun, was to be employed as much as a fighter as in its intended role. A fighter version, the Blackburn Roc, was ordered in 1937; like the Boulton-Paul Defiant, it had four guns in a power-operated turret. It entered service in 1940, and then equipped only two land-based squadrons.

FRENCH MONOPLANES

France's first cantilever low-wing monoplanes were those of the handsome, all-metal D.500 series, evolved in response to a 1930 requirement for a machine to replace the biplanes and parasol monoplanes then in service. The prototype D.500 flew on 18 June 1932, and development culminated in the D.510, which first flew in August 1934. The first French monoplane fighter with a retractable undercarriage and enclosed cockpit was the Morane-Saulnier MS.405, the production version of which, the MS.406, flew in January 1939. The MS.406 was a rugged, cannon-armed fighter, and 225 had been delivered to the Armée de l'Air by August 1939, equipping four Escadres de Chasse (Fighter Wings). Each Escadre comprised three Groupes de Chasse, each with an establishment of 25 aircraft. In terms of all-round performance, the Morane was inferior to its British and German counterparts, the Hawker Hurricane and Messerschmitt Bf 109E. The Armée de l'Air's other first-line fighter was an American type, the Curtiss

■BELOW: A formation of USAAC Curtiss P-36A Hawk fighters. Hawks in the French Air Force service gave an excellent account of themselves in the Battle of France.

Hawk 75A. An initial order for 100 of these machines had been placed in May 1938, and in 1939 – when it was at last obvious that the French industry was in no position to match German fighter production – follow-on orders were placed for a further 100 Hawk 75A-2s and 135 Hawk A-3s. Two French fighter units began conversion to the type in March 1939, and by the end of August 100 Hawks were operational. French pilots spoke highly of the American fighter's handling qualities; it had a longer range and climbed faster than the Morane 406, although its armament of two 0.30in (7.62mm) and one 0.5in (12.7mm) machine guns left a lot to be desired. The modern fighter equipment that the Armée de l'Air was still eagerly awaiting in August 1939 included two French-built types, the Bloch MB.151/152 series and the Dewoitine D.520. The Bloch fighters had been beset by a spate of teething troubles; 200 151s had been scheduled for delivery by April 1939, but the fighter's performance was so disappointing that

deliveries were suspended while modifications were carried out. In the event only 140 Bloch 151s were completed, and during the summer of 1939 Marcel Bloch's production line was occupied primarily with turning out a more powerful variant, the Bloch 152, for which initial orders totalling 288 machines had been placed. At the end of August 120 Bloch 151s and 152s were on the Armée de l'Air inventory, but of these 95 had no propellers and the rest had no gunsights. It was to be the end of the year before any units were fully operational on the type. The Dewoitine 520 was by far the most promising of the French-designed fighters from the viewpoint of manoeuvrability and all-round performance; 200 were ordered in April 1939, followed by a further 400 in June. Subsequent orders called for the production of 2200 D.520s for the Armée de l'Air and 120 for the Aéronavale (France's naval air arm), but it would be January 1940 before the first examples were delivered, and three more months

Nakajima Ki-27

Type: single-seat fighter
Country of origin: Japan
Powerplant: one 780hp (581.6kW)
Nakajima Ha-1b nine-cylinder radial
Performance: maximum speed

292mph (470km/h)
Weights: empty 2447lb (1110kg);
maximum take-off 3946lb (1790kg)
Dimensions: wing span 37ft 1in
(11.31m); length 24ft 8in (7.53m);

height 10ft 8in (3.25m)
Armament: two 7.7mm (0.303in)
machine guns in upper forward
fuselage, plus 220lb (100kg) of
external ordnance

before the type began to reach the Groupes de Chasse. France's fighter aviation was beginning to shake off the shackles of obsolescence which had bound it for so long, although the process of expansion and modernisation was painfully slow and it would be months before the force was up to effective combat strength. By then, it would be too late.

PEASHOOTER

The United States, the nation that produced France's Curtiss Hawks, took its first step on the road of monoplane fighter design with the Boeing P-26, which first flew in March 1932. Deliveries of production P-26As to the USAAC began at the end of 1933, and pilots soon gave the little fighter the affectionate nickname 'Peashooter'. The P-26 became standard pursuit equipment in Hawaii and the Panama Canal area, and in 1940 surplus American P-26s were used to form the Philippine Army Air Force. A further 11 P-26s (P-26Bs) were supplied to China, and these saw action against the Japanese in Manchuria in 1937. The Army Air Corps' first modern fighter aircraft was the Seversky P-35, development of which originated in 1935. Designed by Alexander Kartveli, it flew

for the first time in August 1935 and an order for 76 production models was placed by the Air Corps in June 1936, delivery taking place between July 1937 and August 1938. Of the 177 P-35s built, 40 were exported to Sweden and 60 were used in the Philippines at the time of the Japanese attack at the end of 1941. Also exported in large numbers was the Curtiss P-36, the A and C models of which were delivered to USAAC fighter squadrons in 1938–39. Designed in 1934, the P-36 was not an outstanding aircraft. Neither was the Republic P-43 Lancer, a development of the P-35. Inadequate as a fighter, it was later converted to the photo-reconnaissance role. Total production of the P-43 was 272 aircraft, of which 103 were sent to China; these were the only Lancers to see action. Another export fighter developed in the USA was the Curtiss Hawk 75, 112 of which were delivered to the Chinese Air Force in 1938 as Hawk 75Ms. A further 25 generally similar Hawk 75Ns were produced for Thailand, and 30 Hawk 75Os for Argentina. The Hawk 75A, also built for export, featured a retractable undercarriage and other improvements; as mentioned earlier, this version was ordered by France, which placed orders totalling 730; deliveries were still

incomplete when France was invaded in May 1940, and the remaining aircraft were diverted to the RAF, in whose service the aircraft was known as the Mohawk. Also from the Curtiss stable came the P-40 Warhawk, which for the first two years of the war against Japan was to be the most important fighter in the American arsenal. Derived from the P-36A, the prototype XP-40 flew in October 1938 and the fighter was ordered into production on 27 April 1939. Contemporary with the P-40 was the Bell P-39 Airacobra, which flew in its original form in April 1938. The P-39 featured a 37mm (1.45in) cannon installed in the extreme nose and firing through the hub of the propeller shaft, the engine being positioned behind the pilot. Another feature, novel for its time, was a tricycle undercarriage. The P-39 underwent numerous modifications, not all of them for the better, before it was ordered into mass production in August 1939. But the shape of the future lay in another American fighter which flew for the first time in January 1939, having been conceived two years earlier. Distinctive with its twin engines and twin tail booms, the Lockheed Model 22, which was later to become the P-38 Lightning long-range tactical fighter, was to have a profound effect on the course of the coming air war.

RED RATAS

On 31 December 1933, two months after the appearance of the I-15, a new Polikarpov fighter made its first flight. This was the I-16 or TsKB-12, a low-wing monoplane with a retractable undercarriage, two wing-mounted 7.62mm (0.3in) guns and a large 480hp (358kW) M-22 engine. The I-16 was the first Soviet fighter to incorporate armour plating around the pilot's cockpit. The first production versions, the I-16 Types 4, 5 and 10, were fitted with a 750hp (559.2kW) M-25B, increasing their top speed to around 290mph (466km/h). On these variants, wheels and flaps had to be wound down by hand, which required some mild gymnastics on the part of the pilot. During the mid-1930s, the basic I-16 design was progressively modified to carry out a variety of different tasks. Among the variants produced was the TsKB-18, an assault version armed with four PV-1 synchronised machine guns, two wing-mounted machine guns and 225lb (100kg) of bombs. The pilot was protected by armour plating in front, below and behind. In 1938 the I16 Type 17 was tested, armed with two wing-

mounted cannon. This version was produced in large numbers. Then, with the cooperation of the armament engineer B.G. Shpitalnii, Polikarpov produced the TsKB-12P, the first aircraft in the world to be armed with two synchronised cannon firing through the propeller arc. The last fighter version of the I-16 was the Type 24, fitted with a 1000hp (745.7kW) M-62R engine which gave it a top speed of 325mph (523km/h). Altogether, some 20,000 I-16s of all types were built. The stubby little fighter never had an official name; its nickname Rata (Rat), acquired during the Spanish Civil War, was only one of many applied to it. Concurrently with the I16, Andrei Tupolev developed the I-4, a low-wing single-seat monoplane which was the first Soviet aircraft to feature stressed-skin construction, and in 1934 the Grigorovitch design bureau produced the IP-1 fighter, armed with two machine guns and two DRP-76 recoilless cannon. The IP-1 and the IP-4, a modified version, were produced in fairly large numbers.

BEAUTY

It was not until 1939–40 that the prototypes of three Soviet fighters that could really be classed as modern made their appearance. The first was the

LaGG-3, which took its name from the initials of the three engineers who conceived it: Lavochkin, Gorbunov and Gudkov. It was a remarkable little aircraft, built entirely of wood and bearing a strong resemblance to France's Dewoitine D.520. It was armed with one ShVAK 20mm (0.78in) cannon, two ShKAS 7.62mm (0.3in) machine guns and one 12.7mm (0.5in) BS (Beresin) machine gun. The LaGG-3 flew for the first time in March 1939. The second type, the MiG-1, which flew in March 1940, was the fruit of collaboration between the two aero-engineers Artem I. Mikoyan and Mikhail I. Gurievitch. An open-cockpit single-seater, it was not a particularly successful design, though over 2000 were built before it was replaced by the much improved MiG-3. The third type, the Yak-1 Krasavyets (Beauty) made its first public appearance during an air display on 7 November 1940. It was Aleksandr S. Yakovlev's first fighter design, and it earned him the Order of Lenin, the gift of a Zis car and a prize of 100,000 roubles. The fighter was powered by a 100hp (74.5kW) M-105PA engine and carried an armament of one 20mm (0.78in) ShVAK cannon, two 7.62mm (0.3in) ShKAS machine guns and sometimes six RS-82 rockets. The Yak-1 was of mixed

Mitsubishi A5M

Type: single-seat fighter
Country of origin: Japan
Powerplant: one 785hp (585.4kW) Nakajima Kotobuki 41 9-cylinder radial

Performance: maximum speed 270mph (435km/h)
Weights: empty 2874lb (1236kg); maximum take-off 4017lb (1822kg)
Dimensions: wing span 36ft 1in

(11.00m); length 24ft 10in (7.56m); height 10ft 7in (3.24m)
Armament: two 7.7mm (0.303in) Type 89 machine guns; 66lb (30kg) of external ordnance

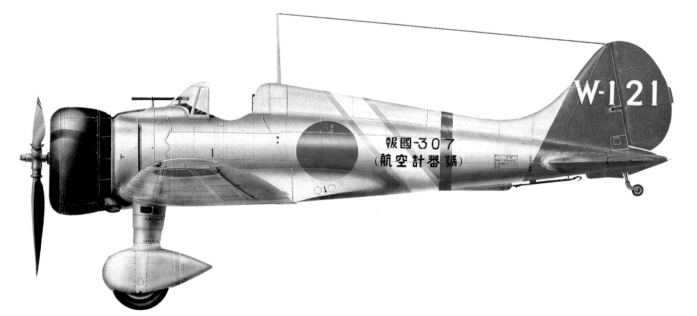

construction, fabric and plywood covered; it was simple to build and service, and a delight to fly. Maximum speed was 360mph (580km/h), about the same as the early model. Series production of all three types was begun in 1940–41.

In both Japan and the USSR, the development of monoplane fighters proceeded on more or less parallel lines in the early 1930s, although there were separate requirements for the Imperial Japanese Navy and Army. These resulted, respectively, in the Mitsubishi A5M and the Nakajima Ki-27, both of which were powered by radial engines and had fixed undercarriages. Both types had been in service for only a short time when their merits were put to the test in combat.

INVASION

In July 1937 the Japanese launched a full-scale invasion of China, quickly capturing urban centres along the Chinese coast and pushing rapidly along the Yangtse river as Chinese forces retreated westward. During the initial period of operations, the Imperial Japanese Army left the brunt of the air fighting to the Navy, limiting its own activity to air support of ground operations along the Manchurian border while new units were formed. The IJN was well placed to conduct offensive air operations. Its first-line fighter squadrons were now equipped with Mitsubishi A5Ms, its carrier-based attack squadrons with the Yokosuka B4Y bomber and its

land-based bomber squadrons with the twin-engined Mitsubishi G3M (later to be code-named Jean and Betty by the Allies).

In August 1937, following the conclusion of a non-aggression pact between China and the Soviet Union, the Soviet Central Committee agreed to supply quantities of aircraft and equipment for use by the Chinese Central Government. The first contingent of Soviet Air Force personnel arrived in China during the last week of September, and by the beginning of 1938 there were over 350 Russians serving in the country, a total that included 80 fighter pilots. Although their task was ostensibly to give flying instruction to Chinese aircrew converting to Russian types, their real purpose was to fly four squadrons of Polikarpov I-152 (I-15bis) fighters in combat against the Japanese. Two squadrons of SB-2 bombers also arrived at the same time, and they, too, were manned by Russian crews. Operational flying began almost immediately from bases in the vicinity of Nanking, the Chinese capital, which by that time was coming under heavy Japanese air attack. In January 1938, two I-15 squadrons, supplied to the Chinese some time earlier, were pulled out of the front line and replaced by two fresh units operating I-16s, which proved able to meet the Japanese A5M fighters on more equal terms. The Soviet contingent was commanded by Lieutenant Colonel Stepan P. Suprun. Meanwhile, Chinese

units had begun to receive the first of 400 I-152s and I-16s promised by the Soviet government, and Russian-trained Chinese pilots were flowing through the flying and technical schools at Nanchang, Langchow and Hami at a fast rate – so fast, in fact, that many of them were far from ready to take on the highly skilled Japanese aircrews in combat. Nevertheless, so desperate was the situation that they were immediately sent into action in the defence of Nanking, replacing the Soviet squadrons. That was in mid-November. Four weeks later, their pilots completely outclassed by the Japanese, the Chinese squadrons had been decimated and had to be withdrawn to Nanchang, leaving the capital naked to air attack.

AIR RAIDS

The Russian squadrons, meanwhile, had regrouped near Langchow, where a new batch of crews had arrived to start their four-month tour of duty in China. There was little air activity on either side during the spring of 1938, but in April and May, Japanese reconnaissance aircraft began to appear in increasing numbers over Langchow and other places in northwest China, where the combat

■**BELOW: Spanish Republican I-16 Ratas preparing for take-off. The I-16 was superior to every fighter in the Spanish Civil War except the Messerschmitt Bf 109.**

■ABOVE: The Fiat CR.32, seen here in Spanish Nationalist colours, was the principal Italian type used in the civil war. A strong, agile little aircraft, the CR.32 was well liked by its pilots.

aircraft being supplied by Russia were assembled. The first heavy air raids on these centres were carried out late in May and continued for five weeks, heavy losses being inflicted on the attacking Mitsubishi G3M bombers – which had a very long range but poor defensive armament – by the defending fighters.

Two months later, in July 1938, a major clash occurred between Soviet and Japanese forces after Russian troops occupied a strategic ridge near Lake Khasan on the Soviet-Manchurian border. The Japanese claimed that the ridge was theirs and attacked the Russian positions on 29 July, capturing the objective. During the bitter fighting that followed, four squadrons of TB-3 heavy bombers, escorted by I-152s, repeatedly pounded the Japanese positions. While Soviet infantry and tanks fought their way back towards the ridge, I-16s and I-152s strafed ahead of them. Japanese attacks

the next day were also broken up by Soviet aircraft about 180 of which were committed to the battle. On 11 May 1939 the Japanese, anxious to avenge their defeat at Lake Khasan, launched a major offensive into Mongolian territory at Khalkhin-Gol. There was sporadic air fighting during the opening weeks of the battle, but the battles of August were to be marked by the biggest air confrontation the world had seen since World War I. During July, the Japanese had assembled a total of 475 aircraft of all types in Manchuria, including considerable numbers of Mitsubishi A5M and Nakajima Ki-27 fighters. There were also some bomber squadrons equipped with Mitsubishi Ki-21s, fast twin-engined bombers which had entered service with the Japanese Army Air Force the previous year and which were later to be known by the Allied code-name of 'Sally'. The Russians, meanwhile, had been

pouring troops and equipment into Mongolia, and the First Army Group – commanded by General Georgi K. Zhukov, who was to achieve fame during World War II – was rapidly deployed along the disputed frontier.

CLASHES

At his disposal, at the end of July, Zhukov had 580 aircraft operated by both Soviet and Mongolian squadrons. The total included 150 I-16s and 200 I-15s/152s. The I-15s had already clashed with Japanese fighters on several occasions, and had proved inferior to the Nakajima Ki-27; during subsequent operations they were relegated mainly to the ground

attack role, leaving the I-16s and I-152s to engage the enemy. During August, four of the Red Air Force squadrons exchanged their I-15s for the more modern I-153, with a retractable undercarriage, and the appearance of these aircraft over the Khalkhin-Gol took the Japanese fighter pilots by surprise, especially as the Russians evolved tactics which were deliberately designed to mislead the enemy. They would approach the combat area with their undercarriages lowered, giving the impression that they were slower I-15s or I-152s and inviting the Japanese to attack. The Ki-27s suffered some losses before their pilots realised what was happening. Combats over the Khalkhin-Gol sometimes involved as many as 200 aircraft. The Japanese usually emerged the worse from these encounters; although the Ki-27 could hold its own against the I-153 and was superior to the I-152, it was outclassed in speed and firepower by its most frequent opponent, the I-16, which the Japanese nicknamed 'Abu' (Gadfly). Figures of the air losses sustained by both sides are vague and conflicting. The Russians were reported to have lost 145 aircraft of all types between 11 May and 15 September 1939, when a ceasefire was arranged. The Japanese are said to have lost 600, 200 of them during the last ten days of the fighting, but these figures seem over-optimistic. What is certain is that very heavy aircraft losses were suffered by both sides, and particularly by the

Japanese. Although there had not been a great deal of difference in terms of skill between Russian and Japanese pilots, the Russian tactics had been better. So had the armament – four machine guns (MGs) mounted in both the I-16 and I-153, compared to the twin MGs carried by the Ki-27 and A5M.

ROCKETS

The air battles over the Khalkhin-Gol produced an interesting and novel incident. On 20 August 1939, five I-16s, led by Lieutenent N.I. Zvonarev and armed with RS-82 air-to-ground rocket projectiles, fired their salvoes of these at a formation of Japanese aircraft and brought down two of them in what was the world's first aircraft-to-aircraft rocket engagement. (Le Prieur aircraft rockets had been used in World War I, but only against balloons.)

The Japanese Army Air Force's poor showing in the fighting against the Russians, and the clear superiority of Russian equipment and tactics, led the Japanese High Command to consider the USSR as the principal potential enemy, and equipment planning was influenced by the requirement to be prepared for a renewed conflict on the Manchuria-Siberia border. New combat aircraft were developed to carry out tactical missions in cold weather, so that they were poorly suited to long over-water missions among the Pacific islands in the coming war of 1941–45. The Imperial Japanese Navy, on the other hand, bore the brunt of long-

■ABOVE: The Heinkel He 100D was a better all-round performer than the Messerschmitt 109, but fell victim to politics. It was originally sanctioned under the designation Heinkel He 113.

range operations against Chinese targets, the aircraft industry developing bombers for missions at extreme range and also a fighter capable of escorting them to the target and back. The result was one of the finest aircraft of all time, the Mitsubishi A6M Zero. This superb fighter first flew on 1 April 1939 and ,after 15 aircraft had been evaluated under combat conditions in China, the type was accepted for service with the Japanese Naval Air Force in July 1940, entering full production in November that year.

Meanwhile, Soviet fighters had been in action in an environment far different from that of the barren Khalkhin-Gol, and against a far different foe. When civil war broke out in Spain in July 1936 there were some 200 military aircraft in the country, most of them obsolete or obsolescent types. The bulk remained in the hands of the air arm of the Republican government, and only a very few found their way to the Nationalist commanders, General Franco in North Africa and General Mola in northern Spain. It was the Nationalists who were the first to receive substantial aid from overseas. On 26 July 1936, Franco sent emissaries to Adolf Hitler, who promised German support for the Nationalist cause, and by the end of the month 85 Luftwaffe personnel and six Heinkel He 51 fighters sailed from Hamburg, bound for Cadiz. The ship also carried spare parts for 20 Junkers Ju 52 bomber-transports, which had reached Spain by way of Italy. They were used to airlift thousands of Nationalist troops from North Africa to the Spanish mainland. Further air reinforcements for the Nationalists came in August, with the arrival of nine Italian SM.81 bombers and an initial batch of Fiat CR.32 fighters.

FIRST COMBAT

In the meantime, the Soviet government had been making plans to assist the Republicans by supplying arms and military advisers. By the end of October 1936, 30 Polikarpov I-15 fighters had arrived in Spain, along with 150 Russian personnel. The group included 50 fighter pilots under the command of Colonel Yakob Shmushkievich, who was known as 'General Douglas' throughout Russia's commitment in Spain, and it was in their hands that the I-15 – dubbed Chato (Snub-nose) by the Spaniards – made its operational debut on the Madrid front. The I-15's first combat over Spain took place on 4 November 1936, when ten fighters, all flown by Russian pilots, attacked an Ro 37 reconnaissance aircraft of the Italian Legion over the Manzanares river. The Ro 37 escaped, but two Fiat CR.32s escorting it were shot down. The I-15s were soon reinforced by the first batch of I-16s, which went into battle on 15 November 1936, providing air cover for a Republican offensive

against Nationalist forces advancing on Valdemoro, Sesena and Equivias. The I-16 – nicknamed Mosca (Fly) by the Republicans and Rata (Rat) by the Nationalists – proved markedly superior to the Heinkel He 51. It was also faster than its most numerous Nationalist opponent, the Fiat CR.32, although the Italian fighter was slightly more manoeuvrable and provided a better gun platform. Apart from that, the Nationalists' tactics were better; the Republicans tended to stick to large, tight, unwieldy formations that were easy to spot and hard to handle.

CONDOR LEGION

As the Russians continued to step up their aid to the Republicans, increasing numbers of German personnel were arriving in Spain to fight on the Nationalist side, their presence a closely-kept secret. Luftwaffe personnel assigned to the Condor Legion, as the German contingent was known, reported to a secret office in Berlin where they were issued with civilian clothing, Spanish currency and papers. The main body of the Condor Legion sailed for Spain during the last days of November 1936. It consisted of three squadrons equipped with He 51s, four bomber-transport squadrons operating Ju 52/3ms, a reconnaissance squadron equipped with Heinkel He 70s, a seaplane squadron with He 59s and He 60s, six anti-aircraft batteries, four signals companies and a repair section. After settling in, the Legion began a series of bombing raids on Mediterranean ports held by the

Republicans, but the Ju 52s encountered severe icing difficulties over the Sierra Nevada and were later transferred to Melilla in Spanish Morocco, from where they made attacks across the straits. One of the most active elements of the Condor Legion was Jagdgruppe J/88, comprising the three He 51-equipped fighter squadrons. However, the Heinkel fighter's limitations soon became apparent; it proved incapable of intercepting the Republicans' Russian-built Tupolev SB-2 bombers even under the most favourable conditions, and was forced to avoid combat with I-15s and I-16s. By the spring of 1937 the He 51 could no longer carry out its task as a fighter without suffering unacceptable losses, and from March onwards, fitted with bomb racks, it was confined to close support duties. Throughout the spring of 1937 the Republicans, thanks to the influx of Soviet aircraft, retained air superiority over the vital Madrid battlefront. They had concentrated some 200 I-15s, I-16s, R-Zs (observation and ground attack aircraft) and SB-2 bombers in the Madrid area, and the five fighter squadrons assigned to the Jarama sector inflicted heavy losses on the Nationalist Ju 52 units engaged there. Following the failure of the Nationalist offensive at Jarama, the Republican Air Arm was substantially reorganised, with many of the I-15 and I-16 units which had hitherto been staffed exclusively by Russian personnel now being turned over to the Spaniards. The first all-Spanish I-16 unit was Grupo 21, which began to exchange its Breguet XIXs for Ratas just

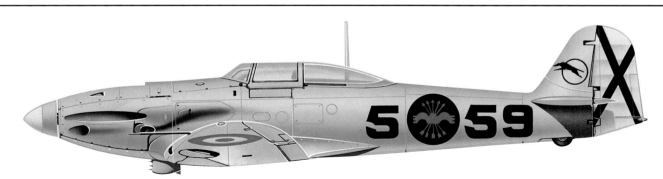

Heinkel He 112

Type: single-seat fighter
Country of origin: Germany
Powerplant: one 680hp (507kW) Junkers Jumo 210Ea 12-cylinder inverted Vee-type engine
Performance: maximum speed

317mph (510km/h)
Weights: empty 3571lb (1620kg); maximum take-off 4960lb (2250kg)
Dimensions: wing span 29ft 10in (9.10m); length 30ft 6in (9.30m); height 12ft 7in (3.85m)

Armament: two wing-mounted 20mm (0.78in) FF cannon; two 7.9mm (0.31in) machine guns in sides of forward fuselage.
Provision for three 22lb (10kg) bombs under each wing

in time to take part in the final stage of the Republican counter-attack. The other I-16 squadron which featured prominently in the strafing attacks on the Nationalists was a Red Air Force unit based at Barajas, which was also the base of the Voluntary International Squadron commanded by Andre Malraux and equipped with I-15s.

THE MESSERSCHMITTS ARRIVE

By the summer of 1937 there were 13 Republican fighter squadrons – six I-16s and seven of I-15s – opposing eleven Nationalist, ten of which were equipped with Fiat CR.32s. The 11th Nationalist fighter squadron, the Condor Legion's 1 Staffel, J/88, had just received the first examples of a combat aircraft which was to become one of the most famous fighters of all time: the Messerschmitt Bf 109. German monoplane fighter development had been progressing at a fast pace since the Nazis' rise to power, and fell into two categories: the single-engined air superiority fighter and the twin-engined, long-range escort fighter, the so-called 'Destroyer' (Zerstorer). Messerschmitt designs were chosen in both cases, the twin-engined requirement being met by the Bf 110. (The prefix Bf, incidentally, denotes Bayerische Flugzeugwerke, or Bavarian Aircraft

■BELOW: Mechanics at work on one of the He 100 prototypes. What looks like a radiator under the nose is part of the loosened engine cowling; the He 100 had an enclosed cooling system.

■ABOVE: The Heinkel He 178 was the first aircraft in the world to fly solely on the power of a turbojet engine. It first flew from Marienehe airfield on 27 August 1939.

Factories. A company designation, it was never used by the Luftwaffe, who referred to the aircraft as Me 109 and Me 110.) There were other contenders for the Luftwaffe contracts; these included the Heinkel He 112, a batch of 30 undergoing Luftwaffe evaluation in 1938. Seventeen of these saw service with Grupo 5-G-5 of the Spanish Nationalist Air Force in the closing stages of the Spanish Civil War. The He 112, which was well liked by its pilots, saw no operational service with the Luftwaffe, although 24 were delivered to the Romanian Air Force in 1939, and these were used for a brief period in the war with Russia. Heinkel's other single-engined fighter design was the He 100 (originally He 113), which the firm developed as a potential successor to the Bf 109. The aircraft, which flew for the first time in January 1938, was very fast, with a top speed of 416mph (670km/h) at 13,000ft (3962m), and the prototypes established a number of speed records, but the type did not go into service.

It was, however, cleverly manipulated by the German propaganda machine, the 12 aircraft that were built for evaluation being painted in a variety of spurious markings, with the result that in the first year of World War II many Allied pilots reported having encountered the 'He 113' in combat. Meanwhile, the Messerschmitt 109 had seen considerable action in Spain, equipping three Nationalist squadrons, and their pilots had continued to develop the tactics that would enable them to gain air superiority in the early air campaigns of World War II. The air battles over Spain saw the first use of the tactical formation known as the Schwarm (swarm). This comprised four aircraft, made up of two sections of two called a Rotte. The aircraft were positioned about 650ft (200m) apart, the four assuming a formation that resembled the fingertips of a hand when spread out flat and controlled with the aid of FuG 7 radio telephony equipment. This loose formation, which enabled one fighter to protect another's tail, was ideal for aerial combat. It would soon be put to the test in a greater arena than Spain.

But, even as German forces were massing for the invasion of Poland, the event that would precipitate World War II, another event passed unnoticed except to a select band of aircraft engineers, Luftwaffe officers and representatives of the German Air Ministry. On 20 August 1939, a diminutive aircraft, the Heinkel He 178, took off from the company's airfield at Merienehe. It was the world's first turbojet-powered aircraft, and within five years its successors would change the face of aerial combat forever.

CHAPTER 3
WORLD WAR II: THE GREAT ARENA

World War II was the showcase for some of the most famous aircraft ever built. It was also a great leap forward. At its beginning biplanes served in many air forces; by its end, jets were on active duty with the RAF and Luftwaffe.

At the end of August 1939, the Polish Air Force possessed some 436 operational aircraft and a personnel strength of 15,000. In the spring of that year, the first-line units had been reorganised around a combat nucleus consisting of a pursuit and a bomber brigade under the direct command of the C-in-C of the Polish armed forces, the remainder being split up among the six Polish Army regions. The Pursuit Brigade, whose main task was the defence of Warsaw, was equipped with four squadrons of PZL P-11c fighters and one squadron of even older P-7as; eight more P-11c and two more P-7a squadrons served with the Army Air Force. Powered by a Bristol Jupiter radial engine, the gull-winged PZL P-7a was one of the leading fighter aircraft of the inter-war years; deliveries had begun in the latter half of 1932 to the Eskadra Kosciuszkowska (Kosciuszko Squadron), and by the end of 1933 all first-line fighter squadrons of the Polish Air Force's 1st, 2nd, 3rd and 4th Air Regiments were equipped with it. Its successor, the PZL P-11, was basically a more powerful derivative which first flew in September 1931, with deliveries beginning in 1934. Most P-11s were powered by Bristol Mercury engines, built under licence by Skoda; the definitive version of the fighter was the P-11c, of which 175 were built. The P-11 was to have been replaced by a low-wing fighter

■LEFT: Spitfire pilots sprint for their aircraft in response to what was probably a practice 'scramble' for the the camera. According to the wartime caption, the pilots were Free French.

monoplane, the P-50 Jastrzeb (Hawk), as part of a major expansion scheme, but cuts in the military budget resulted in the cancellation of an order for 300 P-50s, and more P-11s were purchased instead. A similar fate befell the twin-engined Wilk (Wolf), which was to have fulfilled the dual role of heavy long-range fighter and dive-bomber. Such, in brief, was the state of Poland's fighter defences at dawn on 1 September 1939, when the Germans attacked. The first few hours of the German offensive were marked by bad weather, which curtailed operations, but this cleared at noon and the Luftwaffe directed its main attacks against Polish troop concentrations. It was in the late afternoon that the onslaught began in earnest, with all 20 groups of Luftflotte (Air Fleet) 1 carrying out heavy attacks on airfields, ammunition dumps, railway and factory installations and the Baltic ports.

MASSACRED
At 5pm on 1 September, three groups of Heinkel He 111 bombers escorted by twin-engind Bf 110 fighters headed for the Polish capital, Warsaw. They were intercepted by two squadrons of P-11cs; the latter shot down two Heinkels and a Bf 110, but five of their own number were also destroyed. Ninety minutes later the Luftwaffe attacked Warsaw again; two more Heinkels were destroyed, but the Poles lost four PZLs. In less than two hours the two Polish squadrons lost nearly half their aircraft. It was the same story with the Polish bomber squadrons. Several of these carried out determined attacks on enemy columns, but without

Fokker D.XXI

Type: Single-seat fighter
Country of origin: Netherlands
Powerplant: one 830hp (618.9kW)
Bristol Mercury VIII nine-cylinder
radial

Performance: maximum speed
286mph (460km/h
Weights: empty 3197lb (1450kg);
maximum take-off 4519lb (2050kg)
Dimensions: wing span 36ft 1in

(11.00m); length 26ft 10in (8.20m);
height 9ft 8in (2.95m)
Armament: two 7.9mm (0.31in)
machine guns in forward fuselage;
two 7.9mm (0.31in) guns in wings

fighter cover they were massacred. Eleven more P-11s were lost on 4 September in combat with Bf 109s, although the Polish airmen had some success against German observation aircraft on this day. The Poles fought on; in the first six days of the battle the four PZL squadrons of the Pursuit Brigade, defending Warsaw, shot down 42 enemy aircraft for the loss of 37 of their own aircraft. The final air defence sorties were flown over Warsaw on 14–15 September by the so-called 'Deblin Group', a scratch unit composed of P-7as, the surviving P-11cs and the prototype PZL P-24, an improved version of the P-11. On 17 September, in accordance with a secret German-Soviet agreement on the partition of Poland, Soviet forces invaded the country from the east, effectively sealing its fate. The brief campaign had cost the Polish Air Force 327 aircraft, of which 260 were lost in action. Air combat losses, however, were only about 70, the remainder being destroyed on the ground. The Luftwaffe, for its part, lost 285 aircraft, of which about 90 were claimed by anti-aircraft fire. Polish fighter pilots claimed 126 victories, but in view of the overall German loss figure their actual score must have been much greater. In addition, over 200 German aircraft were

so badly damaged that they had to be withdrawn from operations. And, although Poland had been overwhelmed, many of her airmen escaped. In due time, fighting alongside the French, British and Russians, they would make a great contribution to the ultimate Allied victory.

FIGHTERS OVER FINLAND

On 30 November 1939, as Allied and German fighter pilots tentatively sparred with one another over eastern France in the early engagements of the so-called 'Phoney War', a savage conflict broke out in the far north between the Soviet Union and Finland. The small Finnish Air Force operated a miscellany of combat aircraft, the most modern of which were 31 Fokker D.XXI monoplanes with fixed, spatted undercarriages. Designed in 1935, the D.XXI was originally intended for the Royal Netherlands East Indies Army Air Service, but instead 36 examples were ordered for the home air force. Seven Dutch-built D.XXIs were supplied to Finland, which built 38 more under licence. The other 120 or so aircraft available to the Finns included Fokker CV.Xs and C.VEs, Blackburn Ripon floatplanes, Junkers K.34s and Bristol Bulldogs. Against these, the Soviet Air Force had four bomber and two fighter

brigades totalling about 750 aircraft. The main equipment of the fighter units was the I-15 and I-152, with only a small number of I-153s and I-16s. Because of their conviction that there would be no serious opposition from the Finns, the Russians had not thought it necessary to commit their more modern fighter types to the battle. Despite the odds against it, the Finnish Air Force proved a formidable opponent, just as the Finnish Army did on the ground. By mid-December the Russian offensive had been halted and the Soviet Air Force, its casualties mounting, switched its attacks from towns and communications to Finnish airfields, whereupon the Finns began operating from frozen lakes. Early in the new year a Swedish volunteer squadron, Flygflottilj 19, joined the Finns in action; equipped with 12 Gloster Gladiators and four Hawker Harts, it operated from a frozen lake at Kemi. Although 150 targets in Finland were repeatedly bombed by the Russians, the latter completely failed in their primary objective, which was the neutralisation of a major part of the Finnish war effort. Because of the inefficiency of their navigation and poor bombing accuracy, the Russians persisted in daylight attacks until the very end of the campaign, and it cost them dearly. By the time an armistice brought the 'Winter War' to an end on 12 March 1940, 280 Russian aircraft had been shot down by Finnish and Swedish fighters, and a further 314 had been destroyed by anti-aircraft fire. Against this staggering total the Finns lost only 62 aircraft in combat, although 69 more were so badly damaged that they could no longer operate.

When Britain and France declared war on Germany on 3 September 1939 both countries anticipated massive air attacks from the start of hostilities, but the waves of German bombers never came. It was RAF Bomber Command that struck the first blow, when ten Bristol Blenheim bombers carried out a daylight raid on units of the German fleet in the Elbe estuary on 4 September. No significant damage was caused, and five Blenheims were shot down by flak. Later in the day, the Luftwaffe scored its first victory of the war against the RAF when a

Wellington bomber of No 9 Squadron was shot down in the same area by Corporal Alfred Held, flying a Messerschmitt Bf 109 of III/JG77. In the first weeks of the war, RAF bombers, attempting to attack enemy warships in harbour and in

■**BELOW: A formation of Polish Air Force PZL P.7 fighters. It was a developed version of this fighter, the PZL P.11c, that was pitted against the Luftwaffe in September 1939.**

daylight, suffered terrible losses at the hands of the Messerschmitts, one of the reasons being that the RAF aircraft were not fitted with self-sealing fuel tanks. One of the most important lessons absorbed by the Luftwaffe from its experiences in the Spanish Civil War was the extreme vulnerability of light alloy aircraft fuel tanks to bullets and shell fragments. In the worst case, red-hot ammunition might ignite the layer of fuel vapour above the liquid, causing explosion and fire; at best, fuel might be lost at such a rapid rate that the aircraft would be forced down. The German response to the problem was to construct fuel tanks of compressed cellulose fibre with 2mm (0.078in) thick walls and an outer covering comprising a series of layers; 3mm (0.12in) of chrome leather, 3mm of unvulcanised rubber, two layers of lightly vulcanised rubber 0.5mm (0.019in) thick, and an outer layer of highly vulcanised rubber, 3mm thick. When the tank wall was pierced and fuel ran out, a chemical reaction occurred, causing the layer of unvulcanised rubber to swell up and seal the hole. In September 1939 only the Luftwaffe was equipped with self-sealing tanks, and the RAF suffered a spate of tragic and unneccessary losses before it, too, learned the lesson.

EARLY BATTLES

Meanwhile, on Germany's western frontier, the initial alarms that had followed the outbreak of hostilities had given way to the unreal period known as the 'Phoney War'. The British and French armies on the one hand, and the Germans on the other, settled in behind their static defence lines to wait out the long winter months. Only in the air was there any real activity, as British, French and German fighters met in frequent skirmishes over the threatened borders. During these battles the Messerschmitt 109's performance proved superior to that of the Hawker Hurricane, which equipped four RAF squadrons in France, and the French Morane 406 and Curtiss Hawk fighters. It was certainly superior to that of the Gloster Gladiator biplane, which equipped two fighter squadrons assigned to the British Expeditionary Force; yet it was the Gladiator that had to hold the line for the Allies when, on 9 April 1940, the Germans launched an invasion of Norway. The Norwegians, who also had a few Gladiators, fought back hard, but under relentless enemy pressure they were steadily forced to yield ground. In an effort to redress the situation the Allies landed an expeditionary force of British, French and Polish troops at Namsos and Andalsnes between 14 and 19 April; air cover for the force was provided by 18 Gloster Gladiators of No 263 Squadron RAF, operating from a frozen lake under appalling conditions. They shot down four enemy bombers, but

■BELOW: A Messerschmitt Bf 109F at its French airfield. Because of a series of accidents caused by weakness of the rear fuselage, the F model did not enter service until May 1941.

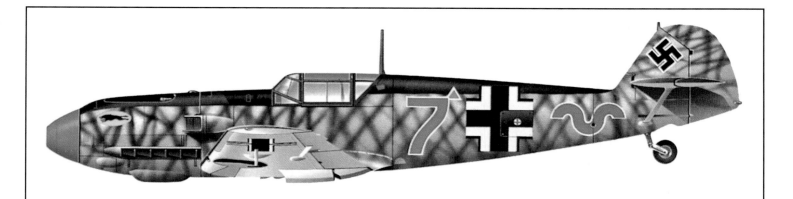

Messerschmitt Bf 109E-3

Type: single-seat fighter
Country of origin: Germany
Powerplant: one 1150hp (857.5kW)
Daimler-Benz DB 601A inverted
Vee-type engine
Performance: 357mph (575km/h)

Weights: empty 4685lb (2125kg);
maximum take-off 5875lb (2665kg)
Dimensions: wing span 32ft 4in
(9.87m); length 28ft 4in (8.64m);
height 11ft 2in (3.40m)
Armament: two 7.9mm (0.31in) MG

17 machine guns in upper front
fuselage; two wing-mounted MG
FF 20mm (0.78in) cannon; one
nose-mounted MG FF 20mm
(0.78in) cannon firing through
propeller boss

all were soon destroyed. The squadron, with new Gladiators, returned to Norway in May, operating this time from Bardufoss, and in the next two weeks the RAF pilots shot down 21 enemy aircraft, but on 7 June the Norwegian campaign came to an end with the Germans everywhere victorious, and the surviving Gladiators, together with a few Hawker Hurricanes which had taken part in the battle, landed on the aircraft carrier HMS *Glorious*, bound for Scapa Flow in the Orkneys. The next day, she was intercepted by the German battlecruisers *Scharnhorst* and *Gneisenau* and sunk, most of the RAF personnel being lost with her.

BLITZKRIEG

At dawn on 10 May 1940, while the fighting in Norway still raged, the Germans launched their offensive against France, Belgium and Holland, attacking 72 Allied airfields. The Luftwaffe's main effort was directed against Holland, where airborne forces had the task of capturing vital strategic points and holding them until the 9th Panzer Division broke through. The German bomber formations were savagely opposed by the Fokker D.XXI fighters – the same type that had fought the Russians in Finland only a few weeks earlier – of the tiny Netherlands Army Air Force, but by noon on 14 May it no longer possessed any airworthy machines. The same was true in Belgium,

where airfields were heavily attacked by the Luftwaffe on the first day and 30 aircraft destroyed on the ground. They included 9 Hawker Hurricanes and 14 Gloster Gladiators, the Belgian Air Force's most modern fighter types. At nightfall on 14 May the entire Belgian fighter force consisted of six Italian-built Fiat CR.42 biplanes, which were evacuated to an airfield in northern France. During the first three days of the invasion the British and French air forces carried out desperate attacks on enemy armoured columns advancing through the Ardennes and across bridges over the River Meuse. Allied losses were fearsome; on the first day alone the squadrons of the RAF Advanced Air Striking Force in France, equipped with Fairey Battle light bombers, lost 23 aircraft out of 64 sent into action, and by the end of the second day the AASF's two squadrons of Blenheim bombers had also been wiped out. On 14 May the Germans forced a crossing of the Meuse near Sedan, and the commander of the reeling French First Army Group asked the RAF to mount an attack on the enemy bridgeheads using all available aircraft. A force of 63 Fairey Battles was mustered, and 35 were shot down. The French day bomber force also suffered heavy losses, and by the end of 14 May was in no position to carry out further attacks. Air cover for the German bridgeheads in the Sedan area was provided by three Geschwader of Messerschmitt 109s and

one of Bf 110s. In all, the German fighters flew 814 sorties and claimed the destruction of 89 Allied aircraft on 14 May; some German pilots flew as many as seven sorties before nightfall.

DUNKIRK

After the breakthrough at Sedan the German armoured columns raced across Belgium and northern France with shattering speed, driving for the Channel coast, and by 23 May it was clear that the Allied armies in Flanders – the Belgian Army, the French First Army and the British Expeditionary Force – were hopelessly trapped, with the BEF beginning its retreat to Dunkirk. On this day the panzers reached the Channel coast at Gravelines and swung northwards; 24 hours later they halted, partly because they had accomplished the major part of their mission and badly needed a rest, and partly because Hermann Göring, the Luftwaffe C-in-C, had indicated that his air power alone was capable of eliminating Allied resistance in and around the main evacuation ports. The Luftwaffe, in fact, was in no position to do anything of the kind. The Ju 87 Stuka dive-bombers of VIII Air Corps, which had supported the German armour in its dash through Belgium and France, was already badly overworked, and a large part of the Luftwaffe's medium bomber and fighter forces was still operating from bases inside Germany. Since Dunkirk and the

Hawker Hurricane Mk I

Type: single-seat fighter
Country of origin: United Kingdom
Powerplant: one 1030hp (768.8kW)
Rolls-Royce Merlin III 12-cylinder
Veetype engine

Performance: maximum speed
324mph (521km/h)
Weights: empty 5085lb (2308kg);
maximum take-off 6661lb (3024kg)
Dimensions: wing span 40ft

(12.19m); length 31ft 4in (9.55m);
height 13ft 4in (4.07m)
Armament: eight fixed wing-
mounted 0.303in (7.7mm) Colt-
Browning machine guns

other ports were within easy reach of fighter bases in southern England, the Stukas could expect strong opposition – and their own fighter escort would be at the limit of its range. The Stukas had a foretaste of things to come on 25 May when 15 of them were attacked by Spitfires over Calais and four were shot down. The day after that the Luftwaffe carried out its first major attacks on Dunkirk; constant defensive patrols were maintained by 16 Spitfire and Hurricane squadrons of No 11 Group, RAF Fighter Command, whose pilots claimed 20 victories in the course of the day. In the air battles that raged over and around the beaches during the nine days of the Dunkirk evacuation the RAF lost 177 aircraft, and the Luftwaffe sustained a comparable loss. Although these losses were roughly similar on paper, the inescapable fact remains that the Luftwaffe had, for the first time, lost the air superiority it had enjoyed since its attack on Poland the year before, and at the hands of the British fighter pilots it had suffered a psychological wound which, before long, would be made deeper and more damaging in the skies over southern England. After Dunkirk the Luftwaffe was heavily engaged in support of the German offensive across the River Somme against the French armies in the south, which fought on for another three weeks before the final collapse. The biggest air battle of this phase was fought on 3 June, when three large formations of German bombers with a

strong fighter escort, some 500 aircraft in total, carried out Operation Paula, a heavy raid on targets in the Paris area. The French put up every available fighter – including their latest Dewoitine D.520s, which were belatedly reaching the Escadres de Chasse – but their efforts lacked coordination; there was no early warning system and no real fighter control, and the enemy bombers often arrived over the French airfields before the fighters could take off. During the battle the French shot down 26 enemy aircraft; but 17 French fighters were destroyed in air combat and 16 more on the ground. The French Air Force fought on gallantly to the last, its situation becoming more hopeless after Italy declared war on the Allies on 10 June 1940 and its efforts crippled by shortages of fuel, ammunition and spares and by the continual need to evacuate its airfields before the Germans overran them. For most of France's fighter pilots, the armistice of 22 June 1940 came as a cruel blow; but many escaped to continue the fight as part of the Free French forces.

CHANNEL BATTLE
In June 1940, while the Battle of France still raged, the Luftwaffe began to turn its attention to 'fringe' targets, such as ports, on the English coast. This was a prelude to larger-scale attacks, starting early in July, on shipping in the English Channel, the aim being to probe Fighter Command's defences and reaction times,

in addition to inflicting physical damage on its fighter squadrons. The convoy attacks continued during July and the first week of August. Although there were several major air battles during this phase, usually in the Dover area, the enemy formations were usually intercepted by only half a dozen British fighters, and were often able to carry out their attack and head for home before any British fighters arrived. But Air Chief Marshal Sir Hugh Dowding, C-in-C Fighter Command, was husbanding his valuable fighter resources; he had earlier turned down repeated requests to send more RAF fighter squadrons to France, knowing that the decisive battle would be fought over the British Isles. His fighter assets at the beginning of July 1940 numbered about 600 aircraft – 29 squadrons of Hurricanes, 19 of Spitfires, seven of Blenheim fighters (most of which were assigned to night defence) and two of Boulton Paul Defiants. One of the latter squadrons, No 141, lost six aircraft in an encounter with Bf 109s on 19 July, and after that the Defiant played no further part in the daylight phase of the battle. Dowding's approach was essentially a scientific one; he believed that Britain's air defences should have the benefit of the very latest technological developments. This was reflected in Fighter Command's operations rooms, linked with one another by an elaborate system of telephone and teleprinter lines to provide an integrated system of control. This enabled fighter aircraft to be passed rapidly from sector to sector and from group to group, wherever they were most needed. It was No 11 Group, in the crucial southeast area of England, that would bear the brunt of the fighting throughout the battle; 29 of Dowding's squadrons were based there, with another 11 in No 12 Group, north of the Thames, and 17 in No 13 Group, covering northern England and Scotland.

RADAR BATTLE

Nowhere was modern technology more apparent in Britain's defences than in the use of radar, or radio direction finding (RDF) as it was then known. Developed by Robert Watson-Watt from earlier experiments in thunderstorm detection by the use of radio waves, the use of radar as an integral part of the British air defence system was laregely the fruit

■BELOW: The Hawker Hurricane was capable of withstanding a high degree of punishment. This particular example is shown after being hit by a German 20mm (0.78in) cannon shell.

of Dowding's initiative; he had worked with Watson-Watt in the 1930s and had not been slow to recognise the potential of the new invention. The Germans knew all about the British warning radar system, and the destruction of the radar stations on the south coast of England was recognised as a vital preliminary to the main air offensive against England. Planning for the offensive was completed by 2 August 1940. Air Fleets (Luftflotten) 2 and 3 were to attack simultaneously, their main tasks being to bring the RAF's fighters to combat, to destroy their airfields and the coastal radar stations, and to disrupt the RAF's ground organisation in southern England. The attacks on the south coast radar stations began on 12 August; one station, at Ventnor on the Isle of Wight, was damaged beyond repair, but although others suffered damage they were operational again within hours. The Germans, it transpired, were unaware of the importance and method of operation of the British radar system, and of its crucial value to the whole British air

defence structure. Attacks on radar sites were therefore sporadic and were soon abandoned, the Germans believing that the radar sites' operations rooms were in bomb-proof underground bunkers and were consequently invulnerable. In fact, they were mostly in huts above ground.

EAGLE ATTACK

The main German air offensive against the British Isles, code-named Adler Angriff (Eagle Attack) was launched on 13 August 1940, and the first days of the attack soon revealed the strengths and weaknesses of both sides. One aspect already appreciated by RAF fighter pilots was the wisdom of arming their Spitfires and Hurricanes with eight machine guns instead of four, as had originally been intended. At first, the idea was that the eight guns would throw out a large bullet pattern, rather like the pellets from a shotgun cartridge, so that the average pilot would stand some chance of striking the enemy, but experience showed that this was a waste of hitting power and eventually the guns were harmonised so

that their bullets converged 250 yards in front of the fighter's nose and then spread out again to a width of a few yards within a distance of 500 yards. In the few seconds available in which to destroy or disable an enemy aircraft, the concentration of eight guns firing 8000 rounds per minute (or 400 per three-second burst, representing a weight of metal of about 10lb (4.5kg) was frequently enough to knock a fatal hole in the wings, fuselage, tail or engine, assuming that the vital cockpit area was not hit. Against this, a three-second burst from a Bf 109's two Oerlikon MG-FF 20mm (0.78in) cannon and two 7.9mm (0.31in) machine guns weighed 18lb (8.16kg). But there was a drawback with the Swiss-designed Oerlikon; when the Germans modified it to make it lighter and faster-firing for use in fighter aircraft, they had to reduce the amount of explosive in the shell's charge, reducing the muzzle velocity (the speed at which the projectile leaves the muzzle of the gun) to 1800 feet (548m) per second, compared with the Browning's muzzle velocity of 2660 feet (810 metres) per second. The result was that the cannon

shells often exploded on impact, causing surface damage but failing to penetrate to a vital part. The Bf 109E-3, the RAF's principal fighter opponent in the Battle of France, had featured four MG17 machine guns, two mounted in the nose and two in the wings, and an engine-mounted FF cannon firing through the propeller boss, but complaints about this arrangement led to the deletion of the nose-mounted cannon, two Oerlikons being installed in the wings of the Bf 109E-4 variant, which equipped most German fighter units during the Battle of Britain. The aircraft's designer, Professor Willi Messerschmitt, had originally intended the 109's thin, frail wings to be left free of guns, but when the Luftwaffe High Command learned that the Spitfire and Hurricane were to be fitted with eight machine guns they insisted that the Bf 109 was to carry wing-mounted guns too. Messerschmitt was therefore forced to design a new wing, with bulges for the ammunition boxes of the 20mm (0.78in) cannon mounted on each side. Further strain was put on the wing when the Bf 109E variant was fitted with a more powerful Daimler Benz 601A engine, as

■ **ABOVE: Messerschmitt Bf 110s with underwing tanks. Designed as a long-range escort fighter and bomber 'destroyer', the Bf 110 was a failure in the Battle of Britain.**

ducted radiators had to be mounted underneath. One innovation, the Bf 109's narrow-track undercarriage, was designed so that the fuselage rather than the wings bore the weight of the aircraft on the ground; but five per cent of all 109s built, some 1750 aircraft, were destroyed in landing accidents.

LONG-RANGE ESCORT

It was soon established that the Bf 109E-4 was superior to the Hurricane on virtually every count except the British fighter's ability to absorb battle damage, and so Fighter Command adopted tactics whereby, in general, Hurricanes would attack the enemy bombers while Spitfires engaged the German fighter escort. The Spitfire was slightly faster than the Bf 109 and certainly more manoeuvrable, although the Messerschmitt had the edge at high altitude. However, the early attacks on targets in southern England brought a growing confirmation of the Bf 109E's most serious deficiency: a combat radius far shorter than was necessary to provide effective escort to bomber formations carrying out a heavy and sustained air assault. During the Battle of France, the Messerschmitt units had been able to provide effective air cover over the rapidly advancing German ground forces only by leap-frogging from one forward airstrip to another, and only a highly efficient Luftwaffe support echelon had kept the fighters effectively in action. A greater endurance and range built into the Bf 109E would have eased tremendously the workload imposed on the Luftwaffe logistics system. What is surprising, given the fact that the Japanese had neatly solved their need for long-range fighter escorts by fitting the Mitsubishi Zero fighters with disposable fuel tanks, was that the Germans did not fit similar tanks, which could be jettisoned just before combat, to their Bf 109s. The answer, no doubt, lay in the Luftwaffe's (or rather Göring's) faith in the twin-engined Messerschmitt Bf 110 Zerstörer (Destroyer), which had performed well enough against unescorted bombers in earlier battles but which was outclassed in fighter-versus-fighter combat. In 1939, the Luftwaffe was the only air force in the world which had tried to confront the problem of creating an escort fighter with sufficient range to accompany bombers to distant targets. Göring considered his Bf 110 units to be an elite force, and some of

Germany's best pilots were assigned to them. The Bf 110's poor acceleration and wide radius of turn made it no match for the Spitfire, but it was a good 40mph (64km/h) faster than the Hurricane and it carried a formidable nose armament of four 7.9mm (0.31in) machine guns and two 20mm (0.78in) cannon, plus a rear-wardfiring MG15 machine gun. If a Bf 110 had an opportunity to make a high-speed attack from high level and break off after a single firing pass, it could be very effective; but such opportunities were rare over England, and the Bf 110 squadrons suffered appalling losses. It was the Bf 109, therefore, that bore the brunt of the escort work, and there can be little doubt that its lack of range was a critical factor in the defeat of the Luftwaffe. The Bf 109E never had more than 20 minutes of combat time in which to protect its bombers, and its combat radius would take it only as far as the northern suburbs of London. Had the 109 been able to extend its time in the combat area by another 30 minutes through the use of external fuel tanks, then the consequences to Fighter Command might have been dire.

NIGHT OPERATIONS

The Luftwaffe's progressive switch to night operations, following its failure to win the daylight battle over England, confronted Fighter Command with a whole new set of problems. The key was airborne radar, which had been the subject of ongoing development in Britain

in the summer of 1940, by which time the RAF had five squadrons assigned to night fighting; these were equipped with Bristol Blenheims and two of them, Nos 29 and 604, were just starting to carry out trials with rudimentary Mk III AI radar. The real pioneering work, however, was undertaken by the Fighter Interception Unit at RAF Tangmere, and on the night of 22/23 July 1940 the long-awaited breakthrough came when a radar-equipped Blenheim of this unit intercepted and destroyed a Dornier Do 17 bomber. Flying Officer G. Ashfield, Pilot Officer G.E. Morris and Sergeant R.H. Leyland were patrolling at 10,000ft (3048m) when the Chain Home (CH) radar station at Poling established contact with a group of enemy raiders crossing the coast at about 6000ft (1829m). Information on the enemy's progress was passed to Tangmere Sector Operations Room where the FIU's CO, Wing Commander Peter Chamberlain, was acting as controller. Following Chamberlain's instructions, Ashfield closed on one of the enemy aircraft, the last phase of the interception being controlled by Morris's AI, and at a range of 400 yards (365 metres) identified it as a Do 17 and opened fire. The bomber, of II/KG3, went down into the sea off the Sussex coast. All four crew members, although wounded, were picked up. This was the first recorded success of a radar-assisted fighter, and although to some extent it was a lucky interception it showed that the concept was feasible, and

Bristol Beaufighter Mk VI

Type: two-seat night fighter
Country of origin: United Kingdom
Powerplant: two 1635hp (1219.2kW) Bristol Hercules VI 14-cylinder radials
Performance: maximum speed

333mph (536km/h)
Weights: empty 14,600lb (6622km); maximum take-off 21,600lb (9798kg)
Dimensions: wing span 57ft 10in (17.63m); length 41ft 8in (12.70m);

height 15ft 10in (4.82m)
Armament: four fixed forward-firing 20mm (0.78in) cannon in forward fuselage underside; six wing-mounted 0.303in (7.7mm) machine guns

the conversion of Blenheims to the night-fighter role continued. However, a few squadrons of Blenheims, converted to carry airborne radar, did not provide a solution to the night defence problem; they were too slow, the equipment was very unreliable, and their operators lacked experience. A solution was on the horizon in the shape of the fast, heavily armed Bristol Beaufighter, which was just entering service; but this aircraft was beset by more than the usual crop of teething troubles. In November and December 1940, Beaufighters and radar-equipped Blenheims flew over 600 sorties, made 71 radar contacts, and succeeded in destroying only four enemy aircraft.

DESPERATE MEASURES

In an attempt to fill the gap Fighter Command was compelled to adopt what might best be described as desperation measures to counter the enemy night raiders, especially when the Luftwaffe began to step up its night offensive against Britain after the failure of its massed daylight attacks in August and September. In the latter month, Air Chief Marshal Sir Hugh Dowding, the AOC-in-C Fighter Command, was ordered by the Air Council to allocate three squadrons of Hawker Hurricanes to night defence, this decision having been taken following the creation of a high-level Night Air Defence Committee earlier in the month. Added to

these were three squadrons of Boulton-Paul Defiants, which, armed solely with a four-gun power-operated turret, had suffered severe losses in the day fighter role during the Battle of Britain. During the closing weeks of 1940, these six squadrons of single-engined fighters flew 491 sorties on 46 nights and destroyed 11 enemy bombers. Operating on a hit-or-miss basis, pilots would seek out enemy bombers trapped in the glare of searchlights and would then go into the attack, risking being shot down by friendly anti-aircraft fire.

While the day fighter pilots struggled in an unfamiliar environment, night fighter developments were making steady progress. Delays in the production of AI Mk IV radar equipment had prevented the full complement of five Beaufighter units (Nos 25, 29, 219, 600 and 604 Squadrons) from becoming operational until the spring of 1941, but despite early teething troubles those that were operational had enjoyed some success. The first AI-assisted Beaufighter kill had been claimed on the night of 19/20 November 1940, when Flt Lt John Cunningham and Sgt Phillipson of No 604 Squadron were credited with the destruction of a Junkers 88, and by the time all five Beaufighter squadrons reached operational status their efficiency was greatly enhanced by the commissioning of six GCI (Ground

Controlled Interception) radar stations on the south and east coasts of England. These could provide fairly wide coverage, and controllers could bring the fighter to within three miles of the target aircraft, at which point the AI Mk IV radar took over. The first GCI-controlled interception was made by John Cunningham on 12 January 1941, but was unsuccessful because the Beaufighter's guns jammed. Then, on 10 May 1941 – the last major Luftwaffe attack on London – GCI-controlled Beaufighters destroyed 14 German bombers, the highest loss sustained by the Luftwaffe on any one night since the Blitz began. From now on, until the arrival of an even more effective night fighter – the de Havilland Mosquito – the fast Beaufighter, with its powerful armament of four 20mm (0.78in) cannon and six 0.303in (7.7mm) machine guns, would be the guardian of Britain's night skies. Thirteen more Beaufighter squadrons were assigned to the night defence of Great Britain in 1941–42, and many of the RAF's night fighter aces scored their early kills while flying the heavy twin-engined fighter. But by now the pressure in Britain's air defences had eased, for Hitler's aggressive intentions had focused on other parts of the arena. At first light on 22 June, 1941, 120 German divisions launched Operation Barbarossa, Hitler's invasion of the Soviet Union. Following the classic tactics

Polikarpov I-16

Type: single-seat fighter
Country of origin: USSR
Powerplant: one 1100hp (820.3kW) Shvetsov M-63 nine-cylinder radial
Performance: maximum speed 304mph (499km/h)

Weights: empty 3285lb (1490kg); maximum take-off 4619lb (2095kg)
Dimensions: wing span 29ft 6in (9.00m); length 20ft 1in (6.13m); height 8ft 5in (2.57m)
Armament: two 7.62mm (0.3in)

fixed forward-firing machine guns in upper part of forward fuselage; two wing-mounted 20mm (0.78in) cannon or 7.62mm (0.3in) machine guns

Mikoyan-Gurevitch MiG-3

Type: single-seat fighter
Country of origin: USSR
Powerplant: one 1350hp
(1006.7kW) Mikulin AM-35A 12-
cylinder Vee-type engine

Performance: maximum speed
398mph (640km/h)
Weights: empty 5721lb (2595kg);
maximum take-off 7385lb (3350kg)
Dimensions: wing span 33ft 5in

(10.20m); length 27ft (8.25m);
height 8ft 8in (2.65m)
Armament: one 12.7mm (0.5in) and
two 7.62mm (0.3in) machine guns
in upper forward fuselage

used during the Battle of France a year earlier, the attack was spearheaded by panzer divisions and an overwhelming concentration of air power, nearly 800 bombers and 480 fighters. During that first morning of the campaign, the Soviet Air Force in the west was decimated as the Luftwaffe attacked its forward airfields. On one airfield alone, German fighter pilots found nearly 100 Russian aircraft lined up in neat rows. Nevertheless, despite the almost total surprise achieved by the Germans, some Russian squadrons took to the air and put up a desperate fight, some Soviet fighter pilots deliberately ramming their opponents. The air fighting was not all one-sided; although the Messerschmitts were faster than the two most numerous Soviet fighter types, the I-16 and I-153, the German pilots often found themselves out-manoeuvred. The Russian pilots fought on the turn and the Germans often found it impossible to keep the nimble enemy in their sights. When a Russian pilot found himself in a difficult spot he would simply pull his aircraft round in a tight turn and race for his attacker head-on. These tactics usually worked, unnerving the German pilots and forcing them to break away sharply. Courage, however, was not enough. By noon on 22 June, 800 Russian aircraft had been destroyed. By nightfall the total had risen to 1489, including 322 shot down by flak and fighters. The Luftwaffe's losses during the day's fighting amounted to a mere 35

aircraft. On the last day of the month the Russians threw every available bomber into action; they were unescorted and the Luftwaffe shot them down in scores. Jagdgeschwader 51, operating in the Minsk area in support of 2nd Panzer Group, destroyed 114 aircraft on 30 June, while further north over the Dvina river the Bf 109s of JG54 accounted for 65. The slaughter went on for days; Luftwaffe fighter pilots who had arrived on the Eastern Front with no combat experience found themselves turned into aces literally overnight. Yet the apparent suicide of the Soviet Air Force was serving a purpose. At the cost of thousands of aircraft and lives, the Russians were buying time. Aircraft factories in the west were dismantled and reassembled in Siberia, beyond the range of the Luftwaffe's bombers, and although this massive evacuation caused a temporary drop in the monthly production total of military aircraft by 50 per cent, the figure would rise to 1000 machines per month by the spring of 1942.

GUARDS REGIMENTS

During the latter half of 1941, Russian fighter production concentrated on the more modern types that had begun to replace the elderly I-16s and I-153s: the Yak-1, MiG-1 and LaGG-3. These aircraft equipped the squadrons that took part in the defence of Moscow, which was subjected to 76 air attacks,

some of them heavy, before the end of 1941. Six Soviet fighter units that particularly distinguished themselves in the battle were designated Guards Regiments. As the war progressed, these and subsequent Guards Regiments would become the elite backbone of the Soviet Air Force, their ranks made up of Russia's best fighter pilots. As the first heavy autumn rains turned the summer dust into clinging mud along the Eastern Front, the Luftwaffe began to encounter improved fighter types in increasing numbers. The MiG-1 was redesignated MiG-3 after the 2100th machine had been produced, the main inmprovements being a fully enclosed cockpit and the addition of an auxiliary fuel tank. Because of the increased combat radius that resulted, MiG-3s were used extensively for fighter reconnaissance. The Yak-1 was also modified, its light 7.62mm (0.3in) machine guns being replaced by one and sometimes two 12.7mm (0.5in) Beresina guns. Its M-105PA engine was also replaced by a 1260hp (939.6kW) M-105PF. The third fighter, the LaGG-3, had proved a disappointment in combat with German fighters. Although its handling characteristics were excellent in level flight, acceleration was poor and the aircraft was sloppy during the tight manoeuvres necessary under combat conditions, with a tendency to spin out of tight turns. A method of overcoming the spinning problem was eventually developed by Lieutenant-Colonel Gruzdev, a Soviet Air Force test pilot, who

■ABOVE: The Bell Airacobra saw extensive service on the Eastern Front as a ground-attack aircraft with the Soviet air arm, despite its being designed as a fighter for the USAAF.

discovered that the aircraft's unpleasant habit could be cured by lowering 10 or 15 degrees of flap, which permitted a pilot to turn as tightly as he wished. Despite its faults, the LaGG-3 enjoyed a better reputation with its pilots than did the MiG-3; conceived as a high-altitude interceptor, the latter suffered a marked drop in performance when circumstances forced it to be adapted to other tasks.

ALLIED HELP

While the Soviet aircraft industry strove to gear up its production lines, help began to arrive from Allied sources. Two RAF squadrons, equipped with Hawker Hurricanes, reached North Russia in September 1941, and after five weeks of successful operations they turned their 24 aircraft over to the Russians – the first of some 2000 Hurricanes of all marks that would be delivered to the Soviet Air Force before the end of 1942. Soon after delivery of the first batch of Hurricanes, 170 Curtiss P-40 Tomahawks arrived in Russia through the northern ports. Russian pilots had no great love for the P-40, whose Allison engine was prone to sudden failure; nevertheless, the number of P-40s eventually handed over to the Russians was 2097, and the type saw service on all fronts. Other types delivered to the Soviet Union by Britain and the United States during the war

included the Supermarine Spitfire (143 Mk VBs and 1186 LF.9s); Bell P-39 Airacobra (4746 delivered); Bell P-63 Kingcobra (2400 delivered); Douglas A-20 Havoc (2908); North American B-25 Mitchell (862); and the Republic P-47 Thunderbolt (195). Altogether, 18,865 aircraft of all types were supplied, a further 638 being lost in transit. There is no doubt that the aircraft delivered by the western Allies played a big part in bringing about the ultimate Soviet victory in the air. But they did not turn the tide, as has often been suggested. The truth is that many of the combat types supplied to Russia during the war were substantially inferior to the combat types being mass-produced by the Soviet industry. The fact that the Russians received over half the total number of P-39 Airacobra and P-63 Kingcobras that were built was due mainly to their lack of success in USAAF service. The Russians adapted both aircraft to close support duties, adding armour and guns, and the Soviet pilots praised them highly – particularly the P-63, which was found to be capable of absorbing tremendous punishment from ground fire.

STALINGRAD

By the summer of 1942 the Soviet aircraft industry's output was beginning to pick up, and more new fighter types were making their appearance. The first of these was the Lavochkin La-5, which was developed from the LaGG-3. Towards the end of 1941, Semyon A. Lavochkin had fitted a standard LaGG-3 airframe with a 1600hp (1193.1kW) Shvetsov M-82A

radial engine, and during flight testing, which began early in 1942, the type was found to be 30mph (48km/h) faster than the Messerschmitt Bf 109F. The improved fighter was extremely promising and was ordered into quantity production, the first examples reaching front-line fighter regiments on the Stalingrad front in October 1942. The other fighter aircraft which made its operational debut on the Stalingrad front was the Yakovlev Yak-9, a progressive development of the Yak-1. From this basic type, Yakovlev had developed the Yak-7B and the Yak-7DI, both of which appeared in action in the summer of 1942. The Yak-7B had the same performance, engine and armament as the Yak-1, but it differed externally in having a redesigned cockpit, which afforded a better view to the rear, and a retractable tailwheel. The Yak-7DI was a long-range fighter version of the Yak-7B, and it was a slightly modified version of this type that served as the prototype Yak-9. The main difference between the Yak-9 and the Yak-7B was that the former had additional fuel tanks to extend its range, and the wing structure was modified to accommodate them. The type was initially built in two versions: the Yak-9D armed with a ShVAK 20mm (0.78in) cannon and a synchronised 12.7mm (05in) machine gun, and the Yak9T, with a 37mm (1.45in) NS cannon in place of the 20mm weapon. But one of the most important fighters on the Soviet inventory at this time was the P-39 Airacobra, and it was while flying this type of aircraft that one of Russia's leading air aces scored the majority of his victories. His name was

Aleksandr Ivanovich Pokryshkin. By the war's end, Pokryshkin would have destroyed 59 enemy aircraft and become a Hero of the Soviet Union three times over. The gold star medal of a Hero of the Soviet Union is Russia's highest award for gallantry, and only one other Soviet fighter pilot was destined to win this honour three times. He was Ivan Nikitich Kozhedub, who later surpassed Pokryshkin to become Russia's (and the Allies') top-scoring ace with 62 victories. Kozhedub did not enter combat until March 1943, which makes his achievement all the more outstanding.

MEDITERRANEAN AIR WAR

On 11 June 1940, the day after Italy's entry into the war on the side of Germany, a radar unit on the island of Malta reported an Italian air raid approaching from Sicily. Despite Malta's importance as a strategic bastion in the Mediterranean, the air defence of the island at this time consisted of only six Gloster Sea Gladiator biplanes, two of which immediately took off to intercept. Before they could reach the Italians, however, the latter had dropped their bombs on Valletta harbour and made their escape. The bombers came back that afternoon, this time escorted by Fiat CR.42 and Macchi C.200 fighters, and once again the Gladiators failed to intercept. During the days that followed, the Gladiator pilots were forced to develop new tactics to cope with their faster opponents; these involved climbing above the enemy formations before the latter reached Valletta and then diving

through them, using the speed of their dive to make one firing pass and upset the Italians' bombing runs. In the first two weeks of the war with Italy, the Italian Air Force (Regia Aeronautica) made seven attacks on Malta, but the Gladiators failed to shoot down any enemy aircraft. The first victory came on 22 June, when a lone Savoia-Marchetti (SM.79) reconnaissance aircraft appeared over the island. A Gladiator was airborne, and managed to get into a good attacking position before the Italian crew sighted it. The SM.79 was shot down into the sea and its crew taken prisoner. The Gladiators shot down two more Italian aircraft that week, and on 28 June Malta's defences received a boost when four Hawker Hurricanes flew in from North Africa. They came just in time, for only two Gladiators were now airworthy. More Hurricanes were flown in from the aircraft carrier HMS *Argus* early in August, and a complete Hurricane squadron was soon operational on the island. In November 1940, when the Italians launched a new series of attacks, several of their aircraft were shot down and the Italians developed new tactics, sending small numbers of fighter-bombers over the island on low level hit-and-run attacks. The RAF countered these by mounting standing patrols, with a flight of Hurricanes patrolling at high level and the two surviving Gladiators lower down. During this period, the principal Italian fighters encountered over the island remained the Fiat CR.42 biplane and the Macchi C.200. The Fiat CR.42 has been called a contemporary of

the Gloster Gladiator, but in fact there was a four-year gap between the first flights of their respective prototypes, the first Gladiator flying in September 1934 and the CR.42 in May 1938. Like the Gladiator, the CR.42 was the subject of substantial export orders, serving with the air arms of Hungary, Belgium and Sweden; but unlike the Gladiator, which was phased out of first-line service in 1941, the Italian fighter remained in full production from February 1939 until late in 1942. Some 300 were in service at the time of Italy's entry into the war in June 1940, and production totalled 1781 aircraft.

The other type, the Macchi MC 200 Saetta (Lightning) was the brainchild of Mario Castoldi, who had designed some highly successful seaplane racers between the wars and who had drawn on experience gained with the M.39, winner of the 1926 Schneider Trophy, and the MC.72, holder of the world air speed record in its class, in the design of his first fighter. Powered by a Fiat A74 radial engine, whose bulk tended to spoil the aircraft's otherwise neat contours, the MC.200 first flew on 24 December 1937, deliveries to the Regia Aronautica beginning in October 1939. About 150 aircraft were in service by June 1940.

MALTA UNDER SIEGE

By the end of 1940, Malta had developed into an offensive base, with island-based bomber squadrons attacking enemy targets in Italy, Sicily and North Africa. Then, in December, came a new development: the Luftwaffe entered the

Yakovlev Yak-1

Type: single-seat fighter
Country of origin: USSR
Powerplant: one 1100hp (820.3kW)
Klimov M-105P 12-cylinder Vee-type engine

Performance: maximum speed 373mph (600km/h)
Weights: empty 5174lb (2347kg); maximum take-off 6276lb (2847kg)
Dimensions: wing span 32ft 10in

(10.00m); length 27ft 10in (8.48m); height 8ft 8in (2.64m)
Armament: one 20mm (0.78in) cannon in nose; two 7.62mm (0.3in) machine guns in fuselage.

battle, the bomber and fighter units of Fliegerkorps X occupying Sicilian airfields in strength. On 11 January 1941 the Luftwaffe began a massive air onslaught against Malta. It continued almost without pause during the first three months of the year, during which period a handful of Hurricanes constituted the island's sole air defence. The fury of the attacks abated somewhat after March 1941, although they never ceased entirely. Meanwhile, the build-up of RAF aircraft on the island continued, and by October 1941 three Hurricane squadrons were based there. Throughout the summer months the Malta-based bomber squadrons had been striking hard at German and Italian shipping in the Mediterranean, and the losses they inflicted were so severe that the Luftwaffe High Command decided to make a final all-out attempt to destroy the island's air capability. For this purpose the Germans assembled 250 bombers and 200 fighters on airfields in Sicily and southern Italy; against this armada the RAF could muster a mere 60 Hurricanes. The renewed German air offensive began a few days before Christmas 1941, with waves of bombers attacking Malta's vital airfields between the rainstorms that lashed the area at this time of the year, and by the second week of January only Luqa was still

serviceable. As a direct result of these attacks the volume of supply traffic crossing the Mediterranean to replenish the enemy forces in North Africa showed a marked increase, and with German and Italian bombers inflicting substantial losses on Allied supply convoys to Malta, the island's position fast became critical. In March 1942, Malta's air defences were reinforced by the arrival of 15 Spitfires, flown off the carrier HMS *Eagle* at enormous risk; they arrived at a time when only 30 serviceable Hurricanes were left. In April, while these aircraft continued the fight, the determined resistance of the island fortress and its people was honoured by the award of the George Cross. On 20 April 1942, 47 more Spitfires reached the island after flying from the aircraft carrier USS *Wasp*; their arrival, however, had been detected by the Germans, and within hours their airfields were under attack. By the end of the next day, after further heavy raids, only 18 of the original 47 Spitfires were still airworthy.

CLIMAX OF THE RAIDS

On 9 May the USS *Wasp* returned, together with HMS *Eagle*, and between them the carriers flew off 64 more Spitfires, which went into action almost immediately. The following day saw a major air battle over the island when the

Lufwaffe made a determined effort to sink the minelayer HMS *Welshman*, which had docked in Valletta harbour, laden with supplies and ammunition. Between them the island's Spitfires and Hurricanes flew 124 sorties that day, destroying 15 enemy aircraft. Three Spitfires were lost, but two of the pilots survived. Seventeen more Spitfires arrived later in May and deliveries of fighter aircraft continued throughout the summer months of 1942; HMS *Eagle* alone delivered 182 Spitfires before she was sunk by a U-boat on 11 July. Most of the ferry work was undertaken by HMS *Furious*, which flew off 37 Spitfires on the day HMS *Eagle* went down, followed by 27 more on 7 August. Several RAF pilots distinguished themselves in the summer of 1942; one of them was Canadian-born Pilot Officer George F. Buerling, who scored 27 victories while flying Spitfires over the island. He survived the war only to be killed while ferrying an aircraft to Israel in 1948. The enemy raids continued, reaching their climax in November 1942, when the Germans subjected Malta to a furious round-the-clock bombardment that lasted ten days. The defenders remained unbroken, and the offensive against the supply convoys ferrying desperately needed supplies and reinforcements to the German and Italian forces in North Africa went on almost

Gloster Gladiator

Type: single-seat biplane fighter
Country of origin: United Kingdom
Powerplant: one 830hp (18.9)
Bristol Mercury IX 9-cylinder radial
Performance: maximum speed

253mph (407km/h)
Weights: empty 3600lb (1633kg);
maximum take-off 4592lb (2083kg)
Dimensions: wing span 32ft 3in
(9.83m); length 27ft 5in (8.36m);

height 10ft 7in (3.22m)
Armament: two 0.303in (7.7mm)
Browning machine guns in sides of
forward fuselage, and two wing-
mounted 0.303in (7.7mm) guns

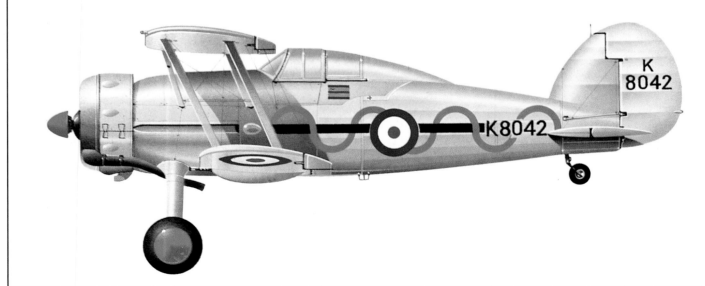

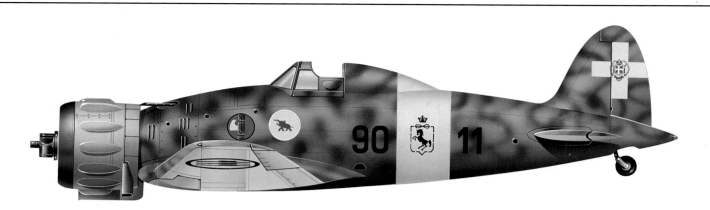

Macchi MC.200 Saetta

Type: single-seat fighter
Country of origin: Italy
Powerplant: one 870hp (648.7kW)
Fiat A.74 RC.38 14-cylinder radial
Performance: maximum speed

312mph (503km/h)
Weights: empty 4451lb (2019kg);
maximum take-off 5597lb (2339kg)
Dimensions: wing span 34ft 8in
(10.58m); length 26ft 10in

(8.19m); height 11ft 6in (3.51m)
Armament: two 12.7mm (0.5in)
Breda-SAFAT machine guns in
upper forward fuselage

unchecked. The battle for Malta was over; by the end of the year most of the Luftwaffe units in Sicily had been withdrawn for service on other fronts. In the early months of 1943, Malta was turned into a major supply base as the Allies built up their resources for the offensive that would take them across the narrow straits to Sicily and, ultimately, the Italian mainland.

NAVAL FIGHTER DEFENCE

Throughout the whole period of the siege of Malta, the greatest threat to the Allied naval forces in the Mediterranean was air attack, once the Italian fleet had been effectively dealt with by the Royal Navy. The standard British fleet fighters at the onset of hostilities with Italy were the Gloster Sea Gladiator, which in effect was a Gladiator with a strengthened rear fuselage and an arrester hook, and the Blackburn Skua, which was not really a fighter at all, but a dive-bomber. A much better proposition, which arrived in the Mediterranean on board the new fleet carrier HMS *Illustrious* in November 1940, was the Fairey Fulmar. Powered by a Rolls-Royce Merlin engine, the Fulmar was armed with eight Browning 0.303in (7.7mm) machine guns, like the Hurricane and Spitfire, and although its maximuim speed of 270mph (435km/h) – a limit partly imposed by the addition of a second crew member – made it a good deal slower than contemporary land-based monoplane fighters, it performed very well in the air battles that raged

over and around the Mediterranean convoys in 1941–2. By 1942 the fleet defence squadrons in the Mediterranean had also begun to receive the Hawker Sea Hurricane, the carrier-based variant of the famous land-based fighter. Its deployment came just in time, for the convoys were now coming under attack from fast Reggiane fighter-bombers, which specialised in making their runs at low level and were difficult to catch. The principal model was the Reggiane Re 2002 Ariete (Ram), which was developed from the Re 2000 export version. Armed with two 12.7mm (0.5in) and two 7.7mm (0.303in) guns, the Ariete could carry a useful load of up to 1433lb (650kg) of bombs. Together with the Fulmar, the Sea Hurricane was active in the desperate air battles of June and August 1942, as the Axis air forces did everything in their power to destroy the supply convoys that were Malta's last hope of survival.

BATTLE FOR GREECE

While the RAF battled in the skies of Malta, the air war had raged no less furiously in other sectors of the Mediterranean theatre. Considerable success had been achieved right at the start of the war with Italy by three squadrons of RAF Gladiator fighters, which saw action over the Egyptian border against the Italian Air Force in June and July 1940; No 33 Squadron, for example, shot down 38 enemy aircraft and destroyed 20 more on the ground in six weeks of combat, while the Gladiators

of No 80 Squadron destroyed nine Italian Fiat CR.42 fighters in a single day for the loss of only one of their own machines. Not long afterwards these two squadrons and the third Gladiator unit in Egypt, No 112 Squadron, were sent to Greece, which had been invaded by the Italians. No 80 was the first to arrive and was detailed to support the Greek Army fighting hard on the Albanian frontier; its pilots had shot down 40 enemy aircraft by the end of the year, when they were joined by their colleagues of No 112 Squadron. In January 1941, when the Gladiators of No 33 Squadron also arrived in Greece, bad weather hampered air operations but, on 9 February, 14 Gladiators of No 80 Squadron, led by Flight Lieutenant M.T.St J. Pattle, engaged 40 Fiat G.50 fighters and shot four of them down for no loss. Pattle, a South African, was credited with the destruction of 30 enemy aircraft – possibly more – during operations in Egypt and Greece; he was shot down and killed on 20 April 1941 while commanding No 33 Squadron. By the end of February 1941 all three RAF fighter squadrons in Greece were rearming with Hurricanes, and these operated side by side with the remaining Gladiators. On 28 February, 16 Hurricanes and 12 Gladiators were patrolling at 14,000ft (4267m) when they sighted a formation of 50 Italian bombers and fighters. While the Gladiators circled round the enemy formation to cut off its escape, the Hurricanes attacked it, and in the ensuing air battle the RAF fighters claimed no fewer than 27 aircraft destroyed – all of which were confirmed by observers on the ground – and a further 11 probably destroyed. The success, however, was to be short-lived, for in April 1941 the Germans entered the battle for Greece. By 19 April, attacks by the Luftwaffe on Greek airfields had reduced the total strength of the RAF fighter squadrons to only 22 aircraft, and a few days later all but seven fighters were destroyed in low-level strafing attacks by Messerschmitts. With this blow, Allied air resistance over Greece ceased to exist. The battle for Greece was followed by the German airborne invasion of Crete, which had no air defences to speak of and which was quickly overwhelmed.

DESERT WAR

In March 1941, while the Allies still fought desperately in Greece, the German

Afrika Korps arrived in Libya under the command of General Erwin Rommel, and the British forces were soon in retreat along the road they had taken in their victorious advance against the Italians a few months earlier. The British garrison at Tobruk was quickly surrounded and, to provide fighter cover, the Hurricanes of Nos 6 and 73 Squadrons were flown in. With their airstrip under continual shellfire, operational conditions were grim, and by 35 April No 73 Squadron was so depleted that it had to be withdrawn, leaving the Hurricanes of No 6 as the only operational aircraft within the Tobruk perimeter. They, too, had to be withdrawn on 10 May. Meanwhile, new Allied squadrons were being formed to challenge the Luftwaffe's air superiority, and in the spring of 1941 the RAF in the Western Desert was joined by air units from Australia and South Africa. The build-up of the Desert Air Force

continued throughout the summer months, in readiness for Operation Crusader – the plan to relieve the Tobruk garrison – and by November there were 40 fighter squadrons in the Middle East, equipped primarily with Hurricanes and American-built Curtiss P-40 Kittyhawks. Operation Crusader began on 18 November, with the British Eighth Army thrusting towards Tobruk. The troops were supported by the Allied fighter and fighter-bomber squadrons, which carried out constant attacks on Rommel's armour. The Afrika Korps fought hard for a week before Rommel broke off the engagement and withdrew to the west, still pounded by the Desert Air Force, and the Germans now worked hard to establish a defensive line based on Gazala. This line was broken in December by a new Eighth Army offensive and the Allied forces pushed on towards Benghazi, but they were halted at El Agheila.

Curtiss P-40 Kittyhawk

Type: single-seat fighter-bomber
Country of origin: USA
Powerplant: one 1200hp
(894.84kW) Allison V-1710-81 12-
cylinder Vee-type engine
Performance: maximum speed

343mph (552km/h)
Weights: empty 6200lb (2812kg);
maximum take-off 11,400lb
(5171kg)
Dimensions: wing span 37ft 3in
(11.37m); length 33ft 4in (10.16m);

height 10ft 7in (3.23m)
Armament: six wing-mounted
0.50in (12.7mm) machine guns,
plus 1500lb (680kg) of external
ordnance

COUNTER-ATTACK

In January 1942 Rommel counter-attacked in strength. The Allied air effort was severely hampered by flooding on the forward airstrips, and for the first 48 hours the fighter-bombers were able to give only limited support to the Eighth Army. Emergency strips were quickly laid, and the Hurricane and Kittyhawk squadrons concentrated on these, carrying out virtually non-stop ground attack operations during the hours of daylight. The Germans, nevertheless, were able to continue their advance, and by February they had pushed the Eighth Army back as far as Rommel's former defensive line between Gazala and Bir Hakeim. The line held firm until May, when three German divisions outflanked Bir Hakeim and cut off the 1st Free French Brigade. The French gallantly resisted every German assault for ten days, and the Desert Air Force threw every fighter it could spare into the battle. The Hurricanes and Kittyhawks wrought great execution among the formations of Ju 87 Stukas that were battering the French stronghold, and No 6 Squadron RAF – now flying tank-busting Hurricane IIDs armed with 40mm cannon – struck hard at the encircling enemy armour and artillery. By

■**LEFT: The Supermarine Seafire, originally converted from a batch of Spitfire VBs, wasn't a great success as a carrier aircraft. It lacked range, and it had a record of landing mishaps.**

10 June, however, the position of the French brigade was hopeless, and the survivors were ordered to fight their way out. By pinning down the German divisions the French had bought time for the Eighth Army to withdraw into Egypt and regroup along a short defensive line from El Alamein to the Qattara Depression; the El Alamein position was attacked in full strength on 31 August, but the Eighth Army held on grimly and inflicted heavy losses on the enemy, while the Desert Air Force continued to increase its overall superiority. By this time the Hurricanes and Kittyhawks which had borne the brunt of Allied fighter operations for so long were being reinforced by more modern combat types, including Spitfires and Beaufighters. No 145 Squadron was the first to receive Spitfires in the desert, in January 1942; it was later joined by Nos 92 and 601 Squadrons. At last, the British could meet the Luftwaffe's Messerschmitt Bf 109Fs on equal terms.

THE STAR OF AFRICA

One of the first Luftwaffe fighter units to arrive in Africa in April 1941 was Jagdgeschwader 27, whose Messerschmitt 109s had been in almost continuous action ever since. Among JG 27's officers was a 21-year-old fighter pilot whose name soon became legendary on both sides of the front: Hans-Joachim Marseille, who flew a Bf 109F with a distinctive yellow '14' painted on its fuselage. In 18 months of operations

Marseille claimed the destruction of 158 Allied aircraft, often shooting down several in a single day. His claims were bitterly disputed by the Allies, and yet all were verified by Marseille's fellow pilots or German ground forces. Before long, the German propaganda machine had nicknamed him the 'Star of Africa'. Marseille attributed his success to his ability to retain full control of his fighter while manoeuvring at low speed, which usually enabled him to turn inside his opponent. He was also an excellent deflection shot. On 5 June 1942, when he landed after shooting down six Kittyhawks of No 5 Squadron, South African Air Force, his astonished armourers discovered that he had used only ten 20mm (0.78in) shells and 180 rounds of machine gun ammunition. No Allied fighter pilot ever brought Marseille to account. On 30 September 1942, while returning to base after an uneventful escort mission, his Messerschmitt caught fire without warning and he baled out. His comrades saw his body strike the tailplane and plummet to earth, his parachute unopened. They buried him where he fell.

By the time of Marseille's death, it was clear that Rommel's offensive – hampered by continual air attack on his overstretched supply lines – had failed,

■**ABOVE: The Blackburn Skua was an excellent dive-bomber, but was never used to its best advantage in this role. It was also used as a fighter, with four wing-mounted machine guns.**

■**LEFT: Fairey Fulmars, with Grumman Martlets in the background, ranged on the deck of the carrier HMS *Illustrious*. In the background, the battleship HMS *Valiant* carries out a practice shoot.**

and the Eighth Army, now commanded by General Bernard Montgomery, prepared a massive counter-attack at El Alamein. This began on 23 October 1942, and the entire strength of the Desert Air Force's fighter-bomber squadrons was turned on the reeling enemy, who finally broke on 4 November. The coastal roads leading to the west were jammed with enemy convoys, which were harried mercilessly by the fighter-bombers during the pursuit into Cyrenaica. Meanwhile, the Allies had launched Operation Torch, a massive landing on the coasts of French Morocco and Algeria by seaborne forces, supported by airborne troops who captured key points inland. Caught between the two Allied pincers, the Germans sought to establish new defences in Tunisia and seized a number of ports, through which they attempted to pour in supplies.

THE END IN AFRICA

In April 1943 the Eighth Army linked up with the American II Corps and the final advance through Tunisia began, with the fighter-bomber units at the forefront of the battle all the way. On occasions RAF Hurricane squadrons operated from temporary landing grounds behind the enemy lines, attacking the Germans from the rear. By May the Afrika Corps was tottering to defeat. In a desperate, last-ditch effort to provide reinforcements, fleets of Junkers Ju 52 and Messerschmitt 323 transport aircraft left Italy and Sicily for the German-held Tunisian airfields; they were caught by formations of Allied fighters, often while still far out to sea, and slaughtered. On 18 April 1943, for example, 47 P-40 Warhawks of the US Ninth Air Force, together with 12 Spitfires of No 92 Squadron RAF, intercepted a formation of 90 Ju 52s escorted by 50 German and Italian fighters and destroyed 77 of them for the loss of six Warhawks and a Spitfire. This great air battle, called the Palm Sunday Massacre, resulted in the destruction of more enemy aircraft than the RAF shot down in one day at the height of the Battle of Britain. On 22

April, RAF Spitfires followed up this success by shooting down 21 massive Me 323 six-engined transports, all heavily laden with troops. It was the end. On 13 May 1943 the remnants of the Afrika Korps finally surrendered. They had fought valiantly to the last, tumbling from the height of victory to crushing defeat; a defeat brought about in no small measure by the Desert Air Force and the RAF and Fleet Air Arm squadrons on Malta, which had battled through fearful odds to win overall air supremacy for the Allied cause in North Africa. The way to the invasion of southern Europe was now open.

PEARL HARBOR

The Axis defeat in North Africa, at long last, seemed to stem the tide of reverses that had overwhelmed the Allies during the first three years of the war. Admittedly, as the bitter year of 1941 drew to a close, Britain and her Commonwealth Allies had seemed to see the first faint glimmer of hope in their struggle against Germany. In North Africa General Erwin Rommel's forces had suffered their first reverse at the hands of the British Eighth Army, while in Russia the German offensive had ground to a halt at the gates of Moscow. Then, on 7 December, had come the first of a series of shattering blows which, in the weeks to come, would alter the whole basis of Allied strategy: the Japanese attack on Pearl Harbor in the Hawaiian Islands, devastating the American Pacific

Fleet and paving the way for further conquests. By the end of December the Japanese had invaded Thailand, Burma and Malaya, had captured Wake Island and Hong Kong, and had carried out a major landing on Luzon, in the Philippines. These early conquests were a triumph of air power, and particularly naval air power; and it was naval aviation that would be the dominant factor in the great battles that were to come. The one significant failure of the Japanese strike on Pearl Harbor was that it had not destroyed the US Pacific Fleet's three aircraft carriers, which had been at sea at the time; these now formed the nucleus of the US Navy's first carrier task force, the forerunner of a mighty weapon that would ultimately carry the war back across the Pacific to the Japanese home islands. The overwhelming superiority of Japanese naval air power came as a complete shock to the Allies, and the nastiest surprise of all was the enemy's ability to provide strong fighter escort for their bombers over enormous distances. On 8 December 1941, for example, 45 Mitsubishi Zero fighters escorted a formation of bombers from Formosa to carry out an attack on the Philippines, a round trip of 1200 miles (1930km). The A6M Zero fighter soon showed itself to be clearly superior to any fighter the Allies could put into the air in the early stages of the Pacific war. Armed with two 20mm (0.78in) cannon and two machine guns, it was highly

Reggiane Re.2000 Falco I

Type: single-seat fighter
Country of origin: Italy
Powerplant: one 985hp (734.5kW) Piaggio P.XI RC.40 14-cylinder radial engine

Performance: maximum speed 329mph (530km/h)
Weights: empty 4585lb (2080kg); maximum take-off 6349lb (2880kg)
Dimensions: wing span 36ft 1in

(11.00m); length 26ft 2in (7.99m); height 10ft 6in (3.20m)
Armament: two 12.7mm (0.5in) Breda-SAFAT machine guns in upper forward fuselage

■ABOVE: The Brewster Buffalo, which equipped several RAF, RAAF and RNZAF squadrons at the time of Pearl Harbor, was completely outclassed by the Japanese Zero fighter.

manoeuvrable and structurally very strong, despite being lightweight. Its main drawback was that it had no armour plating for the pilot and no self-sealing fuel tanks, which meant that it could not absorb as much battle damage as Allied fighters. One well-placed burst of gunfire was usually enough to make the Zero explode in mid-air, and for the pilot that meant certain death, for the Japanese scorned the use of parachutes.

ELITE UNITS

During the first months of the Pacific war the Zeros carved out an impressive combat record. In the battle for Java, which ended on 8 March 1942, they destroyed 550 Allied aircraft. including large numbers of fighters such as the Brewster Buffalo, Curtiss-Wright CW.21, Curtiss Hawk, Curtiss P-40 and Hawker Hurricane. Japanese losses were extremely light. In one big dogfight that took place over Soerabaya on 19 February 1942, 23 Zeros operating from Borneo took on a force of 50 Dutch and American P-36 and P-40 fighters and destroyed more than half of them for the loss of only three of their own number. These remarkable victories earned enormous prestige for the Japanese Navy pilots and tended to overshadow the achievements of their Army colleagues, who fought no less tenaciously albeit with less spectacular success. Throughout the war, the demands of the Navy were to receive priority. Unlike the Army, the Japanese Navy followed the practice of concentrating its best pilots in elite units. One of these was based at Lae in New Guinea in April 1942, and was assigned the task of providing fighter cover for the Japanese drive on Port Moresby, the capture of which was an essential stepping stone to the invasion of Australia. By the end of the month the Lae Fighter Wing included such redoubtable pilots as Saburo Sakai, with 22 victories, Hiroyoshi Nishizawa with 13, and Takatsuka with nine. On 17 May, in a gesture of supreme arrogance that symbolised their complete air supremacy, Sakai, Nishizawa and another pilot named Ota carried out a sequence of aerobatics over the Allied airfield at Port Moresby without being molested. Most of the pilots of the Lae Wing continued to fly the Zero throughout their combat careers. Nishizawa, before being shot down and killed on 26 October 1944, was credited with 94 victories; he destroyed six enemy aircraft in one day over Guadalcanal late in 1942. Another pilot, Kenze Okabe, shot down seven American aircraft in one day over Rabaul in August 1942. Saburo Sakai went on to end the war with 64 victories, making him the surviving Japanese top-scorer. Apart from the Curtiss P-40, the American fighter most often encountered by the Zero pilots was the Bell P-39 Airacobra, which went into action with the 8th Pursuit Group in northern Australia early in 1942, subsequently deploying its aircraft to forward airstrips in New Guinea. Shortly afterwards the unit's designation was changed to the 8th Fighter Group and it was joined by the 35th Fighter Group, also with P-39s. The fighters were a mixture of P-39Ds and Airacobra Mk Is, drawn from a cancelled British order. (The RAF, at first enthusastic about the P-39, soon found it to fall far short of requirements and only one squadron, No 601, was issued with it.) P-39s were also used by the 347th Fighter Group in New Caledonia, with detachments being deployed to Guadalcanal for air defence.

BATTLE FOR BURMA

The Nakajima Ki-43 Hayabusa (Peregrine Falcon) was the Allies' principal opponent in Burma, where air defence was the responsibility of two squadrons of RAF Hurricanes, a few Brewster Buffaloes, and the Curtiss P-40s of the American Volunteer Group (AVG), which had been fighting the Japanese on behalf of the Chinese Government since the summer of 1941, several months before the attack on Pearl Harbor. The Buffalo, which equipped several squadrons of the RAF, RAAF and RNZAF in the theatre, was outclassed by the Zero and the Hayabusa on every count, and had soon been wiped out during the Japanese campaign in Malaya. Only about 40 Hayabusas (the aircraft would soon be given the code-name Oscar by the Allies) were in service with the Japanese Army Air Force (JAAF) in December 1941, and these were deployed to China. As time went by, the type replaced the Nakajima Ki-27, which was in use by the JAAF during the invasion of Burma. Initially, the RAF and AVG, who worked in close concert with Burmese capital, Rangoon, but as the Japanese invasion gathered momentum their story was to be one of endless retreat. At the end of March 1942, starved of reinforcements and supplies, the RAF squadrons pulled back across the Indian frontier and the AVG moved to advanced bases in China, from where the Americans provided air cover for retreating Chinese armies. On 4 July 1942 the American Volunteer Group officially ceased to be an independent fighting unit and became part of the newly activated China Air Task Force, under command of the Tenth Air Force. Meanwhile, April 1942 had seen the RAF's Hawker Hurricanes in action in the defence of Ceylon. Early on April 5, a powerful Japanese carrier task force was sighted heading for Ceylon, and soon afterwards the Japanese launched a strike of 52 Nakajima B5N Kate high-level bombers and 38 Aichi D3A Val dive-bombers, escorted by 36 Zeros, to attack Colombo. Fierce air battles developed over the city and harbour as the raiding force was intercepted by 42 Hurricanes and Fulmars; seven Japanese aircraft were destroyed, but 19 British fighters were shot down. In a second attack four days later, nine out of a defending force of 23 British fighters were shot down. The raids on Ceylon underlined, in almost contemptuous fashion, Japan's air superiority in the early months of 1942; but the situation was about to alter.

CARRIER BATTLES

The Zero retained its overall ascendency during the first two years of the Pacific conflict, even though the Japanese suffered some serious reverses during this period. The first of these was the Battle of the Coral Sea in May 1942, when – in the first naval engagement in history fought without the opposing fleets making visual contact – American carrier forces prevented the Japanese from carrying out their proposed landing at Port Moresby, even though American losses were higher than those of their

Grumman F4F Wildcat

Type: single-seat fighter
Country of origin: USA
Powerplant: one 1200hp (894.8kW)
Pratt & Whitney R-1830-86 Twin
Wasp 14-cylinder radial

Performance: maximum speed
318mph (512km/h)
Weights: empty 5758lb (2612kg);
maximum take-off 7952lb (3607kg)
Dimensions: wing span 38ft

(11.58m); length 28ft 9in (8.76m);
height 9ft 2in (2.81m)
Armament: six wing-mounted
0.50in (12.7mm) machine guns

Mitsubishi A6M Zero

Type: single-seat fighter
Country of origin: Japan
Powerplant: one 950hp (708.4kW)
Nakajima NK1C Sakae 14-cylinder
radial engine

Performance: maximum speed
332mph (534km/h)
Weights: empty 3704lb (1680kg);
maximum take-off 6164lb (2796kg)
Dimensions: wing span 39ft 4in

(12.00m); length 29ft 9in (9.06m);
height 10ft (3.05m)
Armament: two wing-mounted
20mm (0.78in) cannon; two 7.7mm
(0.303in) MGs in forward fuselage

adversary. Then, in June, came the Battle of Midway, when United States carrier aircraft broke up a strong enemy invasion force, sinking two heavy and two light carriers and one heavy cruiser, and destroying 258 aircraft. This battle, in which the Americans lost 132 aircraft and the carrier USS *Yorktown*, marked a definite turning-point in the Pacific war. Not only did it bring an end to Japan's offensive; it also resulted in the loss of a major part of the enemy's carrier attack force and many of the Japanese Navy's most experienced pilots. The standard American carrier-based fighter during the first months of the Pacific war was the Grumman F4F-3 Wildcat, a type that was inferior to the Zero on almost every count. Although very robust and capable of withstanding a tremendous amount of battle damage, it needed a highly experienced pilot at the controls to give the Wildcat a fighting chance of survival in combat with the Japanese fighters. Nevertheless, a number of US Navy pilots scored several noteworthy victories while flying the Wildcat; on 20 February 1942, for example, while flying from the carrier USS *Lexington*, Lieutenant Edward H. O'Hare destroyed five Japanese bombers over Rabaul, while Lieutenant J.G. McCuskey of the USS *Yorktown* also destroyed five during the Coral Sea battle. Another notable Wildcat pilot was Captain Joe Foss, a Marine officer who went on to shoot down 26 enemy aircraft. As the American pilots gained combat experience during 1942, their superior

tactics and teamwork began to have a telling effect on the course of the Pacific air war. Moreover, while the Japanese still relied upon the fighter types with which they had begun the war – the Zero in the case of the Navy, and the Nakajima Ki-43 Hayabusa in the case of the Army – the United States aircraft industry was beginning to produce new combat aircraft which, before long, would enable them to wrest air superiority from the enemy.

FORAYS INTO FRANCE
In northwest Europe, with the Battle of Britain won and Operation Sealion, Hitler's projected invasion of England, postponed indefinitely, RAF Fighter Command began to go over to the offensive. While Blenheim, Hurricane and Defiant intruders prowled around enemy airfields in France and the Low Countries at night, Spitfires and Hurricanes, at first in small numbers, began to make incursions into enemy territory. Their pilots reported that the Luftwaffe was absent from the sky. Encouraged, Fighter Command decided to try something bigger. On 9 January 1941, in brilliant sunshine and perfect visibility, five fighter squadrons penetrated 30 miles into France. There was no sign of movement on the snow-covered airfields they flew over; not a single Messerschmitt took to the air to engage them. Offensive sweeps, usually in concert with small-scale bombing raids, were carried out whenever the weather

permitted during the early weeks of 1941, and Luftwaffe opposition gradually increased. It was clear that the Germans, following the policy adopted by the RAF before the Battle of Britain, were reluctant to commit their fighter defences in strength. But there was also another reason; in January 1941, several first-line Luftwaffe fighter units on the Channel coast had begun to rearm with an improved model of the Messerschmitt, the Bf 109F-1, but early in February three 109Fs were lost when the complete tail assembly broke away, and the remainder had to be withdrawn for structural modifications. By March 1941, fighter sweeps over the continent were becoming organised affairs, with the Spitfire and Hurricane squadrons operating at wing strength. A Fighter Command wing consisted of three squadrons, each of 12 aircraft. There were Spitfire wings at Biggin Hill, Hornchurch and Tangmere, mixed Spitfire and Hurricane wings at Duxford, Middle Wallop and Wittering, and Hurricane wings at Kenley, Northolt and North Weald. The Hurricane wings would soon be rearmed with Spitfires; these were Mk Vs, which had begun to enter service in March 1941. Converted from Mk I airframes, the Mk V was to be the major Spitfire production version, with 6479 examples completed. The majority of Spitfire Vs were armed with two 20mm (0.78in) cannon and four machine guns, affording a greater chance of success against armour plating. The Mk V was powered by a Rolls-Royce Merlin

Nakajima Ki-43 Hayabusa

Type: single-seat fighter
Country of origin: Japan
Powerplant: one 1150hp (857.5kW)
Nakajima Ha-115 14-cylinder radial
Performance: maximum speed

329mph (530km/h)
Weights: empty 4211lb (1910kg);
maximum take-off 6450lb (2925kg)
Dimensions: wing span 35ft 7in
(10.84m); length 29ft 3in (8.92m);

height 10ft 9in (3.28m)
Armament: two 12.7mm (0.5in)
Type 1 machine guns in upper
forward fuselage

45 engine, developing 1415hp (1055.2kW) at 19,000ft (5800m) against the 1150hp (857.5kW) of the Merlin XII fitted in the Mk II. Nevertheless, the Mk V was essentially a compromise aircraft, rushed into service to meet an urgent Air Staff requirement for a fighter with a performance superior to that of the latest model of Messerschmitt. The debut of the Spitfire V came just in time, for in May 1941 the Luftwaffe fighter units began to receive the Messerschmitt Bf 109F, its technical problems now resolved. On 11 May, a group of bomb-carrying Bf 109Fs attacked Lympne and Hawkinge, one being shot down by a Spitfire. The Spitfire V, however, failed to provide the overall superiority Fighter Command needed so badly. At high altitude, where many combats took place, it was found to be inferior to the Bf 109F on most counts, and several squadrons equipped with the Mk V took a severe mauling during that summer.

CIRCUS OPERATIONS
Handling the large fighter formations which were being pushed across the Channel in the sumer of 1941 called for a high degree of skill on the part of the fighter controllers, whose vital role is all too often ignored, or rather eclipsed, in headier tales of air combat. And by July 1941, Circus operations, as these missions were called, were very large affairs indeed, with as many as 18 squadrons of fighters – more than 200 aircraft - covering a small force of bombers. On 12 August, the medium

bombers of the RAF's No 2 Group made their deepest penetration into enemy territory so far when 54 Blenheims bombed two power stations near Cologne. They were escorted by the Westland Whirlwind fighters of No 263 Squadron, the only fighter aircraft with sufficient range to carry out this task. The Whirlwind was highly manoeuvrable, faster than a Spitfire at low altitude, and its armament of four closely grouped 20mm (0.78in) cannon made it a match for any Luftwaffe fighter of the day. As it was, the Whirlwind experienced a spate of troubles with its twin Rolls-Royce Peregrine engines, and only two squadrons were ever equipped with the type. Eventually, it was used in the fighter-bomber role with considerable success. As August 1941 gave way to September, some senior Air Staff members began to have serious doubts about the value of Circus operations. Fighter Command losses were climbing steadily, and the results achieved hardly seemed to compensate for them. The only real justification for continuing the sweeps, apparently, was to ensure that Fighter Command remained in a state of combat readiness. The morale of Fighter Command, however, was soon to take a serious blow. On 21 September 1941, Polish pilots of No 315 Squadron, on their way home, reported being attacked by 'an unidentified enemy aircraft with a radial engine'. All sorts of wild rumours circulated in Fighter Command, the favourite among them being that the

strange aircraft were Curtiss Hawks, captured by the Germans and pressed into service. But after all the available information, including gun-camera shots, was assessed, all speculation was removed. The Focke-Wulf 190 had arrived in France.

FOCKE-WULF FW 190
The Focke-Wulf FW 190 stemmed from a suggestion by the German Air Ministry in 1937 that the company should develop an interceptor fighter to complement the Bf 109. Instead of opting for the Daimler Benz DB601 in-line engine, already in production for the Bf 109, Kurt Tank – Focke-Wulf's technical director – chose the BMW type 139 18-cylinder radial, which was still in the development stage. Three prototypes were built, the first of which flew on 1 June 1939. Apart from some engine overheating problems the flight tests went very well, and construction of the other prototypes was accelerated. The fifth FW 190 was re-engined with the new 1660hp (1237.8kW) BMW 14-cylinder 801C-0 engine, and this met all the Luftwaffe requirements. Its success led to the building of 30 pre-production aircraft designated FW 190A-0, these being followed by the FW 190A-1, which went into service with JG26 at Le Bourget, Paris, in August 1941. As the FW 190 was encountered more frequently it became apparent that it outclassed the Spitfire V in all aspects except radius of turn. The first major operation in which the FW 190 was involved was the famous

'Channel Dash' on 12 February 1942, when the German battlecruisers *Scharnhorst* and *Gneisenau*, together with the heavy cruiser *Prinz Eugen*, made a fast pasage from the French Atlantic port of Brest to northern Germany via the English Channel. To counter the threat presented by the FW 190, the RAF rushed into service its most powerful single-engined fighter aircraft to date, the Hawker Typhoon. This aircraft was designed in response to a 1937 Air Staff requirement for an aircraft capable of taking on heavily armed and armoured escort fighters like the Messerschmitt Bf 110. In fact, two separate designs were submitted, the Type R and Type N. The Type R was powered by a Rolls-Royce Vulture engine; it flew in prototype form as the Tornado, but was abandoned when production of the Vulture was curtailed. The Type N, named Typhoon, was powered by a Napier Sabre engine and flew for the first time on 24 February 1940. The first production aircraft, however, did not fly until May 1941. Delays in production were blamed on the unreliability of the massive Sabre engine, but there were other problems, including structural failures of the rear fuselage.

HIT AND RUN
These problems had still not been cured when No 56 Squadron at Duxford was issued with the Typhoon in September 1941, and several pilots were lost. Moreover, although the aircraft was fast and handled well at medium and low altitudes, its performance at high altitude was inferior to that of both the Focke-Wulf 190 and the Messerschmitt Bf 109F, and its rate of climb was poor. Teething troubles with the type kept the squadron non-operational until the end of May 1942, and at one time there was talk of cancelling the Typhoon programme altogether. It was a change in enemy tactics that brought about the aircraft's reprieve. In the summer of 1942, FW 190s of JG 2 and 26, based on the Channel coast, began carrying out sporadic hit and run attacks on coastal targets in southeast England. This was a prelude to more intensive fighter-bomber attacks on shipping in the Channel, railway installations, harbours and industrial targets. All the raids were carried out at very low level to avoid radar detection and were usually flown by a Schwarm of four aircraft. They were highly successful, and it was fortunate for the British that JG 2 and 26 never had more than about 20 FW 190A-3 fighter-bombers available for operations at any time. The Luftwaffe pilots made full use of the contours of the South Downs, flying that would nowadays be called 'nap of the earth', to pop up and attack coastal targets from the rear. Only the Typhoon was fast enough to catch the elusive intruders, and at low level it was in its element. The original Typhoon squadron, No 56, had now been joined by two more, Nos 609 and 266 Squadrons, and together these formed the Duxford Typhoon Wing. During the summer months of 1942, still suffering from technical problems, they were engaged in air defence duties, although Squadron Leader Roland Beamont's No 609 Squadron, having received the appropriate authority, began to carry out a series of operational trials to investigate the aircraft's usefulness in other roles. These included night interception and, most important of all for the Typhoon's future, ground attack by both day and night. The 12-gun Typhoon MK 1A was now giving way to the Mk 1B, whose four 20mm (0.78in) cannon proved highly effective in the ground attack role.

INTO ACTION
The Duxford Wing's cannon-armed Typhoon 1Bs went into action for the first time in August 1942, when they carried out an uneventful sweep from Dunkirk to Calais as a preliminary to the disastrous Anglo-Canadian landing at Dieppe, which took place the next day. Thirty-six Typhoons took part in the operation, but claimed only two 'probables' and three enemy aircraft damaged. One Typhoon was lost through engine failure and another was shot down (by a Spitfire). The operation served only to underline the complete inadequacy of the Mk I's cockpit canopy design, with its extremely poor pilot visibility, for air superiority fighting. The Typhoon II, which came along later, had a clear bubble-type canopy, which was a vast improvement. Soon after Dieppe the Duxford Wing was disbanded, the three squadrons being dispersed to other locations. Although the Typhoon continued to have problems well

Hawker Typhoon Mk IA

Type: single-seat fighter-bomber
Country of origin: United Kingdom
Powerplant: one 2100hp (1565.9kW) Napier Sabre I 24-cylinder H-type engine

Performance: maximum speed 412mph (663km/h)
Weights: empty 9800lb (4445kg); max, take-off 12,905lb (5853kg)
Dimensions: wing span 41ft 7in

(12.67m); length 31ft 11in (9.73m); height 15ft 4in (4.67m)
Armament: 12 wing-mounted Browning 0.303in machine guns or 4 20mm (0.78in) cannon

into 1943 when they were finally rectified, and its future still hung in the balance, its prowess against the Luftwaffe's low-level intruders had begun to tip the scales in its favour. Since June 1942 the fighter-bomber attacks had been assuming greater proportions, more Focke-Wulf fighter-bombers having been allocated to JG 2 and 26. It was soon apparent that the main line of defence, the Spitfire, was unable to cope with the faster Focke-Wulf FW 190A-4, with which the Jagdgeschwader were now equipped. But on 20 January 1943 the Typhoon at last showed what it could do as an interceptor. On that day 28 enemy fighter-bombers, escorted by single-engined fighters, made a daylight attack on London, causing much damage and many casualties. Little warning had been received of the attack, but as the raiders were making their exit from the target area they were intercepted by the Typhoons of No 609 Squadron. In the ensuing fight Flying Officer J. Baldwin, later to become the top-scoring Typhoon pilot with 15 victories, destroyed three Bf 109Gs, while four FW 190s were shot down by other pilots. Several more successes were achieved against the enemy fighter-bombers by No 609 Squadron in the weeks that followed, and during this period the squadron continued to expand its offensive operations against targets on the Continent. There was no longer any

doubt about the aircraft's effectiveness at low level, and 609 Squadron's performance effectively killed a last-ditch attempt by the Engineering Branch of Fighter Command, early in 1943, to have the fighter axed in favour of the American P-47 Thunderbolt. By the end of the year, with the aircraft's technical problems cured and the growing number of Typhoon squadrons – now carrying a pair of 500lb (227kg) bombs on their aircraft in addition to the built-in cannon armament – striking hard at the enemy's communications, shipping and airfields, the Typhoon was heading for its place in history as the most potent Allied fighter-bomber of all.

SUPER SPITFIRES

It was still the Spitfire, however, that formed the bulk of Fighter Command's offensive and defensive day forces. To counter the activities of high-flying German reconnaissance aircraft the Spitfire Mk VI was produced, with a long, tapered wing and a pressurised cockpit; the aircraft was assigned to one flight of the RAF's home defence squadrons. The Mk VII, also with a pressurised cockpit, was powered by a Rolls-Royce Merlin 60 engine, a two-stage, two-speed, inter-cooled powerplant which was to take development of the Merlin to its ultimate. Early in 1942, the Air Staff envisaged production of both the Spitfire VII and, in much larger numbers, of the Spitfire VIII,

which was basically an unpressurised version of the Mk VII intended for low-level air superiority operations. But the Mk VIII design needed a lot of refinement, including a general strengthening of the fuselage, which meant that production would be delayed for an unacceptably long time, and Air Staff thoughts consequently turned to an interim aircraft: a Mk V Spitfire airframe combined with a Merlin 61 engine. The resulting combination was the Spitfire Mk IX, which for a stop-gap aircraft turned out to be a resounding success. Deliveries to the RAF began in June 1942 and 5665 were built, more than any other mark except the Mk V. From the spring of 1943, the fighter wings of No 11 Group equipped with the Spitfire IX were assigned to escort missions with the US Eighth Army Air Force, which had begun deep-penetration missions into Germany in March. The Spitfires' limited range meant that escort could only be provided for part of the way, leaving the bombers to continue unescorted into Germany, and the Luftwaffe soon shattered the myth that large formations of heavy bombers, without fighter escort and relying entirely on their defensive armament, could operate deep inside enemy territory without suffering serious losses. Originally, it had been planned to provide the American daylight bombers with long-range fighter escorts in the shape of the Lockheed P-38 Lightning, but these

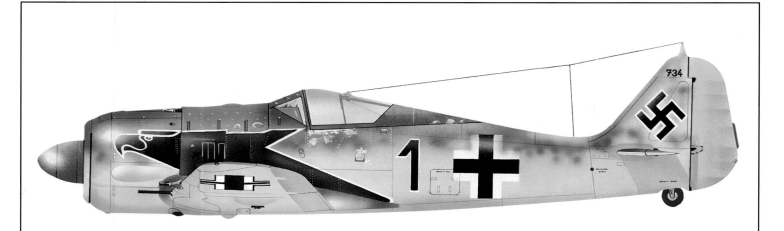

Focke-Wulf FW 190A-4

Type: single-seat fighter-bomber
Country of origin: Germany
Powerplant: one 1700hp (1267.7kW) BMW 801D-2 14-cylinder radial

Performance: maximum speed 383mph (605km/h)
Weights: empty 6393lb (2900kg); maximum take-off 8770lb (3980kg)
Dimensions: wing span 34ft 5in

(10.50m); length 28ft 10in (8.80m); height 12ft 11in (3.95m)
Armament: two wing-mounted 20mm (0.78in) cannon; two 7.9mm (0.31in) MG 17 MGs in fuselage

Supermarine Spitfire Mk IX

Type: single-seat fighter
Country of origin: United Kingdom
Powerplant: one 1565hp (1167kW)
Rolls-Royce Merlin 61 12-cylinder
Veetype engine

Performance: maximum speed
408mph (655km/h)
Weights: empty 5610lb (2545kg);
maximum take-off 9500lb (4309kg)
Dimensions: wing span 36ft 10in

(11.23m); length 31ft (9.46m);
height 12ft 8in (3.86m)
Armament: two 20mm (0.78in)
Hispano cannon and four Browning
0.303in (8.7mm) machine guns

flew only a few escort missions before they were redeployed to North Africa in November 1942 to support the Allied landings there, and it was not until the end of the year that they were replaced by another formidable US fighter, the Republic P-47 Thunderbolt. The P-47 was the culmination of a line of aircraft which had started with the Seversky P-35 of 1936 and which had evolved by way of the P43 Lancer. The prototype P-47 flew on 6 May 1941 and delivery of production aircraft began in March the following year. Production of the Thunderbolt would eventually total 15,683, and the aircraft would justifiably be considered the greatest of the heavy, single-engined fighters built during World War II. The Thunderbolt began combat operations with the 4th Fighter Group, which had been flying Spitfires from Debden in Essex, in the spring of 1943. The USAAF fitted the 4th FG's P-47s with long-range fuel tanks, enabling the fighters to penetrate as far as the German border, but it was not long before the German fighter leaders developed new combat techniques that went a long way towards eliminating the Americans' advantage; the Focke-Wulfs and Messerschmitts would attack the P-47s as they crossed the Dutch coast, forcing them to jettison their auxiliary tanks in order to increase manoevrability. As a consequence the bombers suffered appalling casualties in 1943, particularly on two major raids, the first against Regensburg on 17 August and the second against Schweinfurt on 14

October. On the latter day the Luftwaffe destroyed 60 of the 280 bombers taking part.

AVOIDABLE TRAGEDY
The tragedy for the Americans was that the dreadful losses sustained during the daylight offensive of 1943 might have been avoided, or at least greatly reduced; for a fighter capable of escorting the bombers all the way to their German targets and back already existed. It was the North American P-51 Mustang, produced in response to a 1940 RAF requirement for a fast, heavily armed fighter able to operate effectively at altitudes in excess of 20,000ft (6096m). The first production Mustang I for the RAF flew on 1 May 1941, powered by an 1100hp (820.2kW) Allison V-1710-39 engine. RAF test pilots soon found that with this powerplant the aircraft did not perform well at high altitude, but that its low-level performace was excellent. It was therefore decided to use the type as a high-speed ground attack and tactical reconnaissance fighter, and it was in this role that it entered service with Army Cooperation Command in July 1942. The USAAF, somewhat belatedly, woke up to the the fighter's potential and evaluated two early production Mustang Is under the designation P-51. The RAF suggested that the P-51 would perform much better as a high-altitude interceptor if it were re-engined with the Rolls-Royce Merlin, but the suggestion was initially ignored and the first two Mustang variants, both optimised for ground attack and

designated A-36 and P-51A, were fitted with Allison engines. Trials with Mustangs fitted with Packard-built Rolls-Royce Merlin 61 engines showed a dramatic improvement in performance, maximum speed being raised from 390mph (627km/h) to 441mph (710km/h), and production of the Merlin-powered P-51B finally got under way in the autumn of 1942. Had the decision been taken to install the Merlin engine in a high-altitude interceptor version of the P-51 six months earlier, then the American daylight bombers would have had the benefit of effective long-range escort virtually from the start of their offensive against Germany. As things were, it was not until December 1943 that P-51Bs of the 354th Fighter Group flew their first operational escort mission from England, escorting B-17s to Kiel and back, a round trip of 1000 miles (1600km). More long-range escort missions were flown in January and February 1944 and the results were encouraging, the Mustangs claiming the destruction of over 50 enemy fighters. Even so, one Mustang group was not enough to bring about a dramatic reduction in the losses suffered by the heavy bombers, and early in 1944 these once again reached alarming proportions. On 11 January, for example, 60 out of 238 bombers that attacked aircraft factories at Oschersleben failed to return. The following month there was another tragedy when 430 bombers set out to attack factories in central Germany; shoals of German fighters attacked them

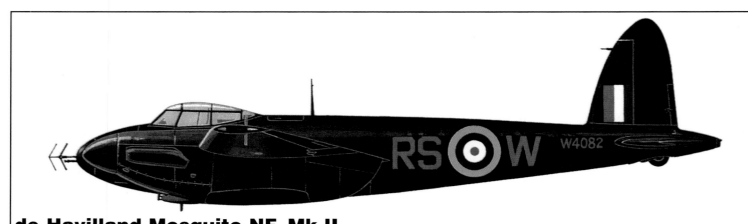

de Havilland Mosquito NF. Mk.II

Type: two-seat night fighter
Country of origin: United Kingdom
Powerplant: two 1480hp
(1103.6kW) Rolls-Royce Merlin 21
12-cylinder Vee-type engines

Performance: maximum speed
370mph (595km/h)
Weights: empty 14,300lb (6492kg);
max. take-off 20,000lb (9072kg)
Dimensions: wing span 54ft 2in

(16.51m); length 42ft 11in
(13.08m); height 17ft 5in (5.31m)
Armament: four 20mm (0.78in)
Hispano cannon and four 0.303in
(7.7mm) Browning machine guns

before they could make rendezvous with their Mustang escort, and 44 Fortresses and Liberators were shot down. The tables, however, were beginning to turn. On 6 March 1944, Mustangs appeared for the first time in the sky over Berlin and took part in one of the most bitterly contested air engagements of the war, between 200 German fighters and 660 heavy bombers and their escort. When it ended, the Americans had lost 69 bombers and all fighters, but the Germans had lost 80 aircraft. The daylight battle over Germany was beginning in earnest.

NIGHT WAR

While the Allies built up their forces to take the air war to Germany, the RAF had slowly but surely been winning the night war over the British Isles. The inauguration of Ground Controlled Interception (GCI) stations, and the conversion of most of Fighter Command's night fighter squadrons to Beaufighters early in 1941, had brought about a dramatic change in the Command's fortunes just in time to counter the Luftwaffe's 'Blitz' on London, Merseyside, Tyneside, Clydeside and other targets. The Hurricane and Defiant squadrons allocated to night defence also added to this change as a result of their increased experience, and because they too derived assistance from GCI. The much more precise information provided by the GCI stations made the task of interception far easier, and matters improved still further with the introduction of AI Mk VII radar,

which had a seven-mile range and a low-level capability. For the first time, the Mk VII, together with information passed on by the Chain Home Low radar stations – the low-level part of the general warning system – gave night-fighter crews the ability to intercept low-flying minelayers and reconnaissance aircraft which had been operating off the north and east coasts almost with impunity. The figures themselves reveal the general improvement in the overall air defence system by the summer of 1941. In February the enemy lost only four aircraft to fighters and eight to anti-aircraft guns but, during March, night-fighters shot down 22 enemy bombers and the AA guns 17. In April the score rose to 48 for the fighters and 39 for the guns, and in the first two weeks of May the loss rate assumed serious proportions, 96 bombers being shot down by fighters and 32 by AA guns. In addition, ten others were lost due to unknown causes. Following a final spate of intense attacks on London, the Midlands and Merseyside, the Luftwaffe's spring 'Blitz' on Britain gradually petered out at the end of May 1941 as the Germans transferred the bulk of their bomber force to the east in readiness for Operation Barbarossa, the invasion of Russia, or to the Balkans. Although

■**RIGHT: The Focke-Wulf FW 190 began to enter Luftwaffe service late in 1940, and in the following year established a measure of air superiority in the Channel area.**

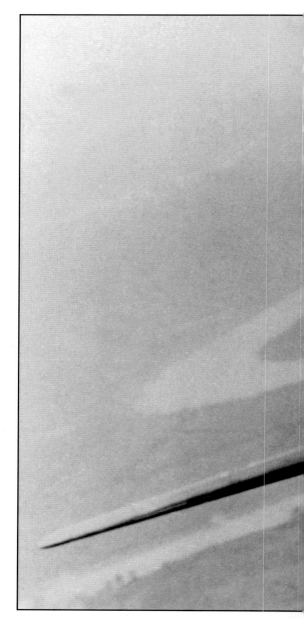

bombing attacks continued on a sporadic basis during 1941, these tended to follow intruder-type tactics, only small numbers of aircraft being involved. Intruder attacks, mostly aimed against the RAF bomber bases in East Anglia and Lincolnshire, continued during June, and on the night of the 13th the intruders suffered a severe setback when three Junkers 88s failed to return, all falling victim to the Beaufighters of No 25 Squadron from Wittering. This was not, however, by any means the beginning of the end for the intruders; Beaufighters accounted for only three more before the middle of October, although others fell to anti-aircraft fire and, in one case, to a Douglas Havoc night fighter of No 85 Squadron.

PROPAGANDA

What dictated the end of intruder operations over England was a personal instruction from Adolf Hitler on 13 October 1941, ordering them to cease. The reason was purely one of propaganda. With the RAF's night-bombing effort steadily increasing, Hitler wanted the German people to see the 'terror bombers' destroyed over the Reich territory; far-away victories over England did nothing to improve their morale. For General Kammhuber, commanding Germany's night defences, it was a bitter blow; what was potentially his most potent weapon had been struck from his hand, and no argument would sway the Führer. What, then, had the intruder force – which never numbered more than 20 or 30 serviceable aircraft – achieved in just over a year of operations? It had certainly destroyed over 50 aircraft over England, together with an estimated 30 more over the North Sea. About 40 others sustained damage as a consequence of intruder attacks. The cost to the Germans was 27 aircraft, plus seven more destroyed in accidents. Had the Luftwaffe been permitted to step up its intruder operations over the United Kingdom in the winter of 1941–42, as RAF Bomber Command prepared to launch a renewed offensive against Germany with its four-engined heavy bombers, it might have dealt a series of damaging blows to the Command, both materially and in terms of morale. It would return to intruder operations later in the war, but by then the intruders would have to contend with air defences vastly superior to those they had encountered previously.

MOSQUITO

Although the Beaufighters and Defiants held the line admirably during the dark months of 1941, the real answer to the prayers of the RAF night

fighter squadrons was the de Havilland Mosquito. Although conceived as a fast day bomber, the Mosquito had too good a turn of speed for its potential as a fighter to pass unnoticed, and the third of three fighter prototypes was completed as a night fighter with AI Mk IV radar in a 'solid' nose. The first Mosquito fighter squadron, No 157, formed at Debden in Essex on 13 December 1941, its first aircraft, a dual-control Mk II, arriving at Debden's satellite airfield, Castle Camps, on 26 January 1942. Seventeen Mk IIs were delivered to Maintenance Units for the fitting of AI Mk V, and by mid-April No 157 Squadron had 19 NF Mk IIs on its inventory, three of them without radar.

■BELOW: **The powerful Hawker Typhoon was rushed into service to counter the FW 190s' hit-and-run attacks on British coastal towns. It would later find its true worth as a close support aircraft.**

By this time No 151 Squadron at Wittering had also begun to rearm with the NF Mk II, with 16 aircraft on strength at the end of April. As the two squadrons built up their night flying hours, practised interceptions and night gun-firing (which revealed the need for flash eliminators on the nose-mounted 0.303in (7.7mm) Browning guns, which when fired blinded the pilot to everything outside the cockpit) the crews became increasingly happy with their new aircraft. Its armament of four 20mm (0.78in) Hispano cannon and four Brownings was formidable, and – unlike the arrangement in the Beaufighter – the radar observer sat facing forwards in the cockpit, on the pilot's right and slightly behind him. It was unfortunate that the Mosquito crews initially had to cope with inadequate AI equipment, for on the night of 23/24 April 1942 the Luftwaffe launched the first of its so-called 'Baedecker' raids against British targets of cultural and

historic value in reprisal for a Bomber Command attack on Lubeck on 28/29 March. The first raid, on Exeter by 45 aircraft – mostly Dornier Do 217s of KG2 – proved abortive and was followed by two on Bath on 25 and 26 April. The city suffered heavily, and in three more successive raids Norwich was attacked twice and York once, the latter city suffering heavy damage from incendiary bombs. The most successful attack was on 3/4 May, when 131 tons of bombs were dropped on Exeter, severely damaging the city centre. During the remainder of the month Cowes, Norwich, Hull, Poole, Canterbury and Grimsby were all raided, but then the emphasis switched to more important strategic targets such as Birmingham, Southampton and Middlesbrough.

The advent of the Mosquito was timely, for KG2's fast Dorniers, which were capable of 300mph (482km/h) at low

Messerschmitt Me 410 Hornisse

Type: two-seat heavy fighter
Country of origin: Germany
Powerplant: two 1750hp
(1304.9kW) Daimler-Benz DB 603A
12-cylinder inverted-Vee engines
Performance: maximum speed

388mph (624km/h)
Weights: empty 16,574lb (7518kg);
maximum take-off 23,500lb
(10,660kg)
Dimensions: wing span 53ft 8in
(16.36m); length 40ft 11in

(12.48m); height 14ft 0in (4.28m)
Armament: Two 20mm (0.78in) MG
151 cannon and two 7.9mm
(0.31in) MG 17 machine guns in
nose; two rearward-firing 13mm
(0.51in) MG 131 guns in fuselage

altitude, were causing problems for the defences. In 1943–44 the Luftwaffe once again mounted frequent intruder operations, using mainly Me 410 and Ju 188 aircraft. The Me 410 Hornisse (Hornet) was descended from the Bf 110 via the Me 210, which was not a success. Only 352 were built before production switched to the Me 410 late in 1942. As well as being used in the fast bomber role, the Me 410 was used as a night fighter and a bomber destroyer, being armed with a 50mm (1.96in) cannon in the latter case. We can see a measure of what they might have achieved, had these aircraft been committed in greater numbers, in one attack on American air bases in East Anglia on 2 April 1944, when intruders destroyed 13 B-24 Liberators and, in the panic, two more were shot down by their own airfield defences. The Germans lost a single Me 410. By the beginning of 1944, however, further improvements in the British air defences had made it hard for the Luftwaffe to penetrate into UK air space at medium and low level. Increased numbers of anti-aircraft guns of all calibres, rocket batteries capable of firing salvoes of 128 missiles, and radar-directed searchlights able to illuminate targets up to 35,000ft (10,600m) all contributed to frustrating the attackers, and the fast enemy bombers now began to penetrate at up to 30,000ft (9150m) before diving on their objectives and making a high-speed exit. These new tactics caused problems for the night

fighters, since following an enemy aircraft in a dive meant that radar contact was often lost because of ground returns. The answer was to extend the night fighter patrol lines well out to sea; many intruders were trapped and destroyed in this way. By the beginning of 1943 the RAF's night fighter squadrons were turning increasingly from defence to offence. The Mosquito's long range and heavy armament of four 20mm (0.78in) cannon made it highly suitable for the night intruder role, as well as for local night air defence. The intruder Mosquitoes (and Beaufighters), although stripped of their AI for operations over enemy territory, were fitted with a device named Serrate, which was developed by the Telecommunications Research Establishment as a result of information on enemy night-fighting radars brought back by special countermeasures aircraft. This enabled the British fighters to home in to the enemy's airborne radar transmissions. It had a range of about 50 miles, and was first used operationally in June 1943 by No 141 Squadron, which scored 23 kills in three months with its help.

WILD BOAR
The Germans, too, were still confident that they could defeat the growing armada of RAF night bombers that were attacking the Reich. By the spring of 1943, General Josef Kammhuber had five Geschwader and 400 twin-engined fighters under his command on bases

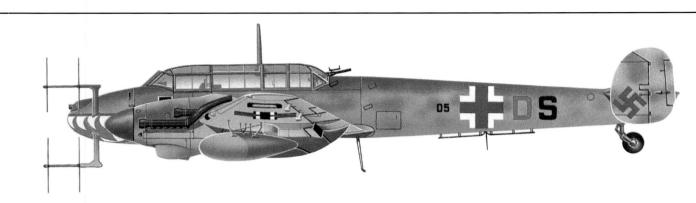

Messerschmitt Bf 110G

Type: two/three-seat night fighter
Country of origin: Germany
Powerplant: two 1475hp (1100kW)
Daimler-Benz DB 605B-2 12-
cylinder inverted-Vee engines
Performance: maximum speed

342mph (550km/h)
Weights: empty 11,230lb (5094kg);
maximum take-off 21,799lb
(9888kg)
Dimensions: wing span 53ft 3in
(16.24m); length 42ft 10in

(13.05m); height 13ft 8in (4.18m)
Armament: two 30mm (1.18in)
cannon in nose, two 20mm
(0.78in) cannon in ventral tray, one
7.92mm (0,31in) twin-barrel
machine gun in dorsal position.

stretching from Holland to the Mediterranean. However, he was the first to realise that 400 night fighters were not enough, and he consequently proposed a major extension of the air defence system, with 18 night fighter geschwader covering the whole of Germany. The aircraft would be fitted with improved AI equipment and the ground radar network would also be modernised. Kammhuber pushed relentlessly for the expansion of his night fighter force, and it was his undoing. Nothing could convince Hitler that the Luftwaffe's night fighters were not already destroying enough enemy bombers to cripple the RAF's night offensive. Kammhuber rapidly began to fall from favour, and his cause was not helped when, during a series of heavy attacks on Hamburg in July 1943, Bomber Command rendered the German air defence radar system virtually impotent by the use of 'window', bundles of tinfoil strips cut to the wavelength of the enemy warning radar and dropped from attacking aircraft to confuse the defences. The paralysing of the air defence system led to the evolution of new tactics, stemming from a proposal made by a Colonel von Lossberg of the General Staff. He recommended that night fighters be released from the confines of their designated patrol areas, which were restricted and susceptible to radar jamming, and instead mix freely with the bomber stream, the pilots making visual attacks. The idea was approved, and it was decided as a first step to increase the strength of

Jagdgeschwader 300, formed a month earlier under the command of Major Hajo Hermann, himself a fighter ace. This was the pioneer Wilde Sau (Wild Boar) unit; equipped with single-engined fighters, its task was to patrol directly over German targets, the pilots endeavouring to pick out enemy bombers in the glare of searchlights and fires. The idea was quickly adopted by other night fighter units, and it achieved considerable success – although at great risk to the attacking fighters, which had to contend with German flak as well as defensive fire from the RAF bombers.

GERMAN AI RADAR

While Wilde Sau operations continued, Telefunken had been hard at work developing a new AI radar that would not be susceptible to 'window' jamming. In October 1943 the night fighter units began to receive the new Lichtenstein SN2 AI radar, which was free from both electronic and 'window' jamming. It had a maximum range of four miles and a minimum range of 450 yards (412m), and it was not long before some night fighter crews began to register a formidable number of sucesses with its help. In the autumn of 1943 two more homing devices were also developed for use by night fighters, the Naxos Z and the Flensburg. The former enabled the fighters to home on transmissions from the RAF's H₂S blind bombing radar, and the latter was designed to lock on to radiations from the 'Monica' tail warning radar carried by the bombers. In the summer of 1943 the

German night fighters also began to receive a new type of armament, which was to prove extremely effective. Devised by an NCO armourer named Paul Mahle and known as Schräge Musik (Slanting Music), it involved the mounting of two 20mm (0.78in) cannon, their muzzles pointing upwards at a fixed angle, on a wooden platform in the upper fuselage of a night fighter. This arrangement enabled the fighter to take advantage of a bomber's blind spot and attack it from directly below with the aid of a reflector sight mounted in the cockpit roof. Schräge Musik was used for the first time on the night of 17/18 August 1943, when two crews of II/NJG5 destroyed six RAF bombers in the space of half an hour. The German airmen reported that the Halifax and Lancaster were extremely vulnerable to this form of attack. The large area of their wings was impossible to miss, and since the wings contained the fuel tanks a relatively short burst was usually enough to set a bomber on fire. It was a terrible irony that the original specification for the Lancaster and Halifax had included a ventral gun turret; it had been dispensed with at an early design stage to permit the carriage of a greater bomb load. As a result of losses caused by fighter attacks from below, some bombers – notably in No 6 (RCAF) Group – were locally modified to incorporate a lower fuselage hatch through which a 0.50in (12.7mm) machine gun could be operated by a crew member. Despite the problems of equipment and organisation that handicapped the German night fighter force, its success rate reached an unprecedented peak in the spring of 1944. In the course of three big air battles over darkened Germany, Bomber Command suffered crippling losses. On the night of 19/20 February, 78 out of a force of 823 heavy bombers despatched to attack Leipzig failed to return; 72 more were destroyed during an assault on Berlin on 24/25 March; and then, five nights later, came the most catastrophic loss of all, and the greatest triumph for the night fighters.

THE NUREMBERG DISASTER

At nightfall on 30 March 1944, 795 heavy bombers set out from their English bases to attack the important industrial centre and railway junction of Nuremberg. The night was cloudless and calm, and across a great arc of Europe stretching across Holland, Belgium, northern France and northwest Germany the Luftwaffe night fighter crews were at cockpit readiness. At 2200 hours reports began to come in of small-scale attacks by Mosquitoes on several airfields in Holland and of minelaying operations over the North Sea, but the GOC I Fighter Corps, Major-General Josef Schmid, realised these were simply diversions and kept his fighters on the ground. Then, at 2230 hours, the German coastal radar stations detected a major raid building up on the other side of the English Channel, and a few minutes later the bomber stream was reported to be heading southeastwards towards Belgium. At 2230 hours Schmid

finally ordered his fighters into the air. This time, instead of carrying out the normal procedure and making several changes of course to confuse the defences, the bomber stream continued due east for 150 miles after making landfall on the enemy coast, and the night fighters had no difficulty in locating their targets. The route to Nuremberg was marked by a series of fiery beacons as one heavy bomber after another fell burning from the sky. From all over Germany the night fighter gruppen converged on the bomber stream, and several pilots scored multiple kills in the battle that developed. The greatest success was achieved by Oberleutnant Martin Becker of I/NJG6, who destroyed six Halifaxes in 30 minutes, between 0020 hours and 0050 hours. Nor was that all; after landing to refuel and rearm, Becker took off again in his Me 110 and shot down a seventh Halifax as it was on its homeward flight. Other pilots who achieved notable successes that night were Oberleutnant Helmut Schulte of II/NJG5, who destroyed four heavy bombers; Leutnant Wilhelm Seuss of IV/NJG5, who also shot down four; and Oberleutnant Martin Drewes of II/NJG1, who destroyed three. For RAF Bomber Command, the cost of the Nuremberg raid was stupendous: 95 bombers failed to return and 71 were damaged. The loss – 11.8 per cent of the attacking force – was the highest ever sustained by the Command. It was the greatest victory achieved by the German

night fighter force during the war, but it was also its last. One by one, the leading German night fighter crews were swallowed up in the cauldron of the air war as 1944 wore on; the Luftwaffe's night fighter resources dwindled steadily through attrition in combat and through Allied bombing. For example, 465 Me 110s, earmarked for night fighting, were destroyed by Allied bombing in February 1944 alone.

LAST GERMAN NIGHT FIGHTERS

In the first half of 1943, General Kammhuber had pressed strongly for the production of new twin-engined types designed specifically for night fighting. At the forefront of these was the Heinkel He 219 Uhu (Owl), the prototype of which had flown in November 1942 after months of delay caused by a lack of interest on the part of the German Air Ministry. By April 1943, 300 examples had been ordered; Kammhuber wanted 2000, but in the event only 294 were built before the end of the war. Formidably armed with six 20mm (0.78in) cannon and equipped with the latest AI radar, the He 219 would certainly have torn great gaps in Bomber Command's ranks had it been available in quantity. It also had a performance comparable to that of the Mosquito, which other German night fighters did not, and therefore could have fought the RAF's intruders on equal terms. Another promising night fighter design that fell by the wayside was the

Heinkel He 219 Uhu

Type: two-seat night fighter
Country of origin: Germany
Powerplant: two 1900hp
(1416.8kW) Daimler-Benz DB 603B
12-cylinder inverted Vee engines
Performance: maximum speed

416mph (670km/h)
Weights: empty 24,692lb
(11,200kg); maximum take-off
33,730lb (15,300kg)
Dimensions: wing span 60ft 8in
(18.50m); length 51ft (15.54m);

height 13ft 5in (4.10m)
Armament: four 20mm (0.78in) MG
151 cannon in ventral pack and
one in each wing root

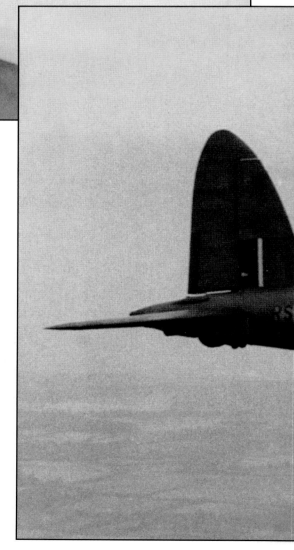

Focke-Wulf Ta 154 Moskito. The Ta 154 was of mixed metal and wood construction, and featured a tricycle undercarriage, with large-diameter tyres to facilitate take-offs from unprepared strips. Powered by two Junkers Jumo 211F engines, the Ta 154 carried a crew of two (pilot and radio/radar operator). Armament comprised two forward-firing 30mm (1.18in) and two 20mm (0.78in) cannon, with a single 30mm cannon mounted obliquely in the rear fuselage. The prototype Ta 154V-1 flew in July 1943 and the type was ordered into production in November, but there were continual delays and in June 1944 the first two production Ta 154A-1s were accidentally destroyed – one when it fell apart because faulty glue had been used in its assembly and the other when its flaps broke away on a landing approach – and as a result the production order was cancelled. Seven more production Ta 154A-1s were completed, however, and these were used operationally for a while by I/NJG3 at Stade and by NJGr10. There is no record

■ABOVE: The Boulton Paul Defiant, a failure as a day fighter, was allocated to the night fighter and night intruder role, in which it enjoyed much greater success.

of their combat achievements, if indeed there were any. The Messerschmitt Bf 110 and the Junkers Ju 88 consequently formed the backbone of the German night fighter force. The Ju 88 was the real mainstay; 4200 were produced as night fighters or converted to the night fighter role. But apart from the He 219, the Germans never fielded a purpose-built night fighter.

TACTICIAN

On the Eastern Front, the Soviet Air Force had developed new tactics in readiness for the planned offensives of 1943. Soviet fighters now operated at full regiment strength, flying in stepped-up battle formation. Usually, they were employed in escorting assault and light bomber aircraft (Ilyushin Il-2s and

Petlyakov Pe-2s) and the ratio of fighters to bombers on these missions depended on the number of bombers engaged. For example, four bombers would be escorted by ten fighters, 16–24 bombers by 20 fighters. Offensive fighter sweeps usually involved one Gruppa (three or four pairs) patrolling within a defined sector, with a second Gruppa at readiness. In this way a fighter regiment with four Gruppi could maintain a constant patrol over the combat area. In addition, ranger patrols (svobodnaya okhota) were frequently carried out by fighters operating in pairs. When escorting ground attack aircraft, the fighter cover was split into two parts, the immediate escort and the assault group. The immediate escort remained constantly near the ground attack aircraft and flew between 300 and 1000ft

■BELOW: A Mosquito FB.VI of No 143 Squadron, RAF Coastal Command. The Mosquito was superb in all the roles it performed during World War II, including that of night fighter.

(90–300m) higher. These fighters had the task of engaging any enemy fighters that managed to break through the forward assault group to present a direct threat to the ground attack formation. They normally broke away over the target and circled out of range of the enemy anti-aircraft defences, ready to take up their original position for the withdrawal flight. Often, if no enemy fighters showed up, the immediate escort would themselves dive down to strafe targets on the ground. The fighters of the assault group flew between 1500 and 3000ft (460–900m) higher than the immediate escort, and either directly above or half a mile ahead of the assault formation. One pair was usually sent out in advance to scout for enemy fighters, while a second pair cruised at high altitude, up-sun of the assault formation, ready to dive out of the sun to surprise attacking enemy fighters. Over the target, the assault group usually went up to 10,000ft (3000m) or so, clear of the light flak, and patrolled the sky over a fixed area

until they were required to cover the withdrawal of the assault aircraft.

GROUND ATTACK

These tactics were first put into practice in January 1943 during the battle for the Kuban peninsula, where the Germans had been building up large forces in readiness for a drive into the Caucasus even as the German Sixth Army, trapped in Stalingrad, stood on the verge of annihilation. By the summer of 1943 they had been further refined and developed, and were to play a decisive part in one of history's greatest land battles. At the beginning of July the Soviet Central Front was in a precarious position, with two German salients at Orel and Kharkov flanking a deep bulge to the west of Kursk. If the Germans could break the Russian defences north and south of Kursk, they would succeed in trapping and destroying the vast Russian forces in the salient. For their planned offensive the Germans assembled nearly a

million men in 70 divisions, supported by large numbers of tanks and 1700 aircraft. The Focke-Wulf 190 had now made its appearance on the Eastern Front, both in the fighter and ground attack roles, and was to play a significant part in the battle. When the German offensive opened on 5 July 1943, however, it was the Soviet Air Force that struck the first blow. At dawn 400 Russian fighters and bombers swept over the front line towards the German-held airfields around Kharkov, where most of the Luftwaffe's squadrons were concentrated. The Russians were intercepted by the Messerschmitts and Focke-Wulfs of Jagdgeschwader 3 and 52, and a tremendous air battle – the biggest of the war, with 500 aircraft involved – took place. The Soviet attack was broken up and the German fighters claimed the destruction of 70 enemy aircraft for the loss of 20 of their own number. The first day of the battle saw both sides throw their air power on a massive scale against tanks and infantry. Much devastation was wrought by the Soviet Air Force's ground attack squadrons, equipped for the most part with Ilyushin Il2 Sturmovik assault aircraft armed with 37mm (1.45in) cannon. On one occasion a formation of these aircraft knocked out 70 German tanks of the 9th Panzer Division in the space of 20 minutes.

BLACK DEVIL

On the second day, Russian fighters once again appeared over the front in strength and more fierce dogfights flared up over the Kursk salient, with heavy losses on both sides. It was on this day that Ivan Kozhedub shot down his first aircraft, a Ju 87 Stuka. He was only one of the Russian fighter pilots who had their baptism of fire over Kursk; another was Guards Lieutenant A.K. Gorovets, who destroyed no fewer than nine Stukas in a single engagement before being shot down and killed.

For a Russian pilot to register such a high score in one air battle was unusual, although a number of Luftwaffe fighter pilots managed to amass an astonishing total of 'kills' while fighting on the Eastern Front, often claiming the destruction of nine or ten enemy aircraft in one day – especially during the early months of the campaign, when the Soviet Air Force was fighting at a disadvantage in every respect. At the top of the Luftwaffe scoreboard was Lieutenant Erich Hartmann, who served with JG52 on the Russian Front from the autumn of 1942 and who went on to claim an incredible 352 victories. Several other German fighter pilots claimed a score that ran into three figures, and although these totals were later disputed, it should be remembered that the staggering number of kills achieved by the Luftwaffe on the Eastern Front were made possible by two principal factors: the inexperience of the rank and file of Soviet pilots, and the fact that many German pilots served almost continuously in action against the Russians for nearly four years, with only short leave breaks. There were no 'rest tours', as in other air forces. The overall result was that as the skill of individual fighter pilots grew, the Eastern Front became the 'happy hunting ground' of air fighting. The Russians themselves held the top German fighter pilots in considerable awe; they dubbed Erich Hartmann 'Cherniye Chort' (Black Devil) and offered a reward of 10,000 roubles to anyone who shot him down. Hartmann, in fact, survived the war only to be handed over to the Russians, spending a harrowing ten years in prison before his eventual release.

AIR SUPERIORITY

There is no doubt that Kursk was the decisive battle of the Eastern Front. Within eight days the German offensive had been broken and the Russians had begun a series of strong counter-attacks, exploiting their success all along the line. In August 1943, supported by 100 air divisions totalling 10,000 aircraft, the whole Soviet battlefront began to roll forward in a relentless drive that would not cease until it reached the heart of Germany. In three weeks the Russians captured Orel, Belgorod and Kharkov, and in September they established a bridgehead on the Dnepr in readiness for an assault on Kiev. This city was taken after bitter fighting in November, before the grip of winter brought a halt to further major offensive action.

By the beginning of 1944 the Soviet Air Force had established definite air

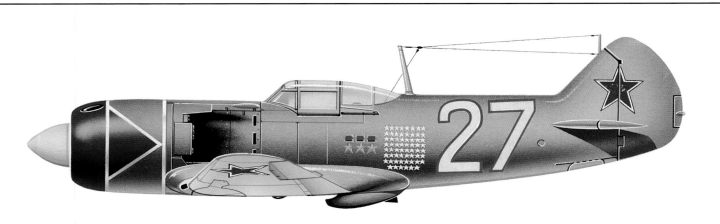

Lavochkin La-5

Type: single-seat fighter
Country of origin: USSR
Powerplant: one 1630hp
(1215.5kW) Shvestsov Ash-82FN
14-cylinder radial

Performance: maximum speed
403mph (648km/h)
Weights: empty 5743lb (2605kg);
maximum take-off 7198lb (3265kg)
Dimensions: wing span 32ft 2in

(9.80m); length 28ft 5in (8.66m);
height 8ft 4in (2.54m)
Armament: two 20mm (0.78in)
ShVAK or 23mm (0.9in) NS cannon
in upper forward fuselage

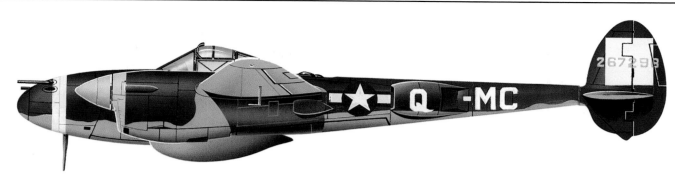

Lockheed P-38 Lightning

Type: single-seat fighter-bomber
Country of origin: USA
Powerplant: two 1600hp
(1193.1kW) Allison V-1710-111/113
12-cylinder Veetype engines
Performance: maximum speed

414mph (666km/h)
Weights: empty 12,800lb (5806kg);
maximum take-off 21,600lb
(9798kg)
Dimensions: wing span 52ft
(15.85m); length 37ft 10in

(11.53m); height 12ft 10in (3.91m)
Armament: one 20mm (0.78in)
cannon and four 0.50in (12.7mm)
machine guns in nose; up to
4000lb (1814kg) of external
ordnance

superiority, and although the Luftwaffe was still a force to be reckoned with, the calibre of its aircrews was beginning to show a marked decline. Russian equipment, moreover, was improving; new fighters were making their appearance, while ground radar supplied by the Americans was introduced and pioneered into use by Aleksandr Pokryshkin's fighter regiment on the Crimean Front in January 1944. In March 1944, Soviet forces under Marshal Koniev set foot on Romanian soil, and in an effort to dislodge them the Germans launched a strong counter-offensive at Iasi (Yassy). To provide air cover the Luftwaffe had assembled some of its finest fighter units, opposed on the Russian side by a number of Guards Fighter Regiments. As these units met in combat, the battle of Iasi was marked by air fighting of a savagery unmatched since Kursk. It was the last time that the Luftwaffe made a serious attempt to gain air superiority over the battlefield on the Eastern Front, and it ended in failure. The Russian fighters enjoyed overwhelming numerical superiority, and Luftwaffe losses were high. In April 1944 the Soviet Army liberated the whole of the Crimea; this was followed by a major offensive on the Byelorussian Front, which was to end with the encirclement and annihilation of 30 German divisions in the Minsk sector. By the middle of July the German Army Group Centre had virtually ceased to exist, and the Russians were advancing into Poland.

HELLCATS AND LIGHTNINGS
Thousands of miles from the carnage of the Russian Front, the tide of the air war in the Pacific was at last beginning to turn against the Japanese. Taking note of the lessons learned in action by the Wildcat squadrons, the Grumman Aircraft Company designed a larger and more powerful version, the F6F Hellcat, which entered service in 1943 and which at last gave the US Navy pilots a chance to meet the Zeros on more or less equal terms. Before the war ended, the Hellcat squadrons would be officially credited with the destruction of nearly 5000 enemy aircraft, or 80 per cent of all the kills registered by American carrier pilots during World War II. Another new American type that made its appearance in the Pacific theatre in 1943 was the twin-engined, twin-tailed Lockheed P-38 Lightning. Already in service in Europe, the long-range Lightning substantially increased the radius that could be covered by land-based American fighter squadrons. One of the most famous of all operations carried out by the Lightning took place on 18 April 1943, when P-38s of the 339th Fighter Squadron, USAAF, shot down a Japanese bomber carrying Admiral Isoroku Yamamoto, the Japanese Navy Commander-in-Chief. To do the job, the Lightnings made an 1100-mile (1770km) round trip from Guadalcanal to intercept Yamamoto's aircraft over Kahili Atoll. The two top-scoring American pilots of the Pacific war, Major Richard I. Bong and Major Tommy McGuire, both flew P-38s; Bong ended the war with a score of 40 enemy machines destroyed, while

McGuire shot down 38 before his death in action over the Philippines in January 1945.

WHISTLING DEATH
Early in 1943 some US Navy and Marine squadrons began to rearm with a powerful new carrier-borne fighter, the Chance Vought F4U Corsair. One pilot in particular achieved spectacular successes while flying this type; he was Lieutenant Bob Hanson, a member of Marine Squadron VMF-215, and he rose to fame in the embattled sky over Rabaul. On 14 January 1944, Hanson fought the first of a series of combats that would set a record, destroying five out of a formation of 70 Zeros that were trying to intercept American bombers. His next five sorties over Rabaul netted him one Zero, three Zeros, four Zeros, three Zeros and four Zeros, which brought his score to over 20 enemy aircraft destroyed in a period of only 17 days. Later in the war, when Britain sent a carrier task force to join the US Navy in the Pacific, squadrons of the Royal Navy's Fleet Air Arm were also equipped with the Corsair, and the type was used by the Royal New Zealand Air Force. The Japanese called it the 'whistling death' because of the characteristic note of its powerful Double Wasp radial engine. From the spring of 1943 onwards, American and Allied pilots began to notice a marked decline in the standard of their opponents; the loss of the nucleus of the Imperial Japanese Navy's best pilots, many of whom had seen extensive combat in China before the start of the Pacific war in 1942, was

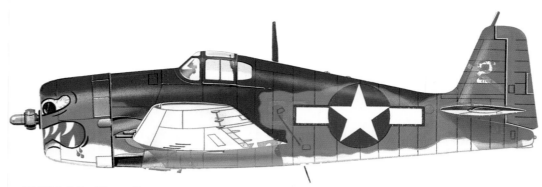

Grumman F6F Hellcat

Type: single-seat fighter
Country of origin: USA
Powerplant: one 2000hp
(1491.4kW) P&W R-2800-10 Double
Wasp 18-cylinder radial

Performance:maximum speed
375mph (603km/h)
Weights: empty 9101lb (4128kg);
max. take-off 15,487lb (7025kg)
Dimensions: wing span 42ft 10in

(13.06m) length 33ft 7in (10.24m);
height 13ft 1in (3.99m)
Armament: six wing-mounted
0.50in (12.7mm) MGs; up to 1000lb
(454kg) of external ordnance

at last beginning to have its effect. As new American fighter types arrived in the Pacific, the Japanese began to suffer combat losses that were little short of staggering, and the US pilots, now skilfully led by veterans with two years of experience behind them, rapidly assumed a superiority that would never be lost, gaining formidable successes in dogfights that were often unbelievably one-sided. In April 1943, for example, four P-38 Lightnings were carrying out a sweep over Guadalcanal at 31,000ft (9450m) when they sighted three Zeros lower down. The P-38s dived to the attack and shot all three Zeros down in quick succession. Climbing again, the American pilots sighted a formation of Zeros attacking some Wildcats at 28,000 feet (8534m). The Lightnings burst through the middle of the fight at high speed in a shallow dive, knocking down two Zeros as they went. The Japanese broke in all directions and took evasive action, but two more Zeros went down in flames. In less than 20 minutes the four P-38s had accounted for seven of the enemy with no loss or damage to themselves. Even the Curtiss P-40, a type which had suffered heavily in combat in the early days of the war in the Far East, was now capable of beating its opponents as superior American tactics, leadership and teamwork decided the outcome of battles. This was superbly demonstrated one day in January 1944, when 16 USAAF P-40s encountered 36 Japanese fighters and dive-bombers off Saidor, New Guinea. The P-40s shot down three enemy aircraft on their first pass; the remainder scattered,

and in the ensuing battle the Japanese lost 18 fighters and one dive-bomber. The P-40s suffered no loss. The American pilots observed that although the Japanese pilots seemed aggressive enough and eager to fight at the beginning, they quickly lost their discipline and cohesion and tried to break off combat, leaving themselves exposed and vulnerable.

DEVASTATING LOSSES
In another major air battle of 1944 the Japanese lost 114 aircraft to the guns of the US Navy's Hellcats; the Americans lost only nine fighters. It happened on 24 June, during a long-range fighter sweep against the island of Iwo Jima. During the first mission of the day 48 Hellcats encountered more than 100 enemy fighters over Iwo Jima and destroyed 33 of them in the course of just a few minutes. Japanese torpedo aircraft tried to break through to the US task force cruising off the island, but more Hellcats were waiting for them and they were massacred. One US fighter squadron, VF-2 from the carrier USS *Hornet*, destroyed 67 enemy machines in the course of the day – a record for a Navy unit. By the end of the day, Iwo Jima's fighter defences had been annihilated and the island lay naked. But the Americans would not be in a position to invade Iwo

■RIGHT: The Chance Vought F4U Corsair was a key aircraft in the Pacific war. This one, a Goodyear-built FG1D, had eight underwing RPs and two 1000lb (454kg) bombs.

Jima until the following year, by which time the Japanese had poured troops and equipment into its defence. It was in June 1944, too, that the Japanese suffered their most devastating loss of the entire Pacific war in the Battle of the Philippine Sea, when carrier-borne aircraft of the US Task Force 58 provided air cover for the occupation of the Marianas. During the first major fighter sweep over the islands, on 11 June, the carrier aircraft destroyed one-third of the defending air force. On the 19th, with the amphibious invasion in full swing, large numbers of Japanese bombers and torpedo bombers made a series of desperate attempts to hit the task force; they were detected by radar at a range of 150 miles (240km), and the carrier fighters were waiting for them. The great air battle that followed was a one-sided massacre that would go

down in history as 'The Great Marianas Turkey Shoot'. The agile Hellcats swarmed all over the attackers before they even sighted the carriers, and of the 200 Japanese aircraft in the first two strike waves, only 30 escaped. At the close of the day, the Japanese had lost a staggering 402 aircraft.

FIGHTERS OVER ITALY

In July 1943, as the Americans, Australians and New Zealanders made preparations for their first major counter-offensives in the Pacific, the Allies invaded Sicily as a stepping stone to the invasion of the Italian mainland, which took place in September. At this time, the Italian Air Force, the Regia Aeronautica, was in the throes of re-equipment. The main Italian fighter type in 1943 was the Macchi MC 202 Folgore (Thunderbolt),

which was a derivative of the MC 200 Saetta fitted with a Daimler-Benz DB601 engine. It had seen action in North Africa, on the Russian Front and over Malta, where British fighter pilots developed a healthy respect for it, but it was underpowered and was being replaced by a much-improved variant with a DB605A engine, the MC 205 Veltro (Greyhound). The MC 205 went into operational service in April 1943 and was used mainly in the Mediterranean and in Sicily. When the Italian Government concluded a separate armistice with the Allies on 8 September 1943, some 40 aircraft re-mustered with the Italian Co-Belligerent Air Force, which fought on the Allied side, and saw active service until the end of the war, mainly on the Yugoslav Front. About 30 more escaped to join the Aviazione

Nazionale Repubblicana (ANR), which continued to fight on the side of the Germans, and the ANR also acquired 112 more Veltros which were built up to May 1944. Another new fighter that served mainly with the ANR was the Fiat G.55 Centauro, the prototype of which first flew on 30 April 1942 and entered service with the Regia Aeronautica in June 1943. The G.55 was fast and proved itself to be an excellent high-altitude interceptor, capable of meeting Allied types such as the Spitfire, Thunderbolt, Mustang and Lightning on equal terms. The ANR fighters generally flew in mixed groups with Luftwaffe fighters, their principal targets being the B-17s of the US Fifteenth Army Air Force, operating from bases in Italy. But the air campaign in Italy and the Balkans was one waged primarily by the fighter-bombers of the Allied Tactical Air Forces, drawing on the immense wealth of experience gained in North Africa.

NORMANDY

That same experience was instilled into the RAF's 2nd Tactical Air Force and the USAAF's IX Tactical Air Command, which in the early months of 1944 stood ready to support the biggest seaborne invasion in history. Following the Allied landings in Normandy, the war in the air during the campaign in northwest Europe would be decided by overwhelming tactical air superiority, while the long-range Mustangs, operating

in growing numbers from their English bases, brought the Luftwaffe to battle over Germany itself. The USAAF fighter groups were now armed with the P-51D variant of the Mustang, which featured a 360-degree vision 'teardrop' one-piece sliding canopy and a cut-down rear fuselage. It had six 0.50in Browning air-cooled machine guns in a strengthened wing, and a dorsal fin to compensate for the loss of keel surface after the removal of the upper rear fuselage. Other refinements in the course of production included the addition of two sets of stub rocket launchers under each wing to carry five-inch rockets. The first production P-51Ds to arrive in the United Kingdom in the late spring of 1944 were assigned to group, squadron and flight commanders, who needed better visibility to exercise tactical control of their formations. The P-51D was marginally slower than the P-51B/C, but its six-gun armament was better suited to strafing attacks. The latter, particularly against airfields, were now becoming very costly affairs as the Germans strengthened their airfield defences. While the Mustangs of the 2nd Tactical Air Force and IX Tactical Air Command concentrated on airfield targets in the weeks immediately before D-Day, the Eighth AAF's P-51s ranged farther afield, their long bomber escort missions alternating with attacks on airfields in Germany and the Low Countries. One of the most successful missions flown by

VIII Fighter Command during this period took place on 21 May 1944, when 617 Mustangs, Thunderbolts and Lightnings claimed the destruction of 83 enemy aircraft on the ground, with a further 67 destroyed or damaged in the air. In addition, the fighter-bombers positively destroyed 91 locomotives and attacked 134 other targets, including railway stations and river traffic.

MIGHTY TEMPEST

A new British fighter had its first taste of combat in the weeks before D-Day: the Hawker Tempest. Although it bore some resemblance to the Typhoon IB externally, and was originally named Typhoon II, the Tempest was virtually a new design, developed from the Typhoon and designed to achieve air superiority at low and medium levels. The transition had not been an easy one. The initial contract had called for 400 Tempest Is, powered by the Napier Sabre IV engine, but this was cancelled and the contract amended in favour of the Tempest Mk II, which was to be powered by a Bristol Centaurus radial. Delays in the production of this engine, and the cancellation of the projected Tempest Mks III and IV, which were to have had the Rolls-Royce Griffon engine, meant that the first variant to enter production was the Tempest Mk V, powered by the Napier Sabre II. This gave it an impressive acceleration. The first 100 production aircraft had the Sabre IIA

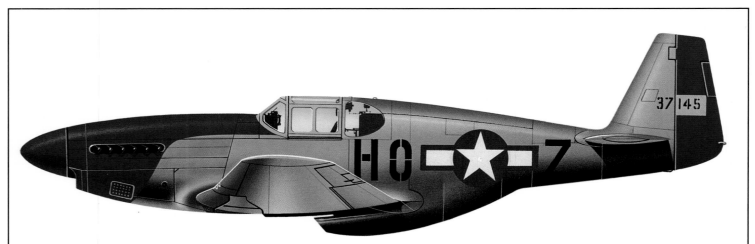

North American P-51B Mustang

Type: single-seat fighter **Country of origin:** USA **Powerplant:** one 1400hp (1044kW) Packard V-1650-3 (RR Merlin) 12-cylinder Vee-type engine	**Performance:** maximum speed 440mph (708km/h) **Weights:** empty 6840lb (3103kg); maximum take-off 11,200lb (5080kg)	**Dimensions:** wing span 37ft (11.80m); length 32ft 3in (9.83m); height 8ft 8in (2.64m) **Armament:** six wing-mounted 0.50in (12.7mm) machine guns

Macchi MC.205V Veltro

Type: single-seat fighter
Country of origin: Italy
Powerplant: one 1475hp (1100kW) Fiat RA.1050 RC.58 Tifone 12-cylinder inverted-Vee engine

Performance: maximum speed 399mph (642km/h)
Weights: empty 5961lb (2581kg); maximum take-off 7514lb (3408kg)
Dimensions: wing span 34ft 8in

(10.6m); length 29ft 0.5in (8.85m); height 9ft 11in (3.04m)
Armament: two 12.7mm (0.5in) MGs, two 20mm (0.78in) cannon plus a 705lb (320kg) bombload

engine and long-barrelled British Hispano Mk II 20mm (0.78in) cannon, and were designated Mk V Series I. Subsequent production aircraft had the Sabre IIB or 'C, the short-barrelled Hispano Mk V cannon fully recessed in the wing leading edge and spring-tab ailerons, and were designated Mk V Series II. At the time it entered service with No 3 Squadron RAF and No 486 Squadron RNZAF (the two squadrons combining to form No 150 Wing) in April 1944, the Tempest was the fastest and most powerful fighter in the world. Below 10,000ft (3000m) it could be dived at up to 540mph (869km/h), far in excess of the speed attainable by any other piston-engined fighter, and its maximum speed, straight and level, was 440mph (708km/h). Combat radius was 500 miles (800km) with external tanks, and its ammunition magazines held 800 20mm (0.78in) shells, enough for 20 seconds of firing time. The two initial Tempest squadrons flew many cross-Channel sorties before and during the invasion of Normandy and, in their first encounter with the Luftwaffe, on 8 June 1944, they destroyed four Messerschmitt Bf 109s, with two more damaged, in exchange for two Tempests damaged.

FIGHTERS V FLYING BOMBS

Soon afterwards, however, the Tempest squadrons were assigned to the air defence of Great Britain, operating against the V-1 flying bombs that were now being launched against London. The Tempest's high speed made it the ideal

interceptor in this new role; No 3 Squadron was the top-scoring unit, with 258 V-1s destroyed, while No 486 claimed 223. As far as individual claims were concerned, no fewer than 52 Tempest pilots shot down five or more flying bombs before the missiles' launching sites were overrun by the advancing Allies. The anti-flying bomb operations, however, revealed some snags with the Tempests' Sabre engines, and the fighters were withdrawn from front-line service for some weeks while the troubles were rectified. The Tempest squadrons subsequently moved to the Continent with 2nd TAF and became a potent addition to the Allies' striking power during the closing months of the war. Other participants in the battle against the V-1 were the Griffon-engined Spitfires XII and XIV. The Mk XII was developed specifically to counter the low-level attacks by Focke-Wulf 190s, and first went into service with No 41 Squadron in February 1943. The Squadron shot down its first FW 190 on 27 April, while operating from Hawkinge. The second unit to re-equip with the Mk XII, No 91, destroyed five enemy fighter-bombers in a running battle over the Channel on 25 May 1943. Only 100 MK XII Spitfires were built, but they were followed by the more numerous Mk XIV. The latter, based on a Mk VIII airframe, was the first Griffon-engined Spitfire variant to go into large-scale production, and the first examples were issued to No 322 (Netherlands) and No 610 Squadrons in

March and April 1944. The Mks XII and XIV performed well against the V-1; in No 91 Squadron, 14 pilots flying the Mk XII destroyed five or more flying bombs, including five with scores of over ten. Both 41 and 91 Squadrons exchanged their Mk XIIs for Mk XIVs before the V-1 offensive was over.

JET FIGHTER GENESIS

In all, 11 RAF fighter squadrons, ten of them equipped with Spitfires Mk IX, XII and XIV, Typhoons, Mustangs, Mosquitoes and Tempests, were assigned to air defence against the V-1s. The eleventh squadron was revolutionary in that it was armed with the RAF's first operational jet fighter, the Gloster Meteor F.Mk.1. The Meteor traced its lineage to the first British experimental jet, the Gloster E.28/39, which flew for the first time on 15 May 1941 under the power of a single Whittle W.2/7000 turbojet. The Meteor was Gloster's answer to Air Ministry Specification F.9/40, calling for a single-seat interceptor powered by gas turbine engines. The low thrust output of the engines available at the time dictated a twin-engine configuration but, apart from the radical nature of its form of propulsion, the Meteor was entirely conventional in design. Twelve prototypes were ordered and eight were completed, the first flying on 5 March 1943. The aircraft was powered by two 1500hp (680kg) thrust Halford H.1 turbojets, but the first 20 production aircraft were fitted with the 1700lb (771kg) Rolls-Royce

Welland. Twelve of these were issued to
No 616 Squadron, which deployed to
Manston and flew its first 'Diver' (anti V-
1) patrol on 27 July. On 4 August, Flying
Officer Dean became the first RAF jet
pilot to destroy an enemy aircraft when
he knocked down a V-1 near Ashford in
Kent; the technique he used was to insert
his Meteor's wing-tip under that of the
flying bomb so that the airflow upset the
missile's equilibrium, turning it over on
to its back so that it dived into the
ground. These tactics were used
frequently by pilots on 'Diver patrols',
and were a good deal safer than
attempting to shoot the missile down;
several pilots had very narrow escapes
when the V-1s they were attacking
exploded, filling the sky ahead with debris.

The Meteor destroyed only 13 V-1s, but
it came very late to the battle and it was
underpowered. The next variant, the
Meteor F.3, was a much better
proposition, using the 2000lb (906kg)
thrust Rolls-Royce Derwent I engine; but
deliveries to No 616 Squadron did not
begin until December 1944. Meanwhile,
one of the Meteor Mk 1 aircraft had been
exchanged for an example of America's
first jet fighter, the Bell P-59 Airacomet,
the protoype of which had flown on 1
October 1942 under the power of two

■ABOVE: A P-51D Mustang of the 364th
Fighter Squadron, 357th Fighter Group,
flown by Captain Richard A. Peterson,
about to touch down at Raydon, Essex,
after a bomber escort mission.

General Electric I-A turbojets, derived
from the Whittle W.2B engine. A higher-
powered engine, the 1400lb (635kg)
thrust I-16, was installed in the 13 trials
aircraft which followed. Two of these
were evaluated by the US Navy, and a
third was sent to the United Kingdom in
exchange for the Meteor. The Airacomet
proved to be underpowered and its
performace fell far below expectations, so
the original order for 100 aircraft was
reduced. Twenty P-59As were built with
J31-GE-3 engines, and 30 P-59Bs with
J31-GE-5s. Although the Airacomet did
not serve operationally in World War II, it
provided the Americans with invaluable
experience in the operation of jet aircraft,
from both the aircrew and engineering
points of view.

JET COMBAT

In the summer of 1944, the Allies were
left in no doubt that the Germans were a
considerable distance ahead of them in
the production of jet fighters. On 25 July
1944, a Mosquito of No 544 Squadron, on

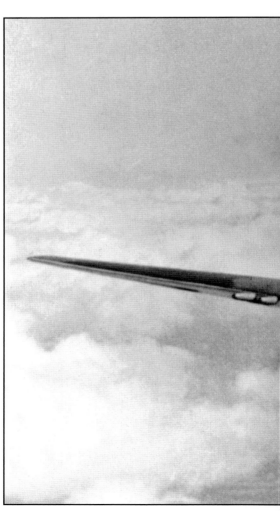

a reconnaissance mission at 30,000ft (9144m) over Munich, was subjected to a series of cannon attacks by an extremely fast enemy aircraft before escaping into cloud. The aircraft was subsequently identified as a Messerschmitt Me 262 jet fighter. Design work on the Me 262 had begun in September 1939, a month after the successful flight of the world's first jet aircraft, the Heinkel He 178, but because of delays in the development of satisfactory engines, the massive damage caused by Allied air attacks and Hitler's later obsession with using the aircraft as a bomber rather than a fighter, six years elapsed between the 262 taking shape on Messerschmitt's drawing board and its entry into Luftwaffe service. It was not until July 1943 that one of the Me 262 prototypes, powered by two Junkers Jumo 004A turbojets, was demonstrated before senior Luftwaffe officials, including Hermann Göring. The latter reported on

■BELOW: The Hawker Tempest Mk V was the fastest and most powerful operational piston-engined fighter of World War II. Its first combat missions were against the V-1 flying bomb.

the aircraft's performance in glowing terms to Hitler, but the Führer refused to increase the fighter's priority rating and forbade any attempt to put the aircraft into mass production, a decision that was to set back the whole German jet fighter programme by six months. Only in November 1943 did Hitler witness the Me 262 in flight, when the Me 262V-6 (the sixth prototype) was flown to Insterburg in East Prussia to carry out a demonstration. In the course of the display, Hitler turned to Göring and asked whether the 262 could be adapted to carry bombs. Göring, who some time earlier had put the same question to Professor Willi Messerschmitt, replied that it was theoretically possible. At this, Hitler became suddenly enthusiastic about the whole project. 'At last,' he exclaimed, 'this is the Blitz (lightning) bomber!' Soon afterwards the Me 262 was ordered into full production by the German Air Ministry, and by the end of 1943 the jet fighter programme had been accorded top priority. December 1943 saw the first flight of the Me 262 V-8, the first of the type to carry a full armament of four 30mm (1.18in) Mk 108 cannon. These

weapons, which were to become standard on the 262, were harmonised at 500 yards and used in conjunction with the Revi 16B gunsight. Mounted in the aircraft's nose, the two upper guns were provided with a magazine of 100 rounds each and the lower guns 80 rounds each. Despite numerous snags, production of the Me 262 began to get into its stride in April 1944, with widely dispersed airframe factories and assembly plants being set up at various locations. The original target was to build up production to the rate of 1000 aircraft per month by May 1945, but it was soon apparent that this figure would never be achieved. In fact, the highest monthly total of Me 262s produced was 280 in March 1945, a remarkable enough figure in view of the fact that by then the German aircraft industry had been forced to abandon many of its factories in the face of the rapid Allied advances. By the end of 1944, 730 Me 262s had been completed, and a further 564 were built in the early months of 1945, making a total of 1294 aircraft. Notwithstanding Hitler's obsession with turning the aircraft into a fast bomber, the Me 262 initially went

into production as a pure fighter, entering service with a trials unit known as Erprobungskommando 262 (EK262) at Lechfeld, near Augsburg, in August 1944. It was originally commanded by Captain Tierfelder, who was killed when his aircraft crashed in flames during one of the unit's first operational missions. His successor was Major Walter Nowotny, who, at the age of 23, was one of the Luftwaffe's top fighter pilots with a score of 258 kills, 255 of them achieved on the Eastern Front. By the end of October the Kommando Nowotny, as the unit had come to be known, had reached full operational status and was deployed to the airfields of Achmer and Hesepe near Osnabruck, astride the main American daylight bomber approach route. Because of a shortage of adequately trained pilots and technical problems, the Kommando Nowotny was usually able to fly only three or four sorties a day against the enemy formations, yet in November 1944 the 262s destroyed 22 aircraft. By the end of the month, however, the unit had only 13 serviceable aircraft out of an established total of 30, a rate of attrition accounted for mainly by accidents rather than enemy action.

ROCKET FIGHTER

On 28 July 1944, the Allies encountered another revolutionary German fighter. Nine P-51 Mustangs of the 359th Fighter Group were escorting B-17s at 25,000ft (7620m) over Merseburg when the pilots spotted two contrails at six o'clock, five miles away and several thousand feet higher up. The Mustang leader's combat report described the ensuing action:

'I identified them immediately as the new jet-propelled aircraft. Their contrails could not be mistaken and looked very dense and white, somewhat like an elongated cumulus cloud some threequarters of a mile in length. My section turned 180 degrees back towards the enemy, which included two with jets turned on and three in a glide without jets operating at the moment. The two I had spotted made a diving turn to the left in close formation and feinted towards the bombers at six o'clock, cutting off their jets as they turned. Our flight turned for a head-on pass to get between them and the rear of the bomber formation. While still 3000 yards from the bombers, they turned into us and left the bombers alone. In this turn they banked about 80 degrees but their course changed only about 20 degrees. Their turn radius was very large but their rate of roll appeared excellent. Their speed I estimated was 500 to 600 miles per hour. Both planes passed under us 1000 feet below while still in a close formation glide. In an attempt to follow them, I split-S'd. One continued down in a 45-degree dive, the other climbed up into the sun very steeply and I lost him. Then I looked back at the one in the dive and saw he was five miles away at 10,000 feet.'

In fact, the attackers were not jet aircraft at all, but early operational examples of the rocket-powered Messerschmitt Me 163 Komet. This remarkable little aircraft was based on the experimental DFS 194, designed in 1938 by Professor Alexander Lippisch and transferred, together with its design staff, to the Messerschmitt company for further development. The first two Me 163 prototypes were flown in the spring

■BELOW: One way of doing it: a Spitfire pilot slips his wingtip under that of a V-1, allowing his slipstream to topple the flying bomb and send it diving into open country.

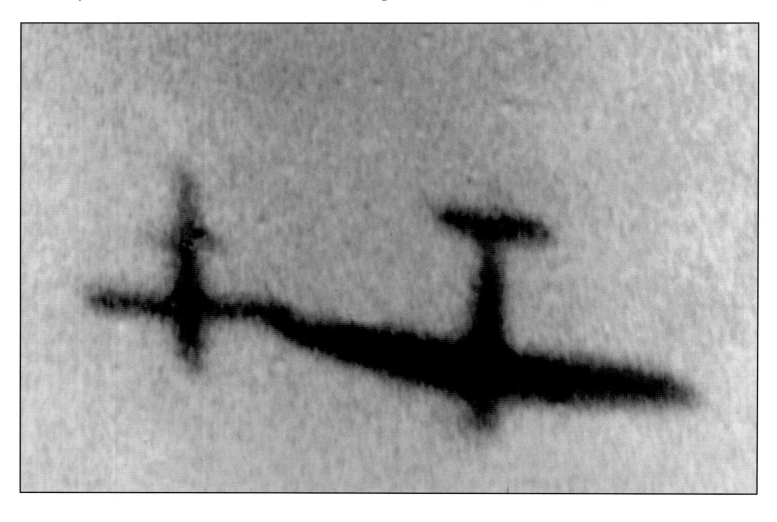

■ABOVE: Britian's first operational jet fighter, the Gloster Meteor F.1, was also sent into battle against the V-1 with No 616 Squadron, but destroyed only 13 of the missiles.

of 1941 as unpowered gliders, the Me 163V1 being transferred to Peenemünde later in the year to be fitted with its 1653lb (750kg) thrust Walter HWK R.II rocket motor. The first rocket-powered flight was made in August 1941, and during subsequent trials the Me 163 broke all existing world air speed records, reaching speeds of up to 620mph (1000km/h). Because of the need for secrecy, these achievements remained unpublicised until after the war. Development of the Me 163 was accelerated, but the programme became protracted because of delays with the production version of the rocket motor, the HWK 509A. The programme entered a new phase early in 1943, when some Me 163s powered by early examples of the HWK 509A were each fitted with two MG151 20mm (0.78in) cannon and assigned to a new unit, Erprobungskommando 16 (EK16) based at Peenemünde West under

the command of Major Wolfgang Späte. EK16's principal function was to pioneer the Me 163B (the fully operational version) into Luftwaffe use, and to train a cadre of experienced pilots. Later, the unit was transferred to Bad Zwischenahn. Halfway through the training programme Späte was inexplicably transferred to command a fighter group on the Eastern Front, his place being taken by Captain Toni Thaler.

In May 1944 an operational Komet unit, JG400, began forming at Wittmundhaven and Venlo, and in June all three Staffeln of this unit moved to Brandis near Leipzig, together with EK16. The task of the Komets at Brandis was to defend the Leuna oil refinery, which lay 55 miles (90km) to the south. Taking off on its jettisonable trolley, the Komet would climb initially at 11,800ft/min (3600m/min), this rate rising to 33,470ft/min (10,200m/min) at 32,800ft (10,000m). Time to the Komet's operational ceiling of 39,690ft (12,100m) was a mere 3.35 minutes. Maximum powered endurance was eight minutes. With its fuel exhausted the Me 163 would make high-speed gliding attacks on its

targets, using its two MK 108 30mm (1.18in) cannon and Revi 16B gunsight. With its 120 rounds of ammunition used up and its speed beginning to drop, the Komet would then dive steeply away from the combat area and glide back to base, landing on a skid. This in itself was a hazardous procedure, as there was always a risk of explosion if any unburnt rocket fuel remained in the aircraft's tanks. Many Me 163s were lost in landing accidents. About 300 Komets were built, but JG400 remained the only operational unit and the rocket fighter recorded only nine kills during its brief career.

STORMBIRDS AND SWALLOWS

It was the Me 262 that remained the principal threat to Allied air superiority during the closing weeks of 1944. Two versions were now being developed in parallel: the Me 262A-2a Sturmvogel (Stormbird) bomber variant and the Me 262A-1a fighter. The Sturmvogel was issued to Kampfgeschwader 51 'Edelweiss' in September 1944; other bomber units that armed with the type at a later date were KG 6, 27 and 54. Problems encountered during operational

Messerschmitt Me 262A-2

Type: single-seat jet fighter
Country of origin: Germany
Powerplant: two 1984lbst (900kg)
Junkers Jumo 004B turbojets
Performance: maximum speed

540mph (870km/h)
Weights: empty 9742lb (4420kg);
maximum take-off 15,720lb
(7130kg)
Dimensions: wing span 41ft

(12.5m); length 34ft 9in (10.60m);
height 11ft 7in (3.84m)
Armament: four 30mm (1.18in)
cannon in nose; 24 R4M air-to-air
unguided rockets

training delayed the aircraft's combat debut, but in the autumn of 1944 the 262s began to appear in growing numbers, carrying out low-level attacks on Allied targets, mainly moving columns. There were also two reconnaissance versions, the Me 262A-1a/U3 and Me 262A-5a. For weeks, these aircraft roved almost at will over the entire battlefront, photographing installations and troop movements deep behind the Allied lines and gradually enabling the German general staff to build up a comprehensive intelligence picture of the Allied order of battle in northern France, Holland and Belgium. Slipping over the front line at low level and hugging the contours of the terain, the 262s usually achieved complete surprise and completed their missions before the Allied defences were able to react. The jets' high speed made it difficult for anti-aircraft guns to track them successfully, and Allied piston-engine fighters could only hope to catch them by means of a dive from higher altitude. In an effort to combat the Me 262 menace the Allied air forces set up so-called 'Rat Patrols', with their latest fighter aircraft – such as the RAF's Hawker Tempests operating in pairs over the front line and a second pair held at cockpit readiness on the ground in the hope of catching the 262s as they slipped across. More often than not, however, the

expertly camouflaged 262s, which were extremely hard to spot from a higher level, eluded this fighter screen and got clean away. The Allies resorted to mounting heavy attacks on the 262s' bases, an extremely hazardous procedure. Not only had the Germans organised 'flak lanes', consisting of strings of 20mm (0.78in) batteries extending for two miles along the approach to an airfield's runways, but a Gruppe of Focke-Wulf 190s (JG54) was assigned to defend the two principal bases at Achmer and Hesepe.

LONG-NOSED FOCKE-WULFS
Jagdgeschwader 54 was now equipped with the FW 190D-9, the final version of this excellent fighter. The BMW radial engine that had powered earlier versions of the FW 190 was discarded and replaced by the 1776hp (1324.3kW) Junkers Jumo 213A-1 engine, a liquid-cooled powerplant whose annular radiator duct gave the 'Dora 9' a radial-engined appearance. The first FW 190D-9s, which were characterised by their long, newly contoured engine cowlings, entered service with JG3 in 1943. The D-9 presented a serious challenge to the latest Allied fighter types, as did its potential successor, the Focke-Wulf Ta 152. This aircraft was a long-span version of the FW 190D-9 and was intended for high-altitude interception. With a top speed of over 460mph (740km/h) at

34,000ft (10,363m), a service ceiling of over 40,000ft (12,192m) and an armament of four 20mm (0.78in) and one 30mm (1.18in) cannon, the Ta 152 might have presented the Allies with serious problems had it become available earlier. As it was, only a small number were in service at the end of the war and it was the workhorse of the German fighter forces, the Messerschmitt 109, that still provided about half the Luftwaffe's piston-engined fighter assets as the war entered its final year. The main Bf 109 variant was the 109G, known as the 'Gustav'. Ongoing development, the installation of a DB605 engine and new equipment had now turned the basic 109 into a heavy aircraft which was relatively easy prey for the latest Allied types. A refined, lighter version, the Bf 109K, saw service only in limited numbers. Many of the Focke-Wulfs and Messerschmitts were now committed to the Eastern Front, where they operated in the fighter-bomber role as the Russians continued their relentless advance.

NORMANDIE-NIEMEN
The German retreat in the east had continued throughout August 1944, by which time the Russians had forced their way to the borders of East Prussia. The Soviet 16th Air Army, which had supported the Russian offensive throughout, was now augmented by three

Polish air regiments, one bomber, one fighter and one ground attack. The 1st Polish 'Warsaw' Fighter Regiment was equipped with the latest Soviet fighter, the Yakovlev Yak-3. Contrary to what might be supposed from its designation, it replaced the Yak-9 in several fighter regiments in the summer of 1944. One of the units to receive the new type was the French Regiment Normandie, whose personnel had reached the Soviet Union by way of Syria and which was now attached to the 3rd Byelorussian Front as part of the 2nd Air Army. Between 22 June and the end of August 1944, while still flying Yak-9s, the French pilots destroyed 30 German aircraft. In September and October, they were engaged in a period of bitter air fighting over the Niemen and East Prussia, where their main opponents were Focke-Wulf FW 190 fighter-bombers. On one memorable day in October, the Frenchmen, led by Lieutenant-Colonel Pierre Pouyade, destroyed 26 enemy aircraft for no loss to themselves. The exploit earned them the honorary title of the 'Normandie-Niemen Regiment' and

they were cited in a special Red Army Order of the Day, an honour reserved for units which had shown an outstanding achievement in battle. The other new fighter type to enter service in the summer of 1944 was the Lavochkin La-7, which was basically similar to the definitive version of the La-5 (the La-5FN), but with aerodynamic refinements that gave it a better combat performance. Production of both types continued in parallel. As well as Soviet units, the La-5FN and La-7 equipped the Czechoslovak Fighter Regiment, which took part in the summer offensive of 1944.

LAST BATTLES IN THE WEST

By the end of 1944 the Russians enjoyed overwhelming air superiority in the east, most of the Luftwaffe's fighter assets having been withdrawn for the defence of the Reich. Me 262 fighters were more in evidence, but attacks on their airfields were taking an increasing toll. During one such attack, on 8 November 1944, Walter Nowotny was shot down and killed by Mustangs while approaching to land at Achmer. Shortly after his death,

one of the Kommando's groups was used to form the nucleus of a new jet fighter unit, Jagdgeschwader JG 7 Hindenburg, under the command of Major Johannes Steinhoff. Although JG 7 eventually comprised three Gruppen, only one of these, III/JG 7, made real and continual contact with the enemy, moving in turn to bases at Brandenburg-Briest, Oranienburg and Parchim. In the middle of February 1945, III/JG 7 took delivery of the first consignment of R4M 5cm (1.97in) air-to-air rockets; the Me 262 could carry 24 of these missiles mounted on simple wooden racks beneath the wings and, when the salvo was fired towards an enemy bomber formation, it spread out rather like the charge from a shotgun, increasing the chances of hitting one or more targets. During their first series of operations using a combination of R4Ms, 30mm (1.18in) cannon and Revi

■ **BELOW: The rocket-propelled Messerschmitt Me 163 Komet was a revolutionary concept, but it had a limited endurance and its volatile fuel resulted in many landing accidents.**

gunsight, in the last week of February 1945, the pilots of III/JG 7 destroyed no fewer than 45 four-engined American bombers and 15 of their escorting fighters for the loss of only four Me 262s. Meanwhile, authority had been given for the formation of a second Me 262 jet fighter unit. Known as Jagdverband 44, and commanded by Lieutenant-General Adolf Galland, it comprised 45 highly experienced pilots, many of them Germany's top-scoring aces. Its main operating base was Munchen-Riem, where its main targets were the bombers of the Fifteenth Army Air Force, coming up from the south, while JG 7 continued to operate from bases in northern and central Germany. On 7 April 1945, JG 7 demonstrated the Me 262's remarkable potential when it took on the American fighter escort and destroyed 28 P-47 Thunderbolts and P-51 Mustangs; but there was no escaping the fact that on that same day, the Luftwaffe lost 183 piston-engined Messerschmitt 109s and Focke-Wulf 190s in what was the last series of major air battles over Germany. Three days later, over 1000 American bombers launched massive attacks on the

Luftwaffe's jet fighter bases. The 262s shot down ten bombers, but with their bases devastated they were compelled to withdraw to airfields as far afield as Prague, the jet units broken up and scattered piecemeal. In the last days of April the remnants of JV 44 moved still further south to Salzburg, but the jets were grounded through lack of fuel. Most of the 262s were destroyed by their ground crews shortly before the airfield was overrun by American tanks on 3 May. Of the total of almost 1500 Me 262s produced before the end of the war, less than a quarter saw combat. Had the figure been higher, the jets would certainly have inflicted severe punishment on the American daylight formations – and probably on the RAF's night bombers too, for the 262's potential as a night fighter was belatedly recognised. As the Allies advanced deeper into Germany, they found plenty of evidence of the devastating weapon the Me 262 might have become. Time and again, during the early days of May 1945, they came upon rows of jet fighters parked in the pine forests that bordered bomb-cratered autobahnen, together with

stockpiles of R4M rockets, all awaiting delivery to Luftwaffe units that no longer existed.

THE END IN THE EAST

At the end of 1944 the Eastern Front ran from Yugoslavia to the Baltic, slicing across Poland and Czechoslovakia and running along the border of East Prussia. The stage was now set for the great Soviet offensive that would take them deep into Germany. For this last mighty thrust they had assembled five million men, and to support it there would be a vast umbrella of 13 air armies totalling 17,000 aircraft, outnumbering the dwindling Luftwaffe by ten to one. In this last phase of the battle the Germans had set up eight lines of defence, and the Russian armies suffered staggering losses as they assaulted them one by one. Over the battlefield massive formations of Soviet fighters operated in three zones, covering the whole front. The forward zone, inside enemy territory, was patrolled by the Guards Fighter Regiments and other crack units, their task being to break up enemy formations before they reached the battle area.

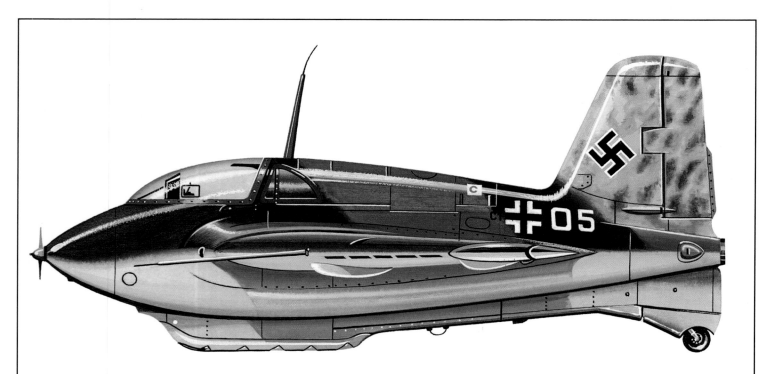

Messerschmitt Me 163 Komet

Type: single-seat rocket fighter
Country of origin: Germany
Powerplant: one 3748lbst (1700kg)
Walter HWK 109-509A liquid-propellant rocket motor

Performance: maximum speed 593mph (955km/h)
Weights: empty 1908kg (4206lb); maximum take-off 9502lb (4310kg)
Dimensions: wing span 30ft 7in

(9.30m); length 19ft 2in (5.85m); height 9ft (2.70m) on take-off dolly
Armament: two 20mm (0.78in) or 30mm (1.18in) cannon in wing roots

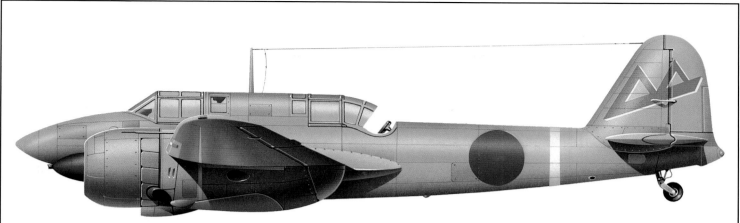

Kawasaki Ki-45 Toryu

Type: two-seat night fighter
Country of origin: Japan
Powerplant: two 1080hp (805.3kW)
Mitsubishi Ha-102 14-cylinder
radial engines
Performance: maximum speed

336mph (540km/h)
Weights: empty 8818lb (4000kg);
max. take-off 12,125lb (5500kg)
Dimensions: wing span 49ft 3in
(15.00m); length 36ft 1in (11.00m);
height 12ft 2in (3.70m)

Armament: one 37mm (1.45in)
cannon under forward fuselage;
two 20mm (0.78in) forward-firing
cannon in central fuselage; one
moveable 7.92mm (0.31in)
machine gun in rear cockpit

Dislocated, the enemy units would then fall prey to other powerful fighter groups patrolling the second and third zones, the latter being directly over the front line. In April 1945 the Russians stood poised on the Oder and Neisse rivers, where the Germans had created their main line of defence. Despite crippling losses, the Luftwaffe continued to throw its dwindling reserves of combat aircraft into the fray, including Messerschmitt Me 262 jets; three of these were shot down by Soviet pilots, one of whom was Ivan Kozhedub. The latter scored his final victories flying an La-7. The Russian armies on the Oder-Neisse front were supported by 8400 combat aircraft, and at dawn on 16 April 1945 these launched an all-out attack on the German positions west of the line. In its wake the Russians launched their offensive, and within a week, after savage fighting at appalling cost, they had succeeded in smashing the German Ninth Army. Then, on 21 April, came the news that the crack Soviet Eighth Guards Army under General Chuikov, the veteran defender of Stalingrad, was fighting in the suburbs of Berlin itself. As the Russian advance rolled forward, the supporting air units operated from stretches of autobahn. The time involved in repairing these was far less than it would have taken to build new forward airstrips, and the forests that bordered the roads provided excellent camouflage for dispersed aircraft. For some time now, the

Luftwaffe had also been operating combat aircraft from this ready-made network of emergency runways. From these forward strips the Soviet fighter formations roved across the sky of the burning German capital. The Luftwaffe fought hard to the last, scraping together its last reserves and flying an average of 1000 sorties a day during the battle. Compared to the Soviet effort, it was a drop in the ocean. In one day alone, during the final assault on the capital, the Soviet air armies flew nearly 17,000 missions. On 2 May 1945, pounded incessantly from air and ground, the last defenders of Berlin surrendered. There was only a few isolated pockets of resistance in the east; the last was Prague, the Czech capital, which held out for a week after the fall of Berlin.

On 9 May, the day of the final German surrender in Prague, Guards Major Viktor Golubev, one of Pokryshkin's pilots and sixteenth-ranking Soviet air ace, shot down a Messerschmitt Bf 109 over the city. It was Golubev's 39th victory, and the last aircraft to be destroyed in combat in the European war.

STRATEGIC AIR OFFENSIVE

The capture of the Marianas was of great significance in the Pacific air war, for the islands provided the USAAF with a springboard to launch a long-awaited strategic air offensive against the Japanese home islands. At Saipan, Tinian and Guam, work went ahead on the construction of new airfields and, by

January 1945, these were ready to receive the strategic bombers, the mighty Boeing B-29 Superfortresses of the US Twentieth Air Force. The first major B-29 attacks on Japanese targets, when the large-scale use of incendiaries caused widespread destruction, revealed the inadequacy of the Japanese air defences. The small night fighter force was severely handicapped by the lack of advanced airborne interception radar. The standard Japanese night fighters of 1945 were the twin-engined Kawasaki Ki-45 Toryu (Dragon Killer) and Nakajima J1N Gekko (Moonlight), known respectively by the Allied code names Nick and Irving. The latter lacked the speed and altitude performance to be very effective, but the Toryu, armed with one 37mm (1.45in) and two 20mm (0.78in) cannon, plus a 7.92mm (0.31in) machine gun, would have been a formidable opponent had it been equipped with anything but the most primitive AI radar. As it was, the Japanese had nothing to compare with America's most potent night fighter, an aircraft that was to make its mark in both the European and Pacific theatres of war.

THE BLACK WIDOW

At the time of the Japanese attack in December 1941, the United States Army Air Corps, as it then was, had no specialised night fighter. In fact, scant thought had been given to night fighting at all until the late summer of 1940, when Lt Gen Delos C. Emmons, commanding general of GHQ Air Corps, visited Britain and saw at first hand the threat posed by night bombers. As a result of his recommendations, the USAAC drew up preliminary specifications for a night fighter and passed them to the Northrop Company, which at that time was working on a night fighter design on behalf of the British Purchasing Commission in the USA. The design that was taking shape involved a radar-equipped aircraft with a crew of two, heavy armament and long endurance, so that incoming bombers could be intercepted long before they reached their targets. Before negotiations could begin with the British on construction of a prototype, the USAAC stepped in and virtually commandeered the project, although British involvement was maintained for the time being; the

RAF relinquished its interest when the Beaufighter began to prove its worth in the night defence role. In January 1941 Northrop received a contract for the construction of two protypes under the designation XP-61. The aircraft would later be called the Black Widow. It was not until the Black Widow began to reach the Pacific theatre in numbers that the USAAF had a really effective night fighter. The 421st NFS was the first to rearm with the new type, operating from Mokmer in New Guinea and, on 7 July 1944, one of its aircraft scored the first P-61 victory in the Southwest Pacific by shooting down a Mitsubishi Ki-46 Dinah over Japen island. The 421st, which was joined in the theatre at later dates by the 418th and 547th NFS, moved to Tacloban, Leyte, on 25 October 1944, and on 29 November the Black Widows were ordered to make a night attack on a

Japanese convoy in Leyte Gulf. The convoy, consisting of two escort destroyers and a number of smaller vessels, was heading towards Ormoc to land reinforcement troops and supplies. The convoy was duly harassed throughout the night, preventing the landing of its troops, and one of the destroyers was sunk by US surface forces at daybreak. In the Central Pacific, the US Seventh Air Force had three Black Widow squadrons, the 6th, 548th and 549th. In June 1944 seven P-61s of the 6th NFS moved to Aslito airstrip on Saipan, and on 27 June one of its aircraft claimed a Nakajima B5N Kate as probably destroyed. There

■ BELOW: The powerful Northrop P-61 Black Widow night fighter, like the P-51 Mustang, started life as a design to meet a Royal Air Force requirement. It served in Europe and the Pacific.

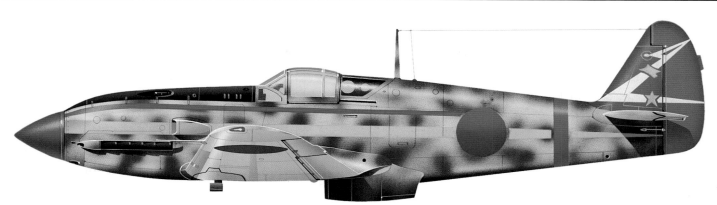

Kawasaki Ki-61 Hien

Type: single-seat fighter
Country of origin: Japan
Powerplant: one 1175hp (876.2kW)
Kawasaki Ha-40 12-cylinder
inverted Veetype engine

Performance: maximum speed
368mph (592km/h)
Weights: empty 4872lb (2210kg);
maximum take-off 7165lb (3250kg)
Dimensions: wing span 39ft 4in

(12.00m); length 28ft 8in (8.75m);
height 12ft 2in (3.70m)
Armament: two 12.7mm (0.5in)
MGs in forward upper fuselage;
two wing-mounted 12.7mm guns

was no doubt about the outcome on 6 July, when two P-61s sent two Mitsubishi G4M Betty bombers down in flames. Two more G4Ms were destroyed on 25/26 December by Lt Dale Haberman (pilot) and Lt Raymond Mooney (RO).

BLACK WIDOW COMBAT

The combat report tells the story:

'Scrambled from Condor Base then to Coral Base and vectored to the north of the island at altitude of 15,000ft. Coral Base ordered figure 8 orbits since they had no Bogies in the vicinity but much Snow (fuzzy radar image) was in the area. Contact made with airborne radar at five miles. Control notified...reported Bogies in vicinity but could give no information. Went into starboard orbit but airborne radar kept picking up Bogie which seemed to be in orbit. Chased Bogie to the north and let down to 9000ft when visual contact was made. Opened fire at 1500ft and closed to 700ft. Bogie made violent turns and hits observed to go into wings and fuselage. Bogie was in a slight dive indicating 300mph. Bogie last seen to roll to port in semblance of Split-S and nose straight down with fires observed coming from the right wing and engine. Visual lost as Bogie was at 6000ft still going straight down, apparently out of control. At the same time the Radar Observer called for a starboard turn as a second Bogie was out about two miles. Closed fast on second Bogie letting down to 4500ft where visual was made at about 2500ft. Closed in to 700ft and opened fire with hits observed to spray the entire

ship. Bogie exploded with its debris hitting P-61 with damage to left cowling. Bogie went down in flames and was seen to hit the water...'

Two more Black Widow squadrons, the 548th and 549th, arrived in the Pacific on 7 and 24 March 1945 respectively, being assigned to the Seventh Air Force on Iwo Jima. The 548th NFS soon moved up to Ie Shima to provide forward air defence and also to carry out night intruder operations over Kyushu, scoring five kills during these operations; the 549th remained on Iwo Jima, sending detachments to Saipan and Guam as required.

There were two Black Widow squadrons in the China–Burma–Índia (CBI) theatre. The first was the 426th NFS, which was activated on 1 January 1944 at Hammer Field, California, and arrived at Chengtu, China, under Fourteenth Air Force command on 5 November 1944. It operated from a number of bases thereafter, mostly in the night ground attack role, as there was virtually no air opposition. The other was the 427th NFS, which was activated on 1 February 1944 and deployed to Myitkyina, Burma, in December by way of Italy and India. During the next few months, under the command of the Tenth and later the Fourteenth Air Force, the 427th flew 73 defensive patrols without encountering a single enemy aircraft and so its aircraft were modified to carry bombs and rockets for intruder operations against Japanese troop concentrations and supply dumps. A

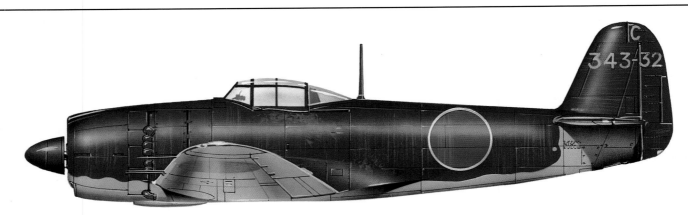

Kawanishi N1K-J Shiden

Type: single-seat fighter
Country of origin: Japan
Powerplant: one 1990hp (1484kW) Nakajima NK9H Homare 21 18-cylinder radial
Performance: maximum speed

361mph (581km/h)
Weights: empty 6387lb (2897kg); maximum take-off 9526lb (4321kg)
Dimensions: wing span 39ft 4in (12.00m); length 29ft 2in (8.90m); height 13ft 4in (4.06m)

Armament: four wing-mounted 20mm (0.78in) cannon; two 7.7mm (0.303in) machine guns in upper forward fuselage

detachment at Kunming, China, did similar work. The hardest-worked P-61 squadron in the Pacific, however, remained the 418th, which saw considerable action against enemy intruders from successive bases in New Guinea, the Schouten Islands, Leyte, Mindoro and Okinawa. A combat report by Lt Beretram C. Tompkins, dated 27 January 1945, describes one of its actions. The squadron was then based on Mindoro.

'Approximately 1½ hours after becoming airborne the GCI controller vectored me onto a Bogey approaching from the northwest. F/O Wertin made radar contact with Bogey at 0010 at a distance of six miles and altitude of 10,000ft on heading of 280 degrees. He directed me to 2000ft directly behind and below Bogey and I obtained a visual and identified it as a Tony (Kawasaki Ki-61). I closed to 150ft and fired one short burst. The Tony exploded and fell burning into the water approximately twenty miles west of base. No evasive action was used by enemy aircraft. Immediately GCI vectored me onto second Bogey, which was twenty miles southeast of me. F/O Wertin made radar contact at six miles and directed me to 3000ft directly behind and slightly below the Bogey, where I got a visual. I closed to 300ft and fired one burst, and enemy aircraft exploded and fell to the water burning. Kill was made approximately five miles west of Mindoro coast. E/A was

identified as a Tony. Violent evasive action was used.'

SWALLOWS AND DEMONS

The Kawasaki Ki-61 Tony, mentioned in the above report, was designed to replace the Nakajima Ki-43 Hayabusa (Oscar) in Japanese army service, and began to reach front-line air units in August 1942. Given the Japanese name Hien (Swallow), it was the only operational Japanese fighter to feature a liquid-cooled engine (a licence-built DB 601), and until Allied pilots became familiar with it its appearance gave rise to erroneous reports that the Japanese were using Messerschmitt 109s. The prototype Hien flew in December 1941 and the aircraft went into full production some six months later. By then and the end of the Pacific war 3078 examples were built, serving in all areas. Also entering service in the summer of 1942 was the Nakajima Ki-44 Shoki (Demon), which was allocated the Allied code name Tojo. It proved to be an outstanding interceptor, due to its excellent speed and rate of climb, although its high take-off and landing speeds, products of its high wing loading, made it unpopular with Japanese pilots until they got used to it. Arguably the best fighter produced by the Japanese in World War II, the most effective version of the Shoki was the heavily-armed Ki-44-IIc, which was used in the air defence of Japan and which achieved some noteworthy successes against the American B-29 bombers. In

all, 1225 examples of the Shoki were built, production being suspended at the end of 1944 in favour of another army fighter type, the Nakajima Ki-84 Hayate (Gale), which was known as Frank to the Allies. The Hayate was more manoeuvrable than the Shoki, and easier to handle; it was also a later design, originating in 1942. Service trials in the autumn of 1943 produced promising results and the fighter was ordered into mass production, about 3500 being completed in the 18 months before the end of hostilities.

IMPROVED JAPANESE FIGHTERS

Although the Mitsubishi A6M Zero remained the principal Japanese naval fighter throughout the Pacific war, two other types were produced which were more suited to meet the Hellcats and Corsairs of the US Navy on equal terms. The first was the Mitsubishi J2M Raiden (Thunderbolt), known to the Allies as Jack, which was the first Japanese naval fighter designed specifically as an interceptor. The first of three J2M prototypes flew on 20 March 1942, and after some necessary modifications the type was ordered into production in October that year. The tubby, radial-engined Jack was used almost exclusively for home defence, although some were encountered during the Marianas campaign in September 1944. Probably the best variant was the J2M5, which had its armament reduced to two 20mm cannon. Its excellent rate of climb made it an ideal high-altitude interceptor, but supply shortages of its Kasei 26a engine resulted in only 35 being built out of a total of about 500. In fact, production of the Raiden was slowed down in the summer of 1944 because of the priority given to another land-based navy fighter, the Kawanishi N1K Shiden (Violet Lightning). Code-named George by the Allies, the Shiden was unique among World War II's landplane fighters in that it was developed from a floatplane

■BELOW: So passed the might of Imperial Japan. Japanese aircraft, including Zero and Raiden fighters, lie derelict on Atsugi airfield in November 1945.

fighter, the N1K1 Kyofu (Mighty Wind). The Shiden, production of which began in August 1943, was one of the finest fighter aircraft to serve in the Pacific theatre and was produced in two models, the N1K1J and the N1K2-J Model 21, the latter having a redesigned airframe that had its wing lowered from the mid-fuselage point to the lower fuselage and modified vertical tail surfaces. Both operational models were prominent in the Philippines, around Formosa and in the defence of the Japanese home islands.

LAST DESPERATE MONTHS
But even aircraft like the Shiden could not stem the bombing storm that

overtook Japan in the last desperate months of the war, when the home islands came within range not only of carrier-based fighter-bombers, but also of P-51D Mustang escort fighters, operating from newly captured Iwo Jima. By July 1945, mastery of the Japanese skies belonged to the Allies. The Japanese fighters that had not been expended in Kamikaze suicide attacks on the Allied fleet lay immobilised through lack of fuel or pulverised by air attack. When the atomic bombs fell on Hiroshima and Nagasaki, they served merely to underline a victory that had already been won by the relentless application of air and naval might.

CHAPTER 4
COLD WAR WARRIORS: DAY AND NIGHT FIGHTERS 1945–65

The Cold War gave new impetus to fighter design, as turbojet engines became more powerful and reliable. Radical new swept-wing fighters like the Soviet MiG-15 were the equal of anything the West could build.

It was only when they had completed their occupation of Germany, and had the opportunity to investigate fully the labyrinth of undergound facilities built by the enemy, that the Allies came to appreciate the staggering technological advances that had been made by German aeronautical science. At Leck, in Schleswig-Holstein, they found some 50 examples of a new jet fighter type, the Heinkel He 162 Salamander, a diminutive aircraft with twin fins and a turbojet mounted in a pod above the fuselage; more aircraft were discovered at Salzburg, where they had been about to go into action alongside the Me 262s of Adolf Galland's JV 44. Developed as a last-ditch air defence fighter in the closing stages of the war, the He 162, also known as the Volksjäger (people's fighter), had progressed from drawing board to first flight in a mere 10 weeks. Most of the examples delivered to the Luftwaffe were assigned to Jagdgeschwader 1, the aircraft having been rushed through its operational trials by a special unit, Erprobungskommando 162, under the leadership of Colonel Heinz Bär, one of Germany's top air aces

with 220 victories. Sixteen of these victories had been gained while flying the Me 262. (In fact, 22 Luftwaffe pilots became jet aces while flying the 262, destroying five or more Allied aircraft.) But aircraft like the Me 262 and the He 162 were the tip of the iceberg; other, even more advanced fighters were either on the drawing board or in various stages of construction, and one – the Dornier Do 335 – was flying in prototype form and had entered production. An unconventional aircraft, the Do 335 was powered by two DB 603 engines mounted in tandem, one forward and one aft with the cockpit in between. Armed with 30mm (1.18in) cannon, the Do 335 was capable of 450mph (724km/h) and would have presented the Allies with a formidable challenge, had it been available in quantity some months earlier.

CONVENTIONAL DESIGNS

Unlike many of their German counterparts, the Allied jet fighter designs that had evolved by the end of the war were strictly conventional. Apart from the fact that it was turbojet-powered, there was nothing at all unconventional about the Gloster Meteor, which apart from one or two idiosyncracies had turned out to be a very good fighter. The Mk 3 version, which eventually equipped 15 squadrons of RAF Fighter Command in the immediate

■ **LEFT: Even at the 11th hour, mass production of German combat aircraft continued. Here, He 162 jet fighter fuselages awaited delivery of other vital components in an underground factory.**

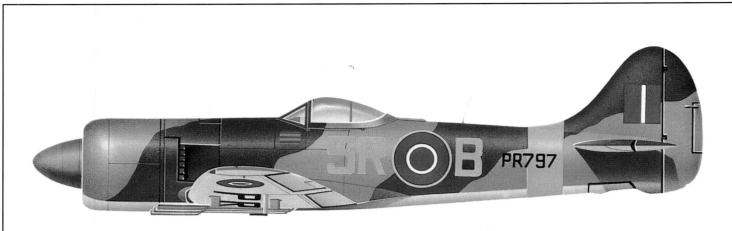

Hawker Tempest Mk II

Type: single-seat fighter
Country of origin: United Kingdom
Powerplant: one 2590hp (1931kW)
Bristol Centaurus V 18-cylinder

Performance: maximum speed
440mph (708km/h)
Weights: empty 9300lb (4218kg);
maximum take-off 13,900lb (6305kg)

Dimensions: wing span 41ft
(12.49m); length 34ft 5in (10.49m);
height 14ft 6in (4.42m)
Armament: four 20mm cannon

post-war years, and which had been operationally tested in a ground attack role in Belgium with Nos 616 and 514 Squadrons in the closing weeks of the war, was followed into service by the Meteor F Mk 4. Powered by two Rolls-Royce Derwent 5s, the F Mk 4 first flew in April 1945 and subsequently, in November, set up a new world air speed record of 606mph (975km/h). The second British jet fighter, the De Havilland Vampire, was also of conventional design, and was of simple configuration, comprising a nacelle housing the engine and cockpit, a very straightforward wing with slightly tapered leading and trailing edges, twin tail booms and twin fins. Design work on the DH.100 Vampire had begun in May 1942, the prototype flying on 20 September 1943, and in the spring of 1944 it became the first Allied jet aircraft capable of sustained speeds of over 500mph (804km/h) over a wide altitude range. The first production Vampire flew in April 1945 and the Vampire F.1 was delivered to Nos 247, 54 and 72 Squadrons in 1946. It was followed by the Vampire F.3, a long-range version with extra internal fuel, underwing tanks and a De Havilland Goblin 2 turbojet. Apart from the Meteor and Vampire, the squadrons of RAF Fighter Command and 2nd Tactical Air Force in Germany in the immediate post-war period were equipped with piston-engined types such as the Tempest Mk 2, which had a Bristol Centaurus radial engine, the Tempest Mk VI, and the later

marks of Spitfire. Perhaps the ultimate in British piston-engined fighter design was the De Havilland Hornet, the fastest twin piston-engined fighter in the world. The Hornet began life as a private venture in 1942 to meet the need for a long-range escort fighter for service in the Far East, but major orders for the Hornet F.1 were cancelled at the end of the war and only 60 were built, entering RAF service in 1946. These were followed by 132 Hornet F.3s, which served with four first-line RAF air defence squadrons until they were withdrawn in 1941. Many were subsequently sent to the Far East, where they were used in the ground attack role against communist terrorists in Malaya.

SHOOTING STAR
As was the case with the RAF, the USAAF's principal fighter assets at the end of World War II comprised the later versions of well-tried piston-engined designs such as the P-51 Mustang and P-47 Thunderbolt. America's first fully operational jet fighter was the Lockheed P-80 Shooting Star, which like its British counterparts was of very conventional design and which was to become the workhorse of the American tactical fighter-bomber and fighter-interceptor squadrons for five years after the war. The prototype XP-80 was designed around a De Havilland H-1 turbojet which was supplied to the United States in July 1943 and the aircraft was completed in just 143 days, making its first flight on 9 January 1944. In April

1945 two YP-80s were sent to England, where they were attached to the Eighth Air Force, and two more went to Italy, but none experienced any operational flying in Europe before the war's end. Early production P-80As entered USAAF service late in 1945 with the 412th Fighter Group, wich became the 1st Fighter Group in July 1946 and comprised the 27th, 71st and 94th Fighter Squadrons. The P-80A was replaced by the P-80B in 1947; the major production version was the F-80C (the P for 'pursuit' prefix having changed to the much more logical F for 'fighter' in the meantime). Some fighter groups equipped with the F-80 were assigned to

■BELOW: The Hawker Tempest II, one of the last of the RAF's piston-engined fighters; the other was the twin-engined De Havilland Hornet. The Tempest II equipped 10 RAF squadrons post-war.

the newly formed Strategic Air Command (SAC), America's nuclear-armed spearhead. At the end of 1947, SAC's assigned fighter resources comprised five groups, each of 75 aircraft, three of which were equipped with F-51 Mustangs and two with F-80 Shooting Stars. The Mustangs equipped the 27th Fighter Group (522nd, 523rd and 524th FS) at Andrews AFB, the 33rd Fighter Group (58th, 59th and 60th FS) at Roswell AFB, New Mexico, and the 82nd Fighter Group (95th, 96th and 97th FS) at Grenier AFB, New Hampshire. The F-80s equipped the 4th Fighter Group (334th, 335th and 336th FS) at Andrews AFB and the 56th Fighter Group (61st, 62nd and 63rd FS) at Selfridge AFB, Michigan. In the third week of July, 1949, the 56th FG demonstrated its ability to reinforce the European theatre when 16 F-80s led by Lt Col David Schilling left Selfridge AFB and flew to Stornoway, in the Western

Isles of Scotland, via Labrador, Greenland and Iceland in a total transatlantic flight time of 5 hours 15 minutes. This was not, in fact, the first transatlantic flight by jet aircraft, as has often been claimed; that was carried out six days earlier by six De Havilland Vampire F.3s of No 54 Squadron RAF. It took the Vampires three hours longer than the F-80s, partly because of their lower cruising speed and partly because they encountered jet streams of up to 200mph (322km/h) as they made the east-west crossing.

ESCORT FIGHTERS

Another F-80 unit, the 1st Fighter Group (27th, 71st and 94th FS) was also assigned to SAC for some months during 1948 and was based at March AFB in California, but in December that year it was re-assigned to Air Defense Command, together with the 4th, 33rd and 56th Fighter Groups. This left the

27th and 82nd Fighter Groups as SAC's only fighter assets. The 82nd FG continued to operate its F-51s out of Grenier AFB until it was re-assigned to Air Defense Command in August 1949, but the 27th FG had begun to rearm with the F-82 Twin Mustang in May 1948 and by the end of the year it had a complement of 81 aircraft.

The North American F-82 Twin Mustang, conceived in 1943 to meet a requirement for a long-range escort fighter for service in the Pacific theatre, was destined to be the last piston-engined fighter ordered by the USAAF. Design was begun in January 1944, the aircraft consisting basically of two F-51H Mustang fuselages joined together by a constant-chord wing centre-section and a rectangular tailplane. The pilot was housed in the port fuselage, the second pilot/navigator in the starboard. The end of the Pacific war reduced an original order for 500 Twin Mustangs to a mere 20 aircraft but, in 1947, orders were placed for a night and all-weather fighter version of the F-82, equipped with AI radar and carrying a radar operator in place of the second pilot. Around 100 Twin Mustangs were completed as F-82Es and were assigned to the escort and ground attack roles. In the night and all-weather fighter roles the F-82 replaced the Northrop P-61 Black Widow with the USAF Air Defense Command, and several squadrons were deployed to Japan for service with the Fifth Air Force. In the escort role, the F-82 was intended as an interim aircraft, for during the period in question the USAF had advanced escort fighter concepts in mind. In 1946, Strategic Air Command had issued a requirement for a so-called 'penetration fighter', intended primarily to escort the Convair B-36 super-heavy bomber, or rather to sweep ahead of the bomber force and tear gaps in the enemy's fighter defences. The Lockheed Aircraft Corporation, whose F-80 Shooting Star was then in full production, put forward a design to meet this requirement. Bearing the Company designation Model 153, and the USAF designation XF-90, it was a very graceful and highly streamlined aircraft featuring a wing swept at 35 degrees. Power was supplied by two afterburning Westinghouse J34-WE-11 turbojets. A substantial fuel load, carried internally and in jettisonable wing-tip tanks, gave the fighter a combat radius of about 1100 miles (1770km) at high altitude, sufficient to penetrate as far as Kiev from bases in West Germany. The XF-90 carried a very heavy armament of four 20mm (0.78in) cannon and six 0.5in (12.7mm) machine guns. Two prototypes were built, the first flying on 4 June 1949, but flight trials revealed that the aircraft was seriously underpowered, with a maximum speed of only 0.9M at sea level and 0.95M at 40,000ft (12,200m). This fact, together with a change in the USAF requirement, led to the project being abandoned in 1950. Another contender was the McDonnell XF-88, prototype construction of which began in 1947 under a USAF contract. The first prototype XF-88 was powered by two Westinghouse XJ34-WE-13 engines, mounted side-by-side and exhausting just aft of the wing trailing edge under a stepped-up rear fuselage. This aircraft flew on 20 October 1948, and in 1950 it was followed by a second prototype fitted with XJ34WE-22 engines equipped with short afterburners that could boost the thrust to 4000lb (1814kg) for combat manoeuvres. The XF-88 had a very thin wing swept at 35 degrees and spanning 38ft 8in (11.8m); length was just over 54ft (16.5m). The first prototype XF-88 reached a maximum speed of 641mph (1032km/h) at sea level and could climb to 35,000ft (10,668m) in four and a half minutes. Combat radius, however, was 850 miles (1368km), much less than the XF-90's, and operational ceiling was only 36,000ft (10,973m). The XF-88 development programme was cancelled in August 1950, when the USAF shelved its long-range heavy fighter plans, but the first prototype – as the XF-88B – went on to have a useful life as a test bed for supersonic propellers. Further experiments were made with other escort fighter concepts, some involving 'parasite' fighters recessed into the bomb-bay of a B-36 mother aircraft, but these proved unworkable. But, the USAF – mindful of the fearful losses suffered by its unescorted bombers over Europe in World War II – persisted with the idea of the escort fighter, and chose another first-generation jet fighter, the Republic F-84 Thunderjet, for this role.

Lockheed F-80C Shooting Star

Country of origin: USA
Powerplant: one 5400lbst (2449kg)
Allison J33-A-35 turbojet
Performance: maximum speed
594mph (966km/h)

Weights: empty 8420lb (3819kg)
maximum take-off 16,856lb
(7646kg)
Dimensions: wing span 38ft 9in
(11.81m); length 34ft 5in (10.49m);

height 11ft 3in (3.43m)
Armament: six 0.50in (12.7mm)
machine guns; two 1000lb (454kg)
bombs and eight rockets

Republic F-84G Thunderjet

Type: single-seat fighter-bomber
Country of origin: USA
Powerplant: one 5600lbst (2542kg)
Wright J65-A-29 turbojet
Performance: maximum speed

605mph (973km/h)
Weights: empty 11,460lb (5203kg);
maximum take-off 28,000lb
(12,701kg)
Dimensions: wing span 36ft 4in

(11.05m); length 38ft 5in (11.71m);
height 12ft 10in (3.90m)
Armament: six 0.5in (12.7mm)Colt-
Browning M-3 MGs; up to 4000lb
(1814kg) of external ordnance

THUNDERBOLT SUCCESSOR

The Republic F-84 Thunderjet, which was to provide many of NATO's air forces with their initial jet experience, began life in the summer of 1944, when Republic Aviation's design team investigated the possibility of adapting the airframe of the P-47 Thunderbolt to take an axial-flow turbojet. This proved impractical, and in November 1944 the design of an entirely new airframe was begun around the Generl Electric J35 engine. The first of three XP-84 prototypes was completed in December 1945 and made its first flight on 28 February 1946. Three prototypes were followed by 15 YP-84As for the USAF. Delivered in the spring of 1947, they were later converted to F-84B standard. The F-84B was the first production model, featuring an ejection seat, six 0.5in M3 machine guns and underwing rocket racks. Deliveries of the F-84B began in the summer of 1947 to the 14th Fighter Group, and 226 were built. The F-84C, of which 191 were built, was externally similar to the F-84B, but incorporated an improved electrical system and an improved bomb release mechanism. The next model to appear, in November 1948, was the F-84D, which had a strengthened wing and a modified fuel system. Production totalled 151 aircraft. It was followed, in May 1949, by the F-84E, which in addition to its six 0.5in (12.7mm) machine guns could carry two 1000lb (453.6kg) bombs, two 11.75in (298mm) rockets or 32 5in (127mm) rockets. With effect from 1 February 1950, the 27th Fighter Group at Bergstrom AFB was re-designated the 27th Fighter Escort

Wing, and shortly afterwards began to convert to the Republic F-84E Thunderjet. On 16 July, Strategic Air Command also assumed control of the 31st Fighter Escort Wing (307th, 308th and 309th FS) which was based at Turner AFB, Georgia, and was equipped with F-84B/C Thunderjets. The third Thunderjet unit to join the SAC order of battle was the 12th FEW, which was activated at Turner AFB on 1 November 1950 and which took its F-84Es to Bergstrom AFB on 5 December. In September and October 1950, the 27th FEW carried out a large-scale reinforcement operation called Fox Able Three, in which it ferried 180 Thunderjets from the United States to Germany. This operation eclipsed a much smaller but extremely significant transatlantic flight made on 22 September 1950. Two specially modified Thunderjets of the 31st FEW, fitted with flight refuelling equipment and designated EF-84Es, staged to RAF Manston in Kent and then took off on a non-stop transatlantic attempt, refuelling three times from KB-29 tankers. The leader, Colonel David Schilling, landed at Limestone, Maine, after a flight of ten hours and ten minutes, but the other pilot, Lt Col William Ritchie, had to abandon his aircraft over Newfoundland when he suffered an engine failure; he was picked up safely by helicopter. Later, the 31st FEW was to pioneer mass non-stop flights over both the Atlantic and Pacific, using flight refuelling. At the end of 1950 all three SAC fighter wings were equipped with the F-84E Thunderjet, 167 aircraft being on the inventory, but during 1952

this model began to give way to the F-84G, the first Thunderjet variant to be equipped for flight refuelling from the outset. It was also the first USAF fighter to have a tactical nuclear capability; atomic weapons development had advanced considerably in the USA since 1950 and the device carried by the F-84G (the Mk 7 nuclear store), although still bulky, weighed less than 2000lb (907kg). On 1 July 1952 a fourth fighter escort wing, the 508th FEW (466th, 467th and 468th FES) was activated at Turner AFB, and by the end of the year SAC had some 230 Thunderjets on charge.

RED ROCKETS

The Soviet Union's road to the production of first-generation jet fighters was much more laborious than that followed by the western nations. That this was so is surprising, because Russian engineers had been experimenting with various forms of reaction engine since the early 1930s, and had tested their first jet engine (the VRD-1, designed by A.M. Lyulka) in 1941. The Russians had also amassed much experience in the development of rocket motors, and work in this field was accelerated soon after the German invasion. In July 1941 two designers, Berezniak and Isayev, submitted details of a proposed rocket interceptor, the BI-1, to the State Defence Committee. The latter approved the design and ordered the construction of five prototypes, the first of which was completed exactly 40 days later. The BI-1 was a single-seat cantilever mid-wing monoplane of mixed construction,

featuring a retractable wheel or ski undercarriage and an armament of two 20mm (0.78in) cannon. It made its first unpowered flight on 10 September 1941, gliding to earth after being towed to altitude behind a Pe-2 bomber, and on 15 May 1942 it flew under the power of its own rocket motor. Several more prototypes were built and delivered to an experimental unit, but during trials the aircraft did not exceed 370mph (595km/h), and after a number of serious snags – including a fatal crash following structural failure – the project was abandoned. The designs of two other experimental rocket fighters, the Polikarpov Malyutka (Baby) and the Tikhonravov 302, also made their appearance at the same time as the BI-1, although neither showed as much promise as the latter aircraft and they were not completed. Apart from these types, only two other experimental Soviet aircraft incorporated reaction engines during the war, and both were mixed-power aircraft, using a combination of conventional piston engines and small turbojets. The first was the Mikoyan-designed I-205(N), which was powered by a VK-107R piston engine coupled with a turbojet which was mounted in the rear fuselage and which reached a speed of 514mph (827km/h) at 26,000ft (7925m) in May 1945. The second aircraft was

the similarly powered, but slightly slower, Sukhoi I-107 (Su-5).

RUSSIA'S FIRST JETS
Of all the aviation booty uncovered by the Russians during their advance into Germany, the most important haul was a large quantity of BMW 003A and Junkers Jumo 004A turbojets, which were distributed among the various aircraft designers for experimental use while the engine manufacturers geared up to produce them in series. One of the designers involved was Aleksandr S. Yakovlev, who set about adapting a standard Yak3 airframe to accommodate a Jumo 004B. The resulting aircraft, designated Yak-15, flew for the first time on 24 April 1946. Deliveries to Soviet Air Force fighter squadrons began early in 1947, production aircraft retaining a tailwheel undercarriage and being powered by the RD-10 engine, as the Jumo 004B copy was known. At the time of its intruduction the Yak-15 was the lightest jet fighter in the world, the lightweight structure of the Yak-3's airframe compensating for the relatively low power of the RD-10 engine. Although the Yak-3 was an interim aircraft, bridging the gap until the advent of more modern jet fighters, it was important in that it provided the Soviet Air Force with the jet experience it badly needed. Although lacking the sophistication of

■ABOVE: A MiG-15 pictured in the markings of the Czech Air Force. The MiG-15 formed the principal jet equipment of all the Soviet 'satellite' air forces in the 1950s.

contemporary western types, it was very manoeuvrable. In 1948 it began to be replaced by the Yak-15, an updated variant with a tricycle undercarriage and redesigned tail surfaces. A two-seat version, the Yak-17UTI, became the Soviet Union's first two-seat jet conversion trainer. Meanwhile, in February 1945, Artem Mikoyan had also begun work on a jet aircraft, the I-300, built around two BMW 003A engines. The prototype I-300 flew on the same day as the prototype Yak-15, and the production version, designated MiG-9, entered service in small numbers in mid-1947. Three other Soviet jet fighter designs, the Sukhoi Su-9, the Lavochkin La-150 and La-152, were test-flown, but failed to meet the necessary requirements and did not enter service. The twin-engined Su-9, in fact, was a much better aircraft than the MiG-9, which had an appalling safety record; but Mikoyan and various other designers, anxious to have their own aircraft accepted, persuaded Stalin that any fighter that resembled the Messerschmitt 262 would be unacceptable because the German fighter had proved dangerous to fly. Stalin was by no means an aviation expert, but he had seen photographs of the Me 262, and possibly a captured example as well, and to his mind the Su-9 was sufficiently like it to be seen in an unfavourable light. So after one brief public appearance at the Tushino air display on 3 August, 1947, development of the Su-9 was abandoned. So was a further development, the Su-11, which flew late in 1947. The aircraft was intended for a close-support role.

BRITISH ENGINES

In the spring of 1947, in a deal seen by many as a misplaced gesture of socialist solidarity, the British Labour Government authorised the delivery of 30 Rolls-Royce Derwent and 25 Nene jet engines to the Soviet Union. The Russians lost no time in applying this technology to their latest fighter designs. By now, Russian designers were overcoming an early aversion to the use of sweepback (an aversion shared by their British and French counterparts), and Lavochkin decided to fit the basic La-152 fuselage with swept flying surfaces. The result was the La-160, which had a wing swept at the optimum 35 degrees and an armament of two NS37 cannon. The aircraft flew for the first time in 1947 and was claimed to be the first post-war swept-wing jet fighter, but in fact it was used purely for aerodynamic research and never went into production. During flight trials, it

reached a speed of 652mph (1050km/h) at 18,700ft (5700m) and yielded a great deal of information that was subsequently applied to the design of more advanced swept-wing jets. The last of Lavochkin's straight-wing designs was the La-174TK, the TK denoting Tonkoye Krylo, or thin wing. Unlike previous Lavochkin jets, which had been powered by copies of German turbojets, the La-174TK used an RD-500 (Rolls-Royce Derwent). It flew early in 1948, but it was an anachronism and contributed nothing to Soviet aeronautical knowledge except to underline the fact that the straight, thin wing offered no advantages over the swept platform. Before the La-174TK even flew, Lavochkin was already studying two much more advanced jet fighter designs. The first of these was the La-168, which was originally intended to be powered by an RD-10 turbojet, but when Lavochkin learned that a rival MiG design was to be powered by a much more effective copy of the Rolls-Royce Nene he realised that the La-168's chances of success were likely to be slim. He therefore set about building a second prototype, similar in configuration to the La-168 but powered by the production version of the RD500 Derwent. Somewhat confusingly, this aircraft was given the designation La-174.

SECOND GENERATION

The rival MiG design, mentioned above, was destined to become one of the most

famous jet fighters of all time. It was the MiG-15. Designed by a Russo-German team headed by Artem I. Mikoyan and Mikhail I. Guryevitch, it flew for the first time on 30 December 1947 and entered series production in the following year. The first MiG-15s were powered by the Rolls-Royce Nene copy, designated RD-45. The prototype crashed during testing, killing its pilot, and the second aircraft was extensively modified, with a strengthened wing featuring slight anhedral and boundary layer fences. Many first-line fighter units of the Soviet Air Force had equipped with the type by the end of 1948, and a number of improvements were made to the basic design. Airframe design progress, in fact, proceeded in parallel with engine development, and from November 1948 the MiG-15's fuselage was modified to accommodate an uprated version of the Nene, designated VK-1 (the engineer responsible being Vladimir Klimov). This engine had re-designed turbine blades, larger combustion chambers and developed 5953lb (2700kg) thrust – 6750lb (3062kg) with water injection. The uprated aircraft was designated MiG-15B, and was serving in large numbers with the Soviet Air Force by the end of 1950. Production of the MiG-15 would eventually total some 18,000 aircraft, this figure including a tandem two-seat trainer version, the MiG-15UTI. Meanwhile, Lavochkin's La-168 had

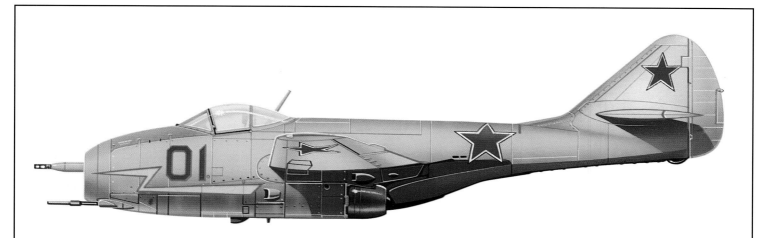

MiG-9

Type: single-seat fighter
Country of origin: USSR
Powerplant: two 1764lbst (7.8kN) RD-20 turbojets
Performance: maximum level speed 565mph (910km/h)

Weights: empty 7804lb (3540kg); maximum take-off 12,125lb (5500kg)
Dimensions: wing span 32ft 10in (10.0m); length 31ft 11in (9.75m); height 10ft 7in (3.22m)

Armament: one 37mm (1.45in) Nudelmann cannon in nose bulkhead dividing the intakes; two 23mm (0.9in) cannon beneath the intakes

been completed with an NII-1 engine, which was the pre-production version of the RD-500. There had been some delay in completion of the aircraft, and by the time the La-168 flew in the summer of 1948 the MiG-15 had already been under test for six months and, despite the loss of the prototype, was working its way through its State Acceptance Trials with remarkably few problems. The prototype of Lavochkin's La-174 flew shortly after the La-168 and, as the La-15, the aircraft went on to enter Soviet Air Force service in 1949. However, its performance proved inadequate for the interceptor role and only a few ground attack units were equipped with it, the MiG-15 becoming the standard Soviet interceptor of the late 1940s. Nevertheless, the La-15 remained in service until 1954, mainly as a combat trainer, and a developed version, the La-176, was evolved from it to meet a specification for a transonic fighter. The La-176 flew in December 1948, powered by an RD-45F turbojet, and on 26 December it became the first Soviet aircraft to exceed Mach One in a dive. The aircraft was re-engined with the Klimov VK1 and flight testing continued. However, it was another Mikoyan design, the MiG-17, that eventually met the Soviet Air Force

requirement for a second-generation swept-wing jet fighter.

THE MAGNIFICENT SABRE
In 1944, before German advanced aeronautical research data became available, the USAAF issued specifications drawn up around four different fighter requirements, the first of which involved a medium-range day fighter that could also serve in the ground attack and bomber escort roles. The first of these requirements awakened the interest of North American Aviation, whose design team was then working on the NA-134, a projected carrier-borne jet fighter for the US Navy. This, like the XP-59A and XP-80, was of conventional straight-wing design and was well advanced, so North American offered a land-based version to the USAAF under the company designation NA-140. On 18 May 1945, North American received a contract for the building of three NA-140 prototypes under the USAAF designation XP-86. At the same time, 100 NA-141s (production developments of the NA-134 naval jet fighter) were ordered for the US Navy as FJ-1s, although this order was subsequently reduced to 30 aircraft. Known as the Fury, the FJ-1 flew for the first time on 27 November 1946 and went

on to serve with Navy Fighter Squadron VF-51 and remained in service until 1949. While construction of the XFJ-1 prototypes got under way, design development of the XP-86 and FJ-1 proceeded in parallel. A mock-up of the XP-86 was built and, in June 1945, was approved by the USAAF. There was, however, one worrying factor. According to North American's estimates, the XP-86 would have a maximum speed of 574mph (924km/h) at sea level, which fell short of the USAAF specification. Fortunately, it was at this point that material on German research into high speed flight, in particular swept-wing designs, became available. North American obtained a complete Me 262 wing assembly and, after carrying out more than 1000 wind tunnel tests on it, decided that the swept wing was the answer to the XP-86's performance problems. The redesigned XP-86 airframe, featuring sweepback on all flying surfaces, was accepted by the USAAF on 1 November 1945 and received final approval on 28 February 1946. In

■BELOW: The North American F-86 Sabre challenged Russia's MiG15 for mastery of the sky in northwest Korea, an area that became known as 'MiG Alley'.

North American F-86F Sabre

Type: single-seat fighter
Country of origin: USA
Powerplant: one 5970lbst (2710kg) General Electric J47-GE-27 turbojet
Performance: maximum speed

678mph (1091km/h)
Weights: empty 11,125lbst (5045kg); maximum take-off 20,611lb (9350kg)
Dimensions: wing span 37ft 1in (11.30m); length 37ft 6in (11.43m);

height 14ft 9in (4.48m)
Armament: six 0.5in (12.7mm) Colt-Browning M-3 machine guns; 1000lb (454kg) of external stores, plus eight rockets

December 1946 the USAAF placed a contract for an initial batch of 33 P-86A production aircraft, and on 8 August 1947 the first of two flying prototypes was completed, making its first flight under the power of a General Electric J35 turbojet. The second prototype, designated XF-86A, made its first flight on 18 May 1948, fitted with the more powerful General Electric J-47-GE-1 engine, and deliveries of production F-86As began 10 days later. These were used for various trials, which were accelerated when east-west tension rose as a result of the Russian blockade of Berlin, and the first operational F-86As were delivered to the 1st Fighter Group early in 1949. As yet, the F-86A was an aircraft without a name, and one of the 1st Fighter Group's acts was to sponsor a competition to find a suitable one. Seventy-eight names were submitted, and one stood out above the rest. On 4 March 1949, the North American F-86 was officially named the Sabre.

COMBAT OVER KOREA

On 25 June 1950, Soviet-backed North Korea invaded the American-backed South, precipitating a war that was to last for three years, cost millions of lives, and witness the first ever jet-versus-jet battles, high in the stratosphere. The chief adversaries were the F-86 Sabre

and the MiG-15, but many other aircraft types were also involved. On 26 June, for example, five F-82 Twin Mustangs of the 68th and 339th Fighter Interceptor Squadrons, covering the evacuation of civilians from the South Korean capital, Seoul, intercepted seven Yak-9s that were strafing Kimpo airfield. In a five-minute air battle three Yaks were shot down, the first by Lt William G. Hudson of the 58th Squadron, to whom fell the distinction of destroying the first communist aircraft over Korea. The other American pilots who scored were Major James W. Little and Lt Charles B. Moran. An hour later the North Koreans launched a second attack, this time with eight Il-10 fighter-bombers. The intruders were sighted over Seoul by the pilots of four F-80s of the 35th Fighter Bomber Squadron, who dived down to intercept. Two Il-10s were destroyed by Lt Robert E. Wayne, while Captain Raymond E. Schilleref and Lt Robert H. Dewald shot down one each. The surviving Ilyushins ran for the 38th Parallel and the Americans, with no orders to pursue, broke off the combat and resumed their patrol. There were no more attempts to interfere with the evacuation during the remainder of that day. In the weeks that followed, Mustangs of the USAF and RAAF, F-80 Shooting Stars and Twin Mustangs joined B-26 light bombers in attacks on

North Korean columns that were advancing relentlessly into the south, inflicting enormous casualties and blunting the attack to the point where it stalled, enabling the Allies to bring in reinforcements and ultimately to launched a series of counter-attacks that drove the North Koreans back towards the Chinese border. During these operations it was the US Fifth Air Force's F-80 Shooting Stars, operating from Japanese bases, which bore the main burden of the ground attack work, completing a good two-thirds of all combat sorties flown, and the pilots quickly built up a high level of experience, particularly in the use of the 5in (127mm) high-velocity aircraft rocket (HVAR) against enemy armour. Each Shooting Star could carry up to 16 of these projectiles, in addition to its primary armament of eight 0.50in (12.7mm) machine guns; in this configuration, and with a full fuel load on take-off, its combat radius was 225 miles (362km) and it had a loiter time over the target of about 15 minutes. The pilots were unanimous in their praise of the F-80 in the ground attack role. Its high speed gave it an important element of surprise and, because there was no propeller torque to cope with, it was a much better gun platform than any conventional propeller-driven machine.

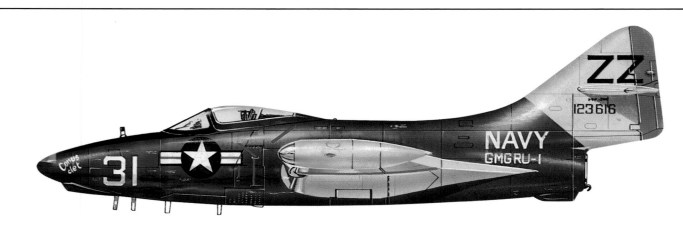

Grumman F9F Panther

Type: single-seat carrier-borne jet
fighter-bomber
Country of origin: USA
Powerplant: one 5000lbst (2270kg)
Pratt & Whitney J42-P-6 turbojet
Performance: maximum speed

526mph (846km/h)
Weights: empty 9000lb (4077kg);
maximum take-off 15,750lb
(7135kg)
Dimensions: wing span 38ft
(11.58m); length 37ft 3in (11.35m);

height 11ft 4in (3.45m)
Armament: four 20mm (0.78in)
cannon; up to 2000lb (907kg) of
external ordnance

The F-80C could also carry a pair of 1000lb bombs in place of its 165-gallon wing-tip fuel tanks, but this reduced its combat radius to about 100 miles (160km). Improvements were clearly necessary, and General Partridge assigned the task of working out a solution to the 49th Fighter Bomber Wing, whose engineers soon provided one by fitting the two centre sections of a Fletcher fuel tank into the middle of the standard Lockheed wing-tip tank carried by the F-80, creating one with a capacity of 265 gallons. By the end of July about a quarter of the Japan-based F-80 units had received the modified tanks, increasing the loiter time in the target area to 45 minutes or thereabouts.

THE US NAVY'S FIGHTERS
As American and British aircraft carriers deployed to battle stations off the Korean coast, activity by naval fighter-bombers increased. On the American side, ground attack missions were flown by piston-engined types such as the Vought F4U Corsair and Douglas AD Skyraider, joined in growing numbers by Grumman F9F Panther jets. The Panther traced its origins back to 1946, when the US Navy signed a contract with the Grumman Aircraft Corporation for the construction of a prototype night fighter, designated XF9F-1 and powered by four Westinghouse J30-WE-20 jet engines. The following October, however, the Bureau of Aeronautics decided to abandon

development of the XF9F-1 in favour of a single-engined day fighter which was to be designated XF9F-2 and powered by a Rolls-Royce Nene turbojet. Two XF9F2 prototypes were ordered, the first of which (Nene-engined) flew on 24 November 1947. The second aircraft, designated XF9F3, flew in August 1948 and was equipped with an Allison J33A-8 engine. The first production batch of F9F-2 Panthers (47 aircraft) featured the Pratt & Whitney J42-P-6 turbojet, the licence-built Nene. It entered service with VF-51 in May 1949, replacing the FJ-1 Fury, and went into action for the first time when aircraft of this unit, operating from the USS *Valley Forge*, flew top cover for strikes on enemy airfields and supply lines near Pyongyang. During this mission, two VF-51 pilots shot down two Yak-9s, the Navy's first kills in Korea. At a later date, the Panther was joined in action by a second jet fighter, the McDonnell F2H Banshee, which was developed from the earlier FH-1 Phantom. The first jet aircraft designed to operate from carriers, the FH-1 originated in 1943. Initially designated XFD-1, it flew for the first time on 25 January 1945, powered by two Westinghouse J30 turbojets. Following carrier trials, an order was placed for 100 production aircraft, but this was cut to 60. On 5 May 1948 Fighter Squadron 17-A, equipped with 16 FH-1s, became the first carrier-qualified jet squadron in the US Navy, operating from the USS *Saipan*.

The type remained in first-line service until July 1950, the last unit to use it being Marine Fighter Squadron VMF-122. The FH-1's successor, the Banshee, stemmed from a 1945 contract for a jet fighter-bomber. The prototype, designated XF2D-1, flew for the first time on 11 January 1947, powered by two Westinghouse J34 turbojets, and the first series production F2H-1s were delivered to Navy Fighter Squadron VF-171 in March 1949. The Banshee went into combat for the first time on 23 August 1941, when F2H-2s of VF-172 (USS *Essex*) struck at targets in northwest Korea.

THE FLEET AIR ARM
Britain's Fleet Air Arm, which had fought its way gallantly through the early years of World War II with a variety of obsolescent equipment, had ended that conflict with carrier aircraft which compared favourably with any the Americans had. The reason was simple: most of them were American, supplied under Lend-Lease. Unlike the US Navy, which had invited tenders for a carrier-borne jet fighter in 1944, the British Admiralty saw little future in jet aircraft operation. A few deck landing

■**RIGHT: The Royal Navy's Hawker Sea
Fury saw action in Korea, its pilots
destroying several MiG-15s. But Korea
proved that the day of the piston-
engined fighter was over.**

trials with a Vampire and Meteor in 1945 had convinced the admirals that jet types had too high a landing speed for safe carrier operation, so when the Fleet Air Arm's combat squadrons re-equipped in the 1940s, it was with piston-engined types, such as the latest versions of the Supermarine Seafire, Fairey Firefly and Hawker Sea Fury. It was the Seafire and Firefly, forming HMS *Triumph*'s air group, that first went into action over Korea.

The Seafire was the Mk 47, the ultimate in a design that stretched back to the prototype Spitfire of 1936 and corresponded to the last of the RAF's Spitfires, the Mk 24. The Firefly was a wartime design, conceived in 1940 as an advanced two-seat fleet fighter; the Firefly FR.1 first went into action in

July 1944, covering air strikes on the German battleship *Tirpitz*, and also served with the British Pacific Fleet in 1945. The version used in Korea was the Mk IV, which operated with considerable success in the ground attack role. *Triumph* was the only carrier to use the combination of Seafire and Firefly; the air groups of other carriers operating in rotation off Korea had the Firefly and the Sea Fury Mk X. The Sea Fury prototype flew on 21 February 1945, and the aircraft arrived too late to take part in the Pacific war, but it proved to be a formidable strike aircraft and served throughout the Korean conflict. An RAF version, the Fury, was cancelled at the end of the war, but a number were sold to Iraq. Both aircraft had

their origin in an Air Ministry requirement of 1942, which called for a new long-range fighter for use against the Japanese.

THE RUSSIAN CONNECTION

The success of the Allied offensives in Korea in the latter half of 1950 led to the direct intervention of Chinese forces on a massive scale, and it was at this point that Soviet fighter pilots entered the battle, flying from bases in China. The Russians were not newcomers to China; long before the Korean War broke out, the Soviet 29th Guards Fighter Regiment, and later the entire 106th Fighter Division, both armed with the MiG-15, were operating in support of the Chinese Communists in their civil war against the Nationalists. The Russians

had few opportunities to engage Nationalist aircraft, but on 28 April 1950 a Major Kelenikov shot down a Nationalist P-38 Lightning, and on 11 May Captain Sinkarenko destroyed a B-24 at night. From the summer of 1950 the 351st Night Fighter Regiment, armed with Lavochkin La-11s, was operating in the Shanghai area; this unit moved to Manchuria in June 1951 and began operating against Allied night bombers. Meanwhile, in 1950, there had been a steady build-up of Soviet fighter units in Manchuria; those involved at this stage were the 151st Guards Fighter Division (28th and 72nd Guards Fighter Regiments) and the 28th Fighter Division (67th and 139th Guards Fighter Regiments). The first operational sorties by both air divisions were flown on 1 November 1950, when MiG-15s crossed the Yalu river and claimed to have destroyed an F-51 Mustang and F-80 Shooting Star, although the Americans admitted no such loss. At dawn on 8 November, 70 B-29s dropped 580 tons of incendiary bombs on Sinuiju, while F-51s and F-80s suppressed flak around the town. Top cover for the mission was provided by two flights of Shooting Stars of the 51st FIW, whose pilots knew what frustration felt like as, powerless to intervene, they watched MiG-15s taking off from Antung airfield just across the river. Six MiGs climbed to 30,000ft (9144m) and dived in pairs towards the F-80s, whose pilots turned to meet the attack head-on. Five of the MiGs, after a

few bursts of inaccurate fire, broke away and climbed back across the Yalu, but the sixth entered a shallow dive and one of the F-80 pilots, Lt Russell J. Brown, seized his opportunity. The F-80 was heavier than the MiG and Brown rapidly overhauled his target, putting a five-second burst into it as it pulled up into a climb. Burning fiercely, the MiG went down to crash on the banks of the river. It was the first jet-versus-jet combat in history. On 9 November, the Yalu bridges between Sinuiju and Hyesanjin, some 200 miles upstream, were attacked by aircraft of Task Force 77, operating from the carriers *Valley Forge*, *Philippine Sea* and *Leyte*. The strikes, by Skyraiders carrying 1000lb bombs and Corsairs armed with either bombs or rockets, were covered by F9F Panthers. The MiGs came up to challenge the US Navy aircraft, and in the ensuing engagement one of the enemy jets was shot down by Lt Cdr W.T. Amen, officer commanding VF-111 aboard the USS *Philippine Sea*, who became the first US Navy pilot to score a jet kill.

THE SABRES ARRIVE

At the end of November 1950 the 64th Fighter Corps was created by amalgamating the 151st Guards Fighter Division and the 28th and 50th Fighter Divisions, but in December the 28th Fighter Division was transfered to central China, where it started training pilots on the MiG-15. Soon afterwards the 151st Guards Fighter Division was assigned a similar task, so that at the

end of the year the only MiG-15 unit taking an active part in the air war over Korea was the 50th Fighter Division, comprising the 29th Guards Fighter Regiment and the 177th Fighter Regiment. The 50th Division was the first unit in China to use the MiG-15B, which it took into action for the first time on 30 November. In the following month it deployed to Antung, where its aircraft were grounded for a time because of elevator defects. In the meantime, the aircraft that was to be the MiG-15's principal adversary, the F-86 Sabre, had arrived in Korea. The unit involved was the 4th Fighter Interceptor Wing, which established its main echelon in Japan and deployed detachments of Sabres forward to Kimpo, the only Korean airfield suitable for F-86 operation. At the same time, F-84 Thunderjets of the 27th Fighter Escort Wing, also newly arrived, deployed aircraft from Japan to Taegu, from where they began armed reconnaissance and close support missions. On 15 December 1950, the 4th FIW's F-86A Sabres carried out their first familiarisation flight from Kimpo and, on the 17th, the Wing mounted its first offensive sweep of the war when four Sabres of the 336th FIS, each carrying two 120-gallon drop tanks to increase its combat radius to 490 nautical miles (907km), headed north towards the Yalu. The American pilots, all of whom were highly experienced – some had already achieved the status of 'aces' by destroying five or more enemy aircraft in

Mikoyan-Gurevitch MiG-15

Type: single-seat jet fighter
Country of origin: USSR
Powerplant: one 5952lbst (2700kg) Klimov VK-1 turbojet
Performance: maximum speed

684mph (1100km/h)
Weights: empty 8820lb (4000kg); maximum take-off 12,566lb (5700kg)
Dimensions: wing span 33ft (10m);

length 36ft 4in (11.05m); height 11ft 2in (3.5m)
Armament: one 37mm (1.45in) N-37 and two 23mm (0.9in) NS-23 cannon

World War II – had given considerable thought to the tactics they would employ. They used the basic and well-tried 'finger four' battle formation which broke down into elements of two upon engaging in combat; the idea was to enter the patrol area at altitudes between 27,000 and 33,000ft (8230 and (10,058m), just below contrail level, so that the pilots could easily spot hostile aircraft above them by their vapour trails. On this first combat mission, however, the Sabre pilots made a mistake that might have cost them dearly had they encountered skilled adversaries. As the distance between Kimpo and the Yalu was 430 miles (690km) and the pilots wanted to extend their patrol time, they entered the combat area at a leisurely, fuel-conserving speed of 0.62M, so that when the Sabre flight – led by Lt Col Bruce H. Hinton – sighted a battle formation of four MiG-15s the F-86s were flying too slowly to achieve maximum effectiveness. Fortunately, the MiGs were below and climbing; their pilots doubtless believed that the American fighters were F-80s, otherwise they would almost certainly have climbed for altitude on the other side of the Yalu. They realised their mistake only when the Sabres came

diving down on them, rapidly gaining speed, whereupon the MiGs broke away and dived for the sanctuary of Manchuria. They were too late. Colonel Hinton's element clung to the tail of the number two MiG and Hinton fired three four-second bursts from his six 0.50in (12.7mm) machine guns. The enemy aircraft burst into flames and went into a slow spin. Its pilot, Major Yefromeyenko, ejected successfully. It was the first of 792 MiGs which were to be claimed by Sabre pilots during the two and a half years of air combat that followed, although this claim would be hotly disputed and later reduced.

COMBAT OVER THE YALU
There were several more encounters between MiGs and Sabres during the next few days, but these were inconclusive and no casualties were suffered by either side. By this time both sides were quickly catching on to the other's tactics and rapidly taking steps to counter them. The Sabre's main drawback was its lack of endurance; patrolling at speeds of 0.85M and higher, the Sabre pilots could afford to spend only 20 minutes in the vicinity of the

■ABOVE: A trio of F-86 Sabres over the mountains of Korea. The Sabres belong to the 51st Fighter Interceptor Wing, which was the second to arrive in Korea.

Yalu before being compelled to return home with a safe margin of fuel. The MiG pilots quickly realised this limitation and exploited it to the fullest advantage, climbing to altitude north of the Yalu and then diving across at high speed to make their attack as the Sabres were withdrawing towards the end of their patrol. The Americans in turn began to mount patrols of 16 aircraft, operating in four flights of four, which arrived in the combat area at various altitudes at intervals of five minutes. In this way the withdrawal of all but the last Sabre flight was adequately covered. On 22 December, eight Sabres led by Lt Col John C. Meyer – one of the USAF's leading fighter pilots, with 24 victories in World War II – were on an offensive patrol at 30,000 feet (10,000m) south of the Yalu when they were engaged by more than 15 MiG-15s. In an engagement lasting 20 minutes and ranging from high altitude to treetop

level, the Sabre pilots claimed six MiGs for the loss of one of their own number, Captain L.V. Bach, who was shot down by Captain Yurkevich of the 29th Guards Fighter Regiment. After this mauling the MiGs were absent from the sky for a week and, the next time they appeared, on 30 December, their pilots showed extreme caution in joining combat. On this occasion 36 MiGs crossed the Yalu and engaged 16 Sabres, but the enemy quickly broke off the action and headed for home. The Sabre pilots claimed two MiG-15s damaged. Both sides were now beginning to assess the relative performances of eath other's aircraft; Russian pilots considered the MiG's cannon armament to be much more effective than the Sabre's 0.50in (12.7mm) machine guns and, although they admitted that the F-86 was the better aircraft in a turning fight, it was nowhere near as good in the vertical as the MiG-15B.

NEW COMBATANTS

At the beginning of 1951 the 50th Guards Fighter Division was recalled to the USSR. Its place in the front line was taken by the 151st Guards Fighter Division, which took over the 50th's MiG-15Bs and relinquished their own earlier-model MiGs to the 3rd Fighter Division of the Chinese People's Air Force. The 151st rotated its regiments to the combat area, sending the 28th Fighter Regiment forward to Antung on 8 February 1951 and two squadrons of the 72nd Regiment in March. In April 1951 the 151st Division was moved to Anshan, where the rest of 64th Air Corps was located, and replaced in the Antung area by the 324th Fighter Division. This unit was very well trained and highly motivated, which was hardly surprising in view of the fact that it was commanded by Ivan Kozhedub, the top-scoring Soviet and Allied fighter pilot of World War II. The Division was armed with 62 MiG-15Bs, and soon began to

■ABOVE: The Supermarine Swift F.1, unsuccessful as a high-level interceptor because of engine flameout problems, performed well for the RAF in its FR.5 fighter-reconnaissance version.

make its presence felt against the US B-29 bombers that were attacking bridges and other strategic targets. On 6 April 1951, before the 324th Division went into combat, B-29s of the 98th and 307th Groups were detailed to attack the railway bridges at Sinuiju and a road bridge at Uiju. The bombers were escorted by 48 F-84s of the 27th Wing, operating out of Itazuke, and these fought a hot engagement with 30 MiG-15s which attacked the B-29s as they were bombing their targets. The Thunderjet close escort proved so effective that only one MiG got through, but this destroyed a B-29 of the 307th Group. The F-84s claimed one MiG destroyed for no loss to themselves. It was a different story on 12 April, when

B-29s of the 19th, 98th and 307th Groups were once again ordered to attack the bridges at Sinuiju, which still refused to collapse despite the battering they had received. Close escort was again provided by the 27th Wing, which put up 39 aircraft, while the Sabres of the 4th Wing flew top cover. With the target still several minutes' flying time away, the bomber formation was attacked by about 40 MiGs of the 324th Division, whose pilots employed new tactics, diving at high speed through the escorting fighters to make their firing passes at the 19th Group's eight bombers. One B-29 was shot down and five more damaged. The attack was scarcely over when 20 more MiGs attacked the 307th Group's twelve aircraft, destroying one of them and badly damaging another. It later crashed and was destroyed while trying to make an emergency landing at Suwon. A small number of MiGs also attacked the 98th Group, which came through unscathed. On the credit side, the Sabres claimed four MiGs destroyed and six damaged, while the Thunderjet pilots claimed three probably destroyed. The B-29 gunners also claimed 10 MiGs destroyed, but in the confusion this was wildly exaggerated; Russian sources admit no losses to the B-29 gunners at all. At the end of April the 324th Division was replaced for a short time by the 151st Division, but this was only a temporary move pending the arrival of the 18th Guards Fighter Regiment of the 303rd Fighter Division, which began operations

from Antung. At the end of May the division's other two fighter regiments, the 17th and 523rd, also arrived. The 303rd Division was commanded by General Georgii Lobov, a World War II ace with 24 victories. The 303rd Division was subsequently moved to a new air base at Miao Kun, making way for the return of the 324th Division to Antung.

MIG ALLEY

Together, these two divisions made a formidable partnership, and it was during their tour of duty that the Americans nicknamed this corner of northwest Korea 'MiG Alley'. The air opposition became so effective that Allied fighter-bombers dared venture into enemy air space only under strong fighter escort. On 9 May, for example, a major attack was carried out against the airfield at Sinuiju, the best-defended target in North Korea. The enemy had 38 aircraft deployed there, all piston-engined types, but concrete revetments had been built around the airfield perimeter and there were indications that these would soon house jet fighters. In the early afternoon of 9 May a maximum-effort operation was launched, with Shooting Stars of the 8th, 49th and 51st Wings, Mustangs of the 18th Wing and Corsairs of the 1st Marine Air Wing – a total of 312 aircraft – pounding Sinuiju for 45 minutes while 4th Wing Sabres, 27th Wing Thunderjets and Panthers of the Marine Air Wing flew top cover. The Shooting Stars went in first to suppress the flak, and the

subsequent attacks destroyed a fuel dump, 26 ammunition and supply dumps, 106 buildings and all the enemy aircraft on the ground. Eighteen MiGs were sighted crossing the Yalu, but most of these avoided combat and the Allied fighter pilots claimed only two damaged. All the Allied aircraft returned safely to base. The air battles of May 1951 saw the emergence of the first Sabre ace, although not, as has often been erroneously stated, of the first jet ace in history; 22 German Me 262 pilots had already claimed that distinction in World War II. He was Captain James Jabara, a pilot with the 334th FIS. On 7 May, when his squadron was rotated back to Japan, Jabara stayed on at Suwon to fly and fight with its replacement, the 335th FIS. At that time his score stood at four MiGs destroyed. On 20 May, a large number of MiGs crossed the Yalu to engage 12 4th Wing Sabres. Two more flights of Sabres, one of which included Jabara, were quickly summoned to the scene of the action. Jabara got on the tail of one of the enemy fighters and saw his bullets registering strikes on the MiG's wings and fuselage. He followed it down to 10,000ft (3000m) and saw the pilot eject, then climbed back to 25,000ft (7620m) and within a couple of minutes was fighting with a second MiG, which he set on fire. He had time to watch it spin down in flames before being forced to break hard as a third MiG got on his own tail. He went into a long dive,

Lockheed F-94A Starfire

Type: two-seat all-weather interceptor
Country of origin: USA
Powerplant: one 6000lbst (2724kg) Allison J33 turbojet
Performance: maximum speed

580mph (933km/h)
Weights: empty 11,090lb (5030kg); maximum take-off 15,710lb (7125kg)
Dimensions: wing span (excluding tip tanks) 38ft 10in (11.85m);

length 40ft 1in (12.2m); height 12ft 8in (3.89m)
Armament: four 0.5in (12.7mm) machine guns

losing the enemy fighters, and returned to base. His two victories were made all the more noteworthy by the fact that one of his wing tanks had refused to jettison, a circumstance that would have compelled most pilots to abandon the mission immediately. Other Sabre pilots claimed one MiG destroyed, with one probable and five damaged. Jabara himself scored no further victories before the end of his current tour, but he returned to Korea later in the war and increased his score to 15.

NEW TACTICS
It was a measure of the MiG pilots' confidently aggressive attitude that on occasions, their aircraft fitted with wing tanks, they now penetrated almost as far south as the 38th Parallel, either singly or in pairs. They also appeared, at last, to be exploiting the advantages of their aircraft, especially the MiG's ability to out-climb the Sabre and out-manoeuvre the American aircraft at high altitude. During this period, UN pilots noted that the enemy was experimenting with new tactics, including one which Sabre pilots nicknamed the 'yo-yo'. A large formation of MiGs would orbit the battle area at maximum ceiling, with small sections breaking off to make high-speed passes at the UN aircraft before zooming up to

altitude again. The MiG-15 was a high-level interceptor and displayed most of its aerodynamic qualities at altitudes of 20,000ft (6096m) or more. Below that, it had dangerous tendencies; on several occasions, UN pilots were mystified to see undamaged MiGs go into a spin during a combat manoeuvre and fail to come out of it, their pilots ejecting. Later, when a MiG-15 fell into Allied hands, thanks to the defection of a North Korean pilot, they had their answer. The cockpit of a MiG-15 featured a white line painted down the middle of the instrument panel and, if the aircraft got into a spin, pilots were directed to shove the control column hard up against it. If the aircraft failed to recover after three rotations, the standard procedure was to eject. The MiG also had a number of other unpleasant shortcomings, including a tendency to oscillate – which made it a poor gun platform – and to pitch up without warning. There was no stall warning device, the cockpit pressurisation worked intermittently, and the emergency fuel pump was prone to explode when turned on, tearing off the rear fuselage. Despite these defects, it was an excellent aircraft, far more robust and easier to service than the F-86, and it came perilously close to gaining air superiority over northwest Korea in the summer of 1951.

■ABOVE: A veteran of the Pacific campaigns of WWII, the Vought F4U Corsair was widely used in Korea. Lt Neil Armstrong, the first man to walk on the Moon, flew one.

SURPRISE ATTACKS
A careful assessment of the Chinese People's Air Force's order of battle, coupled with the knowledge that experienced Soviet aircrew were serving in Manchuria in considerable numbers, pointed to the possibility that the Communists might be planning a series of surprise attacks on Allied air bases in Korea, and possibly in Japan, as a prelude to a new bid for air superiority. On 10 June 1951, General Otto P. Weyland assumed command of the Far East Air Forces, and within a matter of hours, realising the potential seriousness of the situation, he signalled the Pentagon with an urgent request for four jet fighter wings to be sent out to the Far East, one pair to bolster Japan's defences and the other two for deployment to Korea. At the time of the request there were only 89 Sabres in the Far East, including 44 in Korea; Weyland wanted not only more of the Sabres, but new F-86E models to replace the F-86As with which the 4th FIW was then equipped. In fact, the USAF

undertook to replace the FEAF's F-86As with F-86Es on a one-for-one exchange basis, but this process was to take many months. The USAF's objection was that it would be impossible to provide Weyland with a complete wing of F-86Es without depleting Air Defense Command, which was under strength and struggling to meet its commitments. The complacency of the immediate post-war years was having its effect, and it would be some time before the United States' technical prowess could match the Soviet Union's mass production of air superiority fighters. In the meantime, the best that could be done was to increase the number of F-84 Thunderjets in the Korean theatre, something which Weyland's predecessor, General Stratemeyer, had strongly advocated before relinquishing command of the FEAF, and on 1 June 1951 the 27th Fighter Escort Wing began the process of converting pilots of the 49th and 136th Wings, which had been operating F-80s, to the F-84E. As the F-80 pilots qualified on the new type, the 27th Wing's Thunderjets were turned over to the 136th Wing, squadron by

squadron, until by the end of August the 27th Wing's personnel were relieved of duty in the Far East. In addition, the USAF authorised the deployment of one F-84 wing – the 116th – to Japan; the 75 Thunderjets arrived on 24 July and the Wing settled in at Chitose and Misawa Air Bases.

METEORS IN ACTION

One other jet fighter type entered combat in Korea during the summer of 1951. This was the British Gloster Meteor F.Mk.8, which at that time formed RAF Fighter Command's first line of defence in the United Kingdom and which replaced the F-51 Mustangs of No 77 Squadron Royal Australian Air Force in Korea. The Meteor had been tested in mock combat against a Sabre during a two-day series of trials, and among the conclusions drawn was that the Sabre outclassed the Meteor in a steep dive or a long straight and level run, whereas the Meteor was superior in turning, zooming and in a sustained climb. This seemed to indicate that the Meteor would at least be able to hold its own against the MiG

under most combat conditions. After some preliminary sorties from Kimpo, the first real test came on 20 August 1951, when eight Meteors were detailed to escort B-29s and another eight to carry out a diversionary sweep north of Sinanju. At 1120 hours the latter flight, led by Squadron Leader Wilson, spotted six MiGs at 40,000ft (12,200m) over Chongju, 5000ft (1525m) higher than themselves. Keeping the enemy in sight, Wilson manoeuvred his formation up-sun, but as he did so two more MiGs appeared a few thousand feet below. Wilson decided to attack and went into a dive followed by his number two, Flying Officer Woodroffe. As the two Meteors levelled out, however, Woodroffe's aircraft suddenly flicked into a spin (an unpleasant tendency of the Meteor 8, caused by the effects of compressibility, if the aircraft exceeded 0.8M at altitude) and dropped away; the

■ **BELOW: Two VF-721 Panthers from USS *Boxer* move to join in an attack on Wonsan in North Korea on 15 July 1951. Smoke can be seen rising from enemy installations in the city.**

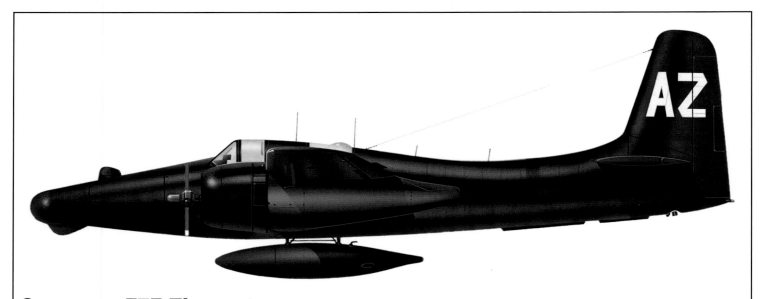

Grumman F7F Tigercat

Type: two-seat night fighter
Country of origin: USA
Powerplant: two 2100hp (1566kW)
Pratt & Whitney R-2800-34W
Double Wasp 18-cylinder radials

Performance: maximum speed
435mph (700km/h)
Weights: empty 16,190lb (7043kg);
maximum take-off 23,881lb
(10,818kg)

Dimensions: wing span 51ft 6in
(15.69m); length 46ft 10in
(14.27m); height 16ft 7in (5.05m)
Armament: four 20mm (0.78in)
cannon

pilot managed to recover several thousand feet lower down, but now Wilson had no one to cover his tail. As he began his approach to attack, a MiG jumped him out of the sun, unnoticed in the 30-degree blind spot caused by the dural structure at the rear of the Meteor's cockpit. The first warning Wilson had of the danger was when cannon shells passed over his wing; he immediately put his aircraft into a maximum-rate turn to shake off his pursuer. He was rescued by Flight Lieutenant Cedric Wilson and Flying Officer Ken Blight, who spotted his predicament and drove the MiG away – but not before cannon shells had shot away Squadron Leader Wilson's port aileron, and punched a three-foot hole in his port wing, puncturing a fuel tank. Despite this, Wilson reached base safely, touching down at 30 knots above normal landing speed.

Meanwhile, a fierce air battle had developed over Chongju as the other Meteors were hotly engaged by 30 MiGs. The weight of the attack fell on 'Dog' section, led by Flt Lt Geoff Thornton; one Meteor was shot down and its pilot, Warrant Officer Don Guthrie, baled out to spend the rest of the war in a PoW camp. After several more bruising encounters with MiGs, the Meteors were assigned to a ground attack role, which they performed very well.

BLACK TUESDAY

On Tuesday, 23 October 1951, the experienced MiG pilots of the 324th and 303rd Air Divisions came close to annihilating the American strategic bombing effort over North Korea. At 0900 hours, eight B-29s of the 307th BW made rendezvous with 55 Thunderjets of the 49th and 136th Wings and set course to attack the airfield at Namsi. Ahead and above, 34 Sabres of the 4th FIW provided distant cover. Suddenly, at 0915 hours, over 100 MiGs swept across the river. Within minutes the Sabres, effectively boxed in, were fighting for their lives. While this battle – in which two MiGs were shot down – was in progress, 50 more MiGs approached the B-29 and Thunderjet formation and circled it at some distance, evidently intent on drawing off the F-84s. The latter, however, refused to take the bait, and after a while the MiGs launched their attack, coming in from all directions. Using their superior speed to good advantage they ripped through the F-84 escort to make several passes at the B-29s as the latter headed towards their target. Two B-29s went down a matter of seconds after they had released their bombs; a third, burning fiercely, staggered towards the coast where its crew baled out – all except the pilot, Captain Thomas L. Shields, who

sacrificed his own life in keeping the crippled bomber flying until the other crew members got clear. One Thunderjet also failed to return from this mission. Four MiGs were claimed as destroyed, three by B-29 gunners and one by an F-84 pilot. The surviving bombers, all but one with battle damage and most with dead and wounded on board, struggled back to emergency landings in Korea and Japan. It was Bomber Command's blackest day since the war began and, although the 307th Wing's subsequent mission report was full of praise for the efforts of the F-84 escort, it also observed that nothing short of 150 Sabres would have been adequate to protect the bombers. According to General Lobov, commanding the 303rd Fighter Division, this date 'meant nothing more or less than the complete collapse of the USAF strategic bombing effort'. It was not far short of the truth. In one week, the USAF had lost five B-29s, with eight others badly damaged and 55 aircrew killed or missing. From then on, the B-29 force was restricted to night bombing operations.

SABRE REINFORCEMENTS

Fortunately for the Allied air campaign, the 324th and 303rd Fighter Divisions were recalled to the Soviet Union in January and February 1952, leaving their aircraft for the 97th Fighter Division (16th Fighter Regiment and 148th Guards Fighter Regiment) and 190th Fighter Division (156th and 821st Fighter Regiments). The latter were inexeperienced, but no time was spent in combat training, or in passing on tactical expertise, and as a consequence there was a marked drop in efficiency to the point where 64th Air Corps lost the initiative which the 324th and 303rd Fighter Divisions had established and was forced on to the defensive. By this time, two Sabre wings were operational in Korea, the 51st Fighter Wing having begun to exchange its F-80s for F-86Es in the previous November. It was commanded by Colonel Francis S. Gabreski, a World War II P-47 ace with 28 victories. The Fifth Air Force now had 165 Sabres in the theatre, of which 127 were in Korea, the others being earmarked for air defence duty in Japan.

■BELOW: Another veteran of World War II, the North American F-51 Mustang served throughout the Korean War on ground attack and armed reconnaissance. Losses were high.

With the F-86E Sabre, the Americans now had the means of taking on the high-altitude MiGs on equal terms, and the 51st FIW's score began to mount steadily. In the spring of 1952 the 4th FIW also began to exchange its F-86As for the later model. The continued presence of these two units in Korea meant that there was always a strong cadre of experienced Sabre pilots at their core, ready to pass on their experience to newcomers. The Russians would have done well to adopt a similar procedure, instead of rotating entire air divisions to and from the Soviet Union. In July 1952, for example, there was a major upheaval when the 133rd Fighter Division (147th Guards Fighter Regiment and 415th and 726th Fighter Regiments) arrived at Antung and Pta-Chu, while in August the 97th and 190th Fighter Divisions left China and were replaced by the 32nd Fighter Division (224th, 535th and 913th Fighter Regiments). Shortly afterwards the 216th Fighter Division also arrived, with the 518th, 676th and 878th Fighter Regiments. It was not until January 1953 that the Russians began to rotate single squadrons, rather than entire air

divisions, but these spent only a short time in China, which was not enough to give their pilots adequate combat experience. The fact was that the Russians, at least up to the middle of 1952, had believed that the communist forces could win the Korean War; now, with the prospect of an armistice on the horizon, they were determined to give as many of their fighter pilots as possible a taste of combat, however meagre.

VETERAN PILOTS

The new pilots were keen and aggressive enough, but their lack of experience was to cost them dearly. The mission of the Fifth Air Force's Sabre wings was now to seek and destroy, rather than to screen and protect, and they modified their tactics accordingly. The Sabres now used up to 98 per cent of their power while awaiting combat; the higher speeds reduced the time they could stay on patrol, but it made catching MiGs easier, and if a MiG attacked, its rate of closure was slower. Between 8 and 31 May, Sabre pilots sighted 1507 MiGs, engaged 537 of them, and destroyed 56 for the loss of only one F-86. In seven instances the

MiGs went into inadvertent spins in combat manoeuvres above 35,000ft (10,675m), and in most cases their pilots were seen to eject. In other cases, the enemy pilots baled out as soon as a Sabre opened fire. The Fifth Air Force's fighter pilots threw everything into the MiG hunt in May 1953, and veteran aces added to their scores. Two pilots, Captain Joseph McConnell and Captain Manual J. Fernandez, had been running neck and neck. With a score of 14½, Fernandez' lead seemed assured, but by 18 May Joseph McConnell had shot down six more MiGs to bring his personal score to 16, a jet combat record that remains unbroken. Fernandez never had a chance to get his revenge, for both pilots were relieved of combat duty on 19 May. Sadly, McConnell was killed on 24 August 1954, while testing a new F-86H Sabre. May 1953 saw the return to combat of Major James Jabara, the original Korean jet ace, whose score stood at seven enemy aircraft destroyed. On the 26th, Jabara shot down his eighth and ninth MiGs; just over a month later he was to become a triple jet ace by destroying his 15th enemy aircraft, moving into second place behind McConnell. In June, Sabres and

MiGs engaged one another in a series of furious combats that resulted in the destruction of 77 enemy fighters, with a further 11 probably destroyed and 41 damaged. There were no Allied losses. The Sabres, meanwhile, claimed 32 MiG-15s in July. On the 11th, Major John F. Bolt, a USMC pilot flying Sabres with the 51st FIW, shot down his fifth and sixth MiGs to become the only Marine Corps ace of the Korean War; on the 15th James Jabara scored his 15th and final victory, putting him in second place. The air war, however, was not yet over. At 1700 hours on 22 July, three Sabres of the 51st FIW led by Lt Sam P. Young entered MiG Alley at 35,000ft (10,700m) on an offensive patrol. Young felt somewhat depressed; in 34 combat missions he had yet to fire his guns in anger, and it was beginning to look as though he would never get his chance. But on this July afternoon, his run of bad luck came to an end. Ahead and below, four MiGs crossed his path at right angles. Young dived down, lined up his Sabre carefully, and shot down the number four MiG with a long burst of fire. It was the last MiG to be destroyed in combat over Korea.

PROFIT AND LOSS

The controversy over actual air combat losses in Korea exists to this day. At the end of the war, the Americans claimed to have destroyed 792 MiG-15s for the loss of 79 Sabres, giving them a ten-to-one kill ratio. Later, they reduced their claim to 379 MiG-15s, while increasing their Sabre casualties to 106. Russian records admit the loss of 335 MiG-15s, which rises to 550 if Chinese and North Korean MiG losses are included. The Russians and their allies, however, claim to have destroyed 181 F-86 Sabres out of a total of 271 UN aircraft, which included 27 Thunderjets and 30 Shooting Stars. Combined Chinese and North Korean losses are said to have totalled 231 aircraft and 126 pilots. Although the true facts may never be etablished, what is a fact is that the top-scoring fighter pilot in the Korean war was not American, but Russian. He was Major N.V. Sutagin, who flew with the 303rd and 324th Fighter

■BELOW: Originally designed as an escort fighter, a role in which it was no match for aircraft like the MiG-15, the F-84 Thunderjet proved to be an excellent strike aircraft in Korea.

■ABOVE: An F-86 Sabre streaks down the runway of a Korean airfield after a combat mission over the Yalu river. Visible just behind the wings are the aircraft's deployed airbrakes.

Divisions and who claimed to have destroyed 22 UN aircraft. In second place was Captain Yevgeni G. Pepelyayev, with 19. In all, 33 Soviet Air Force pilots destroyed five or more UN aircraft. Top-scoring North Korean pilot was Lt Col Kim Ki-ok, with 17 victories, while Tun Wen of the Chinese People's Air Force (which did not have ranks) shot down 10. There is no doubt at all that the communist fighter pilots who took on the United Nations over northwest Korea were worthier opponents than western historians have recorded.

LAST OF THE DAY FIGHTERS

The outbreak of the Korean War, together with fears that it might escalate into a wider conflict, led to the acceleration of combat aircraft re-equipment programmes in both east and west. In Britain, two new swept-wing fighter types, the Hawker Hunter and Supermarine Swift, were to replace the Meteor in the air defence role; their

prototypes flew on 20 July and 1 August 1951 respectively and both types were ordered into 'super-priority' production for RAF Fighter Command. The Swift, however, was found to be unsuitable for its primary role of high-level interception, being prone to tightening in turns and suffering frequent high-altitude flameouts as a result of shock waves entering the air intakes when the cannon were fired. It was later adapted to the low-level fighter/reconnaissance role and, as the Swift FR.5, equipped two squadrons in Germany. The Hunter F.Mk.1, which entered service early in 1954, also suffered from engine surge problems during high-altitude gun firing trials, resulting in some modifications to its Rolls-Royce Avon turbojet, and this – together with increased fuel capacity and provision for underwing tanks – led to the Hunter F4, which gradually replaced the Canadair-built F-86E Sabre (which had been supplied to the RAF as an interim fighter) in the German-based squadrons of the 2nd Tactical Air Force. The Hunter Mks 2 and 5 were variants powered by the Armstrong Siddeley Sapphire engine. In 1953 Hawker equipped the Hunter with the large 10,000lb (4536kg) thrust Avon 203

engine, and this variant, designated Hunter F.MK.6, flew for the first time in January 1954. Deliveries began in 1956 and the F6 subsequently equipped 15 squadrons of RAF Fighter Command. The Hunter FGA.9 was a development of the F6 optimised for ground attack, as its designation implies. In a career spanning a quarter of a century the Hunter equipped 30 RAF fighter squadrons, in addition to numerous units of foreign air forces. The grand total of Hunter production, including the two-seat T7 trainers, was 1972 aircraft, and over 500 were subsequently rebuilt for sale overseas.

ALL-WEATHER FIGHTER

The Hunter was the last of the RAF's pure day fighters. In the late 1950s, it shared the UK air defence task with the Gloster Javelin, developed as a replacement for the night fighter versions of the Meteor, Vampire and Venom aircraft that had equipped the RAF's night fighter squadrons during the first part of the decade. Construction of the Javelin prototype, the Gloster GA5 – the world's first twin-jet delta and an

extremely radical design for its day – began in April 1949, and the aircraft flew for the first time on 26 November 1951, powered by two Armstrong Siddeley Sapphires. The maiden flight was attended by a serious snag in the shape of rudder buffeting, and further flight testing was delayed while modifications were carried out. Then, on 29 June 1952, the protoype lost both elevators and was destroyed in a crash landing at Boscombe Down. (The test pilot, Sqn Ldr W.A. Waterton, was subsequently awarded the George Medal for his action in retrieving the vital flight recorder from the blazing wreckage.) Testing continued with the second prototype, WD808, which flew on 21 August 1952, but this aircraft was also destroyed on 11 June 1953 as the result of a super-stall condition. Three more prototypes had been ordered in the meantime: the third aircraft flew on 7 March 1953 and carried an armament of four 30mm cannon, while the fourth featured a modified wing shape and the fifth, which flew on 20 July 1954, was up to full production standard, with British AI Mk17 radar. As the Javelin FAW1, the new fighter was ordered into 'super-

■ABOVE: Gloster Javelin F(AW)1 all-weather fighter of No 46 Squadron RAF. This unit was the first to arm with the powerful Javelin, receiving its first aircraft in March 1956.

priority' production for the RAF. The first production aircraft flew on 22 July 1954 and deliveries began to No 46 Squadron at RAF Odiham in February 1956. Javelin FAW1s were also issued to No 87 Squadron, which formed part of 2nd TAF in Germany. In October 1955 a new variant, the Javelin FAW2, made its appearance; this was basically similar to the FAW1 apart from its radar, which was the American-designed AI22 (APQ43) and avionics, and replaced the earlier production model in No 56 Squadron. Next on the production line was the FAW4, the prototype of which was the 41st FAW1 with an all-moving tailplane. This variant entered service with No 141 Squadron early in 1957 and, except for the tailplane, was essentially similar to the FAW1. Later that year, No 151 Squadron received the first examples of the Javelin FAW5, which had a modified wing structure and increased internal fuel capacity, and in 1958 the Javelin FAW6 – which was basically an FAW5 with the same radar as the FAW2 – entered service with No 89 Squadron. In November 1956 the Javelin's already formidable combat potential was given an extra boost with the appearance of the FAW7, which was fitted with Sapphire ASSa7R turbojets developing 12,300lb (5579kg) thrust (with reheat) in place of the 8300lb (3765kg) thrust Sapphire ASSa6 engines used in earlier marks. The Javelin FAW7, which incorporated further structural modifications and increased wing fuel tankage, had an armament of two 30mm (1.18in) ADEN cannon and four Firestreak AAMs and entered service with No 33 Squadron at RAF Leeming in July 1958. The FAW8, which flew on 9 May 1958, was externally

similar to the FAW7; it incorporated the US Mk22 radar, a simplified afterburning system, a Sperry autopilot, drooped wing leading edges and dampers on the yaw and pitch axes. The FAW8 was the last production model of the Javelin, the final aircraft being completed in June 1960, but a number of Javelin FAW7s were brought up to FAW8 standard (although with British AI radar) and designated FAW9.

MACH 2 LIGHTNING

Only the RAF, of all the world's air forces, made the jump from subsonic to Mach Two fighter with no Mach One plus intermediary, replacing the Hawker Hunter day fighter and the Gloster Javelin all-weather fighter with the Mach 2 English Electric (later BAC) Lightning. The Lightning had its origin in a Ministry of Supply Specification which was issued in 1947 and called for a manned supersonic research aircraft. English Electric's design, the P.1, submitted in 1949, was quickly seen to

have an operational application, and development of the aircraft for research and military purposes continued in parallel. The first P.1A research prototype flew on 4 August 1954, powered by two Bristol Siddeley Sapphires, and three operational protypes, designated P.1B, were also built. The first of these flew on 4 April 1957, powered by two Rolls-Royce Avons, and exceeded Mach 1.0 on its first flight. On 25 November 1958 it became the first British aircraft to reach Mach 2.0, which it did in level flight. By this time the P.1B had been given the name Lightning and ordered into production for RAF Fighter Command. The first production Lightning F.Mk.1 flew on 29 October 1959, and fully combat-equipped Lightnings began entering RAF service in July 1960. Like the USAF's Lockheed F-104 Starfighter, the Lightning was developed as a supersonic missile-armed interceptor, but it had none of the Starfighter's limitations; in fact the Lightning was the world's only supersonic pure fighter aircraft until the

■BELOW: The Hawker P.1067, prototype of the Hunter. A 'Super Hunter', the Hawker P.1087, was also planned, but was cancelled when the prototype was almost complete.

English Electric (BAC, BAe) Lightning F.Mk. 6

Type: single-seat jet fighter
Country of origin: United Kingdom
Powerplant: two 15,680lbst
(7112kg) Rolls-Royce Avon
turbojets
Performance: maximum speed

Mach 2.3 (1500mph, 2415km/h)
Weights: empty 28,000lb
(12,700kg); maximum take-off
50,000lb (22,680kg)
Dimensions: wing span 34ft 10in
(10.61m); length 55ft 3in (16.84m);

height 19ft 7in (5.97m)
Armament: two Firestreak or Red
Top AAMs; two 30mm (1.18in)
Aden guns in ventral pack

advent of the McDonnell Douglas F-15 and, by the time the latter flew in prototype form, the Lightning had already been in RAF service for 12 years. The Lightning, to be sure, had its fair share of problems – including an inadequate weapon system – but its ability to get off the ground very quickly and climb to 30,000ft (9144m) in a little under two minutes were important assets in an era when it was assumed that an east-west war would begin with a nuclear attack on airfields, with minimum warning time. During the Cold War era the United States and Britain faced an air threat from one main axis, but the British air defences had to expect a much shorter warning time. It was therefore imperative to deploy an aircraft with a rapid reaction time, and in this respect the BAC Lightning was excellent. With the aircraft off the ground, interception was a fairly straightforward matter, even though the main medium between pilot and controller was voice communication. (It had always been intended that the Lightning be equipped with a datalink for the passage of data from a ground-based computer to the aircraft's auto-attack system, but this was never fitted.) In a rear-sector attack, with the Lightning's Firestreak AAM missiles the target would have been well within visual range during the final stage, provided it was daytime, so there was little danger of

engaging a friendly aircraft. The Lightning was constantly improved during its career, culminating in the F6 version. This had a revised wing leading edge designed to reduce subsonic drag and improve range, and was fitted with a large ventral fuel pack with more than double the capacity of earlier packs. The first Lightning F6 flew in April 1964 and entered service in the following year. It was the last jet fighter of purely British design, and it was to serve the RAF well in the front line of NATO's air defences until its eventual retirement in 1976.

US NIGHT FIGHTERS

Although the need for a single fighter type to fulfil the roles of both day and night fighter had been identified by the USAAF before the end of World War II, it was the Korean War that consolidated it. In 1950, the principal night and all-weather fighter in USAF service was the F-82 Twin Mustang, although early night actions over Korea were fought by the F4U-5N night fighter version of the Corsair and the Grumman F7F-3N Tigercat (the latter a twin-engined night fighter that entered service just too late to take part in World War II), both operated by US Navy or Marine Corps squadrons. From November 1952 the night bomber support mission over Korea was assumed by the Douglas F3D Skynight, the first two-seat carrier-borne

jet fighter to be adopted by the US Navy, which replaced the Tigercats of Marine Squadron VMF(N)-513. The most potent night fighter to see service in Korea, however, was the Lockheed F-94C Starfire, which joined the battle early in 1953. The Starfire was one of three aircraft developed to meet a requirement for a two-seat radar-equipped armed with either cannon or machine guns and possessing a top speed of at least 600mph (965km/h) and a ceiling of 40,000ft (12,200m). The first aircraft, the Curtiss XP-87, was the first multi-seat jet combat aircraft designed specifically for a radar intercept role at night, but it was not a success and was abandoned, the funds allocated to it being diverted to the development of the other two aircraft, the Northrop F-89 Scorpion and the F-94 Starfire. The first of two Northrop XF-89 prototypes flew on 16 August 1948 and, after USAF evaluation, Northrop received an order for an initial batch of 48 production aircraft. The first of these flew late in 1950 and deliveries to the USAF Air Defense Command began soon afterwards, the first Scorpion squadrons being assigned to Arctic defence zones such as Alaska, Iceland and Greenland. The first production model of the Scorpion, the F-89A, was powered by two Allison J35-A-21 turbojets with reheat and carried a nose armament of six 20mm cannon. The F-89B and F-89C were progressive developments with uprated Allison engines, while the F-89D had its cannon deleted and carried an armament of 104 folding-fin aircraft rockets (FFAR) in wingtip pods. Additional fuel tanks under the wings gave an 11 per cent range increase over the F-89C and the aircraft was fitted with an automatic fire control system. The F-89H, which followed the F-89D into production, was armed with six Hughes GAR-1 Falcon missiles and 42 FFAR, and could also carry the MB-1 Genie nuclear AAM. The Falcons were housed in the wing-tip pods and were extended prior to firing. The F-89H's armament was fired automatically, a sighting radar and fire control

■BELOW: Although exuding power and purpose, the Lightning also had its graceful moments, as in this fine shot of No 23 Squadron F.6s. The Squadron was based at RAF Leuchars, Scotland.

computer forming a fully integrated attack system.

POTENT STARFIRE
The other night/all weather design conceived in the 1940s, the Lockheed F-94 Starfire, was developed from the T-33A trainer, two production T-33 airframes being converted as YF-94s. The first of these flew on 16 April 1949, and four months later the USAF placed contracts for 17 F-94A-1-LO and 92 F-94A5-LO fighters, together with one YF-94B – the latter having centrally mounted wing-tip tanks instead of underslung tanks.

The F-94A, which incorporated 75 per cent of the components used in the T-33 and F-80 Shooting Star, had 940lb (426kg) of radar equipment in the nose and an armament of four 0.50in (12.7mm) Colt-Browning machine guns. The aircraft was powered by an Allison J33-A-33 centrifugal-type turbojet with reheat. F-94As were fitted with 195-

imperial-gallon (886-litre) Fletcher wing-tip tanks. The F-94A went into production in 1949; 200 were built, the first entering service in June 1950 with the 319th All-Weather Fighter Squadron.

The YF-94B was converted from the 19th F-94A in 1950, and 357 F-94Bs were built. Apart from the revised wing-tip tanks, they differed from the F-94A mainly in having a modified hydraulics system and avionics, including a Sperry Zero-Reader flight recorder. The next variant, the F-94C, differed so extensively from its predecessors that it was originally known as the YF-97A. This designation remained in force from the aircraft's maiden flight on 16 January 1950 until 12 September that year, when the designation YF-94C was officially adopted.

The F-94C was fitted with an afterburning Pratt & Whitney J48P-5, and other changes included an increase in wing dihedral and a reduction in

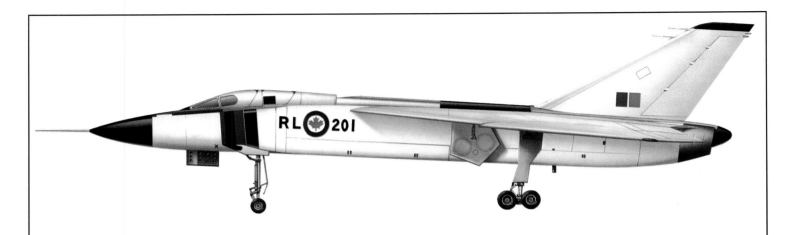

Avro Canada CF-105 Arrow

Type: two-seat supersonic interceptor
Country of origin: Canada
Powerplant: two 49,040lbst (22,244kg) Pratt & Whitney J75-P3 turbojets

Performance: Mach 2.3 recorded during trials
Weights: empty 49,040lb (22,244kg); average take-off during trials 57,000lb (25,855kg)
Dimensions: wing span 50ft

(15.24m); length 77ft 10in (23.72m); height 21ft 3in (6.48m)
Armament: eight Sparrow AAMs in internal bay

thickness/chord ratio from 13 to 10 per cent, the introduction of a swept tailplane, and the replacement of the gun armament by 24 unguided FFAR in a ring of tubes around the nose-cone. Later, provision was made for a further 24 rockets in wing pods. The F-94C carried 1200lb (543kg) of electronics, and two 1000lb (453kg) thrust RATOG (rocket-assisted take-off gear) packs could be fitted under the fuselage. Total production of the F-94C came to 387 aircraft before the series was completed in 1954. Operating in the bomber support role over Korea, flights of four to six F-94s flew barrier patrols about 30 miles (48km) ahead of the bomber stream while F3D Skynights took up position 2000ft to 3000ft (600m to 900m) above the bombers. These tactics quickly produced results, the Skynights scoring two kills in moonlight conditions, one each on the nights of 28 and 31 January 1953.

FIRST KILL IN KOREA

On the night of 30 January, Captain Ben Fithian and Lieutenant Sam R. Lyons scored the F-94's first kill in Korea, shooting down an La-9. Between them, the Skynights and Starfires destroyed 15 enemy aircraft in the first half of 1953. It was a relatively small contribution in terms of enemy aircraft destroyed, but it helped the war-weary B-29s to survive the last months of conflict in Korea. Canada, forming the first line of defence

against the threat of bombers attacking the North American continent across the great wastes of the Arctic, was quick to identify the need for a long-range night and all-weather interceptor during the early post-war years. In response to this requirement, Avro Canada designed the CF-100, at that time the largest fighter aircraft in the world. The prototype CF-100 Mk1 flew on 19 January 1950, powered by two Rolls-Royce Avon RA3 turbojets; production aircraft were fitted with the Avro Orenda.

In September 1950 an order was placed with Avro Canada for 124 CF-100 Mk3s for the RCAF. These were powered by two Orenda Mk8s and armed with eight 0.5in (12.7mm) Colt-Browning machine guns. In fact only 70 were built, the first entering service with No 445 Sqdn. The next production version was the Mk4A, powered by two Orenda 9s and equipped with a Hughes AGP-40 fire control radar. This variant could be armed with 48 'Mighty Mouse' high velocity aircraft rockets (HVAR), eight 0.5in (12.7mm) machine guns or four 30mm cannon in a ventral pack, plus 58 HVAR rockets in wing-tip pods.

The first production Mk4A flew on 24 October 1953 and the aircraft entered service with No 445 Sqdn in the following year. In all, 510 Mk4As and 4Bs (the latter with Orenda 11 engines) were built and, by the end of 1957, nine RCAF squadrons were operating the type, providing round-

the-clock air defence coverage of Canada's far north. Four CF-100 squadrons also served in Germany as part of Canada's NATO commitment, and 53 examples of the last production version, the Mk5, were delivered to Belgium. The CF-100 was to have been replaced in RCAF service by the very advanced Avro Canada CF-105 Arrow delta-wing interceptor, which flew for the first time on 25 March 1958, powered by two Pratt & Whitney J75 turbojets. Four more aircraft were built, designated CF-105 Mk1, and four more – designated Mk2, with 22,000lb (9979kg) thrust Orenda PS-13 engines – were almost complete when the project was cancelled in February 1959. The Arrow was to have been armed with eight Sparrow AAMs.

INTERIM FIGHTER

In 1950, the USAF formulated a requirement for a night and all-weather interceptor incorporating the latest fire control system. This was eventually to emerge as the Convair F-102, whose design was based on experience gained during flight testing of the XF-92 delta-wing research aircraft. Two prototype YF102s were built, the first flying on 24 October 1953. This aircraft was damaged beyond repair only a week later, but testing resumed with the second machine in January 1954. Eight more YF-102s were built for evaluation, and it soon became apparent that the aircraft's performance fell short of expectations.

After substantial airframe redesign the machine re-emerged in December 1954 as the YF-102A, and the type was ordered into full production. The first F-102A was handed over to Air Defense Command in June 1955, but it was another year before the type was issued to squadrons. As an interim measure, Air Defense Command acquired an interim all-weather fighter, the single-seat F-86D Sabre, radar-equipped and mounting a pack of 24 2.75in (69.8mm) FFAR recessed under the fuselage.

TEETHING TROUBLES

The F-86D's innovative weapons system produced some teething troubles, all of which contributed to the slippage of the production programme. On a typical air defence mission beginning with a cold start, once the snags had been eliminated, the F-86D could be off the ground in about four minutes, which included warming up time, and would then take 11 minutes to climb to 45,000ft (13,716m) at full power. The pilot would then initiate the search phase, the AN/APG-36 (AN/APG-37 in later models) radar antenna sweeping an area 68.5 degrees left and right of the centreline in a three-and-a-half second cycle and also, if required, 33.5 degrees up and 13.5 degrees down. When a target was acquired at a range of up to 30 miles (48km) the radar locked on to it and the AN/APA-84 computer then worked out a lead collision course, which the pilot followed by keeping the 'blip' on his radar scope inside a one-inch circle. When the automatic tracking system indicated 20 seconds to go, the system instructed the pilot to turn on to a 90-degree collision course, at which point he elected to launch 6, 12 or all 24 rockets and pressed the trigger switch. The computer controlled the actual firing, extending the rocket pack in half a second and initiating the firing sequence when the target was about 500 yards (457m) away. It took only one-fifth of a second to fire the full salvo of rockets, each weighing 18lb (8kg), the missiles fanning our like a charge of shotgun pellets to make sure of a hit. The rocket pack retracted in just over three seconds, and a symbol on the radar scope, which illuminated at a range of 250yds

(228.6m), warned the pilot to break off. Launching a full rocket salvo presented few problems; these tended to arise when the pilot selected a ripple-firing sequence, a procedure that saw frequent malfunctions. The system was updated and refined, but by the time the snags were ironed out the programme had slipped by two years, and it was not until April 1953 that the F-86D began to enter service with active Air Defense Command units. Thereafter, deliveries proceeded rapidly, and by the end of 1953 600 F-86Ds were in service with the Air Defense Command. Eighteen months later, 1026 –

73 per cent – of the Command's 1405 interceptors were F-86Ds serving with the US Air Forces overseas; some were assigned to the Fifth AF in Korea late in 1953, but the 'Sabre-Dog' was a much heavier fighter than the standard F-86 and it did not take kindly to operations from the still fairly primitive South Korean airfields. It was withdrawn after only a brief period of service in the peninsula. F-86Ds did, however, equip the 199th Fighter Interceptor Squadron of the 154th Fighter Group, Hawaiian Air National Guard, until they were replaced by Convair F-102A Delta Daggers in the early 1960s.

■RIGHT: The F-94 Starfire was originally deployed to Korea to combat piston-engined night intruders, which proved very difficult to catch. F-94 unserviceability was high.

CHAPTER 5

MACH TWO AND BEYOND

Modern fighters are multi-million dollar machines that bear little physical resemblance to the first scouts that flew over the Western Front. Although the Cold War is over, fighter design and development continues apace.

One of the biggest success stories to emerge from the war in Korea was the Republic F-84 Thunderjet, which, although no real match for the MiG-15 in air combat, proved to be a very viable ground attack aircraft. It was the Thunderjet that provided the bulk of NATO's ground attack assests during this dangerous period, and it was followed into service by an equally effective development, the swept-wing F-84F Thunderstreak. The XF-84F, which used about 60 per cent of the F-84's components, flew for the first time on 3 June 1950, only 167 days after it was ordered. It was fitted with an Allison J35-A-25 engine, and flight tests revealed that it was underpowered. Had it not been for the onset of the Korean War, which released emergency funds for combat aircraft development, the F-84F would probably have been abandoned. As it was, the design was modified to take the more powerful Wright J65, the licence-built version of the Bristol Siddeley Sapphire, and the XF-84F flew in this configuration on 14 February 1951. The first production F-84F flew on 22 November 1952 and the type was officially accepted by the USAF in the following month. The first USAF unit to arm with the new type, in 1954, was the 407th Tactical Fighter Wing. The F-84F replaced the Thunderjet in several NATO air forces, giving many European pilots their first experience of modern, swept-wing jet aircraft. In French Air Force service, it saw action during the 1956 Anglo-French operation to secure the

■LEFT: **Symbolising the awesome striking power of the United States Navy, this McDonnell Douglas F/A-18 Hornet prepares for take-off on the steam catapult.**

Suez Canal, which had been closed on the orders of Egypt's President Nasser; in a particularly spectacular mission on 3 November 1956, 20 F-84Fs of the 1ere Escadre, operating from Lydda in Israel, attacked the air base at Luxor in southern Egypt and knocked out 18 Ilyushin Il-28 jet bombers with cannon fire. The Il-28s had been evacuated from Egypt's northern airfields, which were under heavy attack by British and French fighter-bombers.

EARLY FRENCH JETS

It was during the Suez operation, with its associated drive into Egyptian-occupied Sinai by Israeli forces, that French-designed jet fighters saw combat for the first time. At the end of the war in Europe, France's aircraft industry lay in ruins, its factories destroyed or dismantled, its designers scattered far and wide. Its recovery since then had been little short of phenomenal. For the first few years of its post-war existence, the French Air Force had no alternative but to rely on foreign jet aircraft like the de Havilland Vampire for its first-line equipment but, on 28 February 1949, Avions Marcel Dassault flew the prototype of a straightforward, no-frills jet fighter which had begun as a private venture in November 1947. Powered by a Rolls-Royce Nene 102 turbojet, built under licence by Hispano-Suiza, the Dassault MD.450 Ouragan (Hurricane) became the first jet fighter of French design to be ordered in quantity, some 350 production aircraft being delivered to the French Air Force from 1952. The Ouragan was exported to India, where it was known as the Toofani (Whirlwind), and to Israel, which received 75 examples. Although the Ouragan was inferior to the MiG-15, the principal jet

fighter type equipping the Egyptian Air Force at that time, it performed well in the ground attack role, leaving another French-built type to tackle the MiGs. This was the Dassault Mystère IV, one of the finest combat aircraft of its era. Its immediate ancestor was the Dassault MD452 Mystère IIc, a straightforward swept-wing version of the Ouragan which first flew on 23 February 1951. Some 150 Mystère IIcs served with the French Air Force, and Israel had plans to purchase some in 1954–55, but in view of the type's poor service record – several of the earlier French machines having been lost through structural failure – it was decided to buy the Mystère IV instead.

NEW DESIGN

Although developed from the Mystère IIc, the Mystère IV was in fact a completely new design. The prototype Mystère Iva flew for the first time on 28 September 1952, and early trials proved so promising that the French Government placed an order for 325 production aircraft six months later in April 1953. The fighter was also delivered to India, and Israel acquired the first of 60 in April 1956, the type replacing the Gloster Meteor F.8 in Israeli Air Force service. Production of the Mystère IVA was completed in 1958, with the 421st aircraft. A one-off variant of the Mystère IV, the Mystère IVB, was fitted with an afterburning Roll-Royce RA7R turbojet and became the first French aircraft to exceed the speed of sound in level flight. It served as a test-bed for the next Dassault fighter, the Super Mystère B.2. This transonic successor to the Mystère IVA featured a thinner, more sharply swept wing, an improved air intake and

modified cockpit. It flew for the first time on 2 March 1955, powered by the Avon RA7R, and on its fourth flight it exceeded Mach One on the level, becoming the first production aircraft of European design to do so. Super Mystère production totalled 180 aircraft, the type equipping two French Air Force escadres de chasse and two interceptor squadrons of the Israeli Air Force. In both cases, it was replaced by an aircraft that was to prove one of the biggest success stories in the field of post-war combat aircraft design, the Dassault Mirage III, a Mach 2 delta-wing fighter that owed its origin to the Dassault MK550 Mirage I of 1954. This aircraft, developed in response to a high-altitude interceptor requirement, proved too small to carry an effective war load, and its twin Viper turbojets failed to supply the necessary power. Its airframe was substantially redesigned and enlarged and fitted with a SNECMA Atar G1 engine; in this new guise it made its first flight on 17 November 1956 and exceeded Mach 1.5 in level flight on 30 January 1957. Later, equipped with an auxiliary rocket motor, it reached a speed of Mach 1.9. The first production version was the Mirage IIIC, which at 50,000ft (15,240m) was capable of Mach 2.2 in level flight. The French Air Force ordered 100 Mirage IIICs and 72 (as Mirage IIICJs) were ordered by Israel, minus air-to-air missiles and rocket motors. The Mirage IIIE was a long-range tactical strike version that was widely exported, serving with several foreign air forces as well as with the Armée de l'Air, and a variant known as the Mirage IIIO was manufactured under licence in Australia.

Meanwhile, the USAF had progressed via the Republic F-84F Thunderstreak

■ ABOVE: The Dassault MD.450 Ouragan (Hurricane), France's first modern jet fighter, did excellent work with the Israeli Air Force (which received 75 examples) in the war of 1956.

and the last variants of the trusty F-86 Sabre to the first of its so-called 'century' fighters, the North American F-100 Super Sabre. In February 1949 the North American design team had begun work on redesigning the F-86 Sabre with the aim of evolving a fighter that could reach and sustain supersonic speeds in level flight. Originally known as the Sabre 45, the new aircraft bore little resemblance to its predecessor, having a contoured low-drag fuselage, and wings and tail surface swept at an angle of 45 degrees. On 1 November 1951 the USAF awarded a contract for two YF-100A prototypes and 110 F-100A production aircraft; the first prototype flew on 25 May 1953 and exceeded Mach One on its maiden flight. The first F100A Super Sabres were delivered to the 479th Fighter Wing at George AFB, California, in September 1954, but were grounded in November following a series of unexplained crashes. It was established that the vertical tail surfaces were too small to maintain control during certain manoeuvres, and so they were redesigned with 27 per cent more area, the wing span also being slightly increased. With these modifications the F-100A began flying operationally again in February 1955 and 22 examples were built. The next series production variant was the F-100C, which was capable of carrying out both ground attack and interception missions. First deliveries to the USAF were made in July 1955 and total production was 451, of which 260 went to the Turkish Air Force.

The F-100D differed from the F-100C in having an automatic pilot, jettisonable underwing pylons and modified vertical tail surfaces; it was supplied to the USAF Tactical Air Command, Denmark, France and Greece. The TF100C was a two-seat trainer variant and served as the prototype of the TF-100F, which flew in July 1957. Total production of all Super Sabre variants was 2294.

VOODOO: A FIGHTER REBORN

Second of the 'century' fighters was the McDonnell F-101 Voodoo, which was based on the design of the cancelled XF-88 heavy twin-engined escort fighter of 1948. The resurrected design was subjected to a number of changes, including the lengthening of the fuselage by over 13ft (4m) to accommodate extra fuel tankage, and the remodelled aircraft was designated YF-101A. The prototype flew on 29 December 1954 and, although Strategic Air Command had long since abandoned the long-range escort fighter idea, the programme was taken over by Tactical Air Command, which saw the F-101 as a potential replacement for the Northrop F-89 Scorpion. The aircraft went into production as the F-101A, powered by two Pratt & Whitney J57-P-13 turbojets, and the 75 examples built equipped three squadrons of TAC. The next Voodoo variant, the two-seat F-101B, equipped 16 squadrons of Air Defense Command, and production ran to 359 aircraft. This version also equipped three Canadian air

defence squadrons as the CF-101B. The F-101C was a single-seat fighter-bomber version for TAC, entering service with the 523rd Tactical Fighter Squadron of the 27th Fighter Bomber Wing in May 1957. It equipped nine squadrons, but its operational career was relatively short-lived, as it was replaced by more modern combat types in the early 1960s. The first of these was the Republic F-105 Thunderchief, conceived as a successor to the F-84F at a time when the USAF was giving maximum priority to building up its nuclear deterrent. Although beset by continual difficulties during its early development career, the F-105 eventually emerged as the workhorse of Tactical Air Command during the early 1960s. The first of two YF-105 prototypes flew on 22 October 1955, and deliveries of operational F-105Bs began in May 1958 to the 4th Tactical Fighter Wing. Only 75 F-105Bs were built, this variant being replaced on the production line in 1959 by the all-weather ground attack F-105D, of which 610 were produced. In its F-105D version the nuclear-capable Thunderchief served with 13 tactical fighter wings, and in 1962 it was at the spearhead of the American forces poised to launch an attack on Cuba following the discovery of intermediate-range Soviet missiles on the island. On 21 October, soon after the crisis developed, F-105s of TAC's 4th Fighter Wing, the most experienced Thunderchief unit, deployed to McCoy Air Force Base and at 0400 hours the next day began a one-hour alert

status, reduced to 15 minutes in the afternoon. But the F-105s were held back while negotiations (which eventually resulted in the withdrawal of all Russian missiles from Cuba) proceeded, and their activities were confined to patrolling the southern Florida peninsula. The F-105 would have its day in another war, just a few years later.

THE RADICAL F-104

Without doubt, the most revolutionary of the 'century' fighters was the Lockheed F-104 Starfighter. Development of the F-104 was begun in 1951, when the lessons of the Korean air war were starting to bring about profound changes in combat aircraft design. A contract for two XF-104 prototypes was placed in 1953 and the first of these flew on 7 February 1954, only 11 months later. The two XF-104s were followed by 15 YF-104s for USAF evaluation, most of these, like the prototypes, being powered by the Wright J65-W-6 turbojet. The aircraft was ordered into production as the F-104A, deliveries to the USAF Air Defense Command beginning in January 1958. Because of its lack of all-weather capability the F-104A saw only limited service with Air Defense Command, equipping only two fighter squadrons. F104As were also supplied to Nationalist China and Pakistan, and saw combat during the Indo-Pakistan conflict of 1969. The F104B was a two-seat version, and the F-104C was a tactical fighter-bomber,

Dassault Mystere IVA

Type: single-seat jet fighter-bomber
Country of origin: France
Powerplant: one 6280lbst (2850kg) Hispano Suiza 250A (R-R Tay) turbojet

Performance: maximum speed 696mph (1120km/h)
Weights: empty 11,514lb (5875kg); maximum take-off 20,950lb (9500kg)
Dimensions: wing span 36ft 6in

(11.1m); length 42ft 2in (12.9m); height 14ft 5in (4.4m)
Armament: two 30mm (1.18in) DEFA cannon; up to 2000lb (907kg) of external ordnance

the first of 77 examples being delivered to the 479th Tactical Fighter Wing (the only unit to use it) in October 1958. Two more two-seat Starfighters, the F-104D and F-104F, were followed by the F-104G, which was numerically the most important variant. A single-seat multi-mission aircraft based on the F-104C, the F-104G had a strengthened structure and many equipment changes, including an upwards-ejecting Lockheed C-2 seat (earlier variants had a downward-ejecting seat). The first F-104G flew on 5 October 1960 and 1266 examples were produced up to February 1966, 977 by the European Starfighter Consortium and the remainder by Lockheed. Of these, the Luftwaffe received 750, the Italian Air Force 154, the Royal Netherlands Air Force 120 and the Belgian Air Force 99. The F-104G received more than its share of adverse publicity; apart from the fact that it was at the centre of a political row involving allegations of bribery, its new attack role made it heavier than was ever intended, with the result that it had poor low-speed handling characteristics and an appalling accident rate. The basically similar CF-104 was a strike-reconnaissance aircraft, 200 of which were built by Canadair for the RCAF. Canadair also built 110 more F-104Gs for delivery to the air forces of Norway, Nationalist China, Spain, Denmark, Greece and Turkey. Also similar to the F-104G was the F-104J for the Japan Air Self-Defence Force; the first one flew on 30 June 1961 and and 207 were produced by Mitsubishi. The F-104S was an interceptor development of the F-104G, with provision for external stores, and

was capable of Mach 2.4; 165 were licence-built in Italy. While the Starfighter covered the requirement for a multi-purpose strike fighter for NATO, it was too complex an aircraft to be handled by other friendly, foreign air forces. In 1955, therefore, a team of designers and engineers from the Northrop Corporation carried out a fact-finding tour of Europe and Asia, their object being to examine the air defence needs of various nations within the US sphere of influence. As a result, the Northrop N156 was conceived as a relatively cheap and simple aircraft capable of undertaking a variety of tasks. At the end of 1958, Northrop received a Department of Defense contract for three prototypes, the first of which flew on 30 July 1959, powered by two General Electric YJ85-GE-1 turbojets, and exceeded Mach One on its maiden flight. After nearly three years of intensive testing and evaluation, it was announced on 25 April 1962 that the N156 had been selected as the new all-purpose fighter for supply to friendly nations under the Mutual Aid Pact, and the aircraft entered production as the F-5A Freedom Fighter, the first example flying in October 1963. The F-5A entered service with USAF Tactical Air Command in April 1964. The first overseas customer was the Imperial Iranian Air Force, which formed the first of seven F-5A squadrons in February 1965. The Royal Hellenic Air Force also received two squadrons in 1965, and Norway received 108 aircraft from 1967, these being fitted with arrester hooks and rocket-assisted take-off for short field operations. Between 1965 and 1970 Canadair built 115 aircraft for the

Canadian Armed Forces as CF-5A/Ds, these using Orenda-built J85-CAN-15 engines. Other nations using the type were Ethiopia, Morocco, South Korea, the Republic of Vietnam, Nationalist China, the Philippines, Libya, the Netherlands, Spain, Thailand and Turkey. An improved version, the F-5E Tiger II, was selected in November 1970 as a successor to the F-5A series. It served with a dozen overseas air forces, and also in the 'aggressor' air combat training role with the USAF.

DEFENDING NEUTRALITY

While the USA strove to keep its friendly nations supplied with modern combat aircraft, one neutral country – Sweden – had been developing combat aircraft that were a match for any to be found anywhere. Although Sweden had been mostly reliant on foreign combat types before and during World War II, the Swedish aircraft manufacturer, SAAB, had produced an indigenous fighter aircraft, the J-21A. A twin-boom pusher design, powered by a DB605B liquid-cooled engine, the J-21A made its first flight on 13 July 1943, and during trials it reached a respectable top speed of 398mph at 15,000ft (640km/h at 4575m). The J-21A's advanced all-metal flush-riveted stressed-skin wing employed a new high-speed aerofoil section, and other innovations included a cartridge-type ejection seat for the pilot, enabling

■BELOW: A Dassault Mirage F.1 (bottom) in formation with its direct ancestor, the Mirage III. The Mirage line has been a major French success story.

SAAB A/J32 Lansen

Type: all-weather fighter/attack aircraft
Country of origin: Sweden
Powerplant: one 15,190lbst (6890kg) Svenska Flygmotor RM6A (Rolls-Royce Avon)

Performance: maximum speed: 692mph (1114km/h)
Weights: empty 17,600lb (7990kg); maximum take-off 29,800lb (13,529kg)
Dimensions: wing span 42ft 8in

(13m); length 47ft 7in (14.50m); height 15ft 3in (4.65m)
Armament: four 30mm (1.18in) Aden guns; four Sidewinder AAMs or FFAR rocket pods

---

him to clear the propeller blades and tail unit. The new aircraft entered service with the Royal Swedish Air Force late in 1945, 298 production aircraft being delivered. By this time SAAB was working on a jet-powered version, the J-21R. This flew on 10 March 1947 but, because of many modifications that had to be made to the airframe, production deliveries did not take place until 1949, and an order for 120 aircraft was cut back to 60. SAAB's efforts were now concentrated on the much more modern J-29, an aircraft that had the distinction of being the first swept-wing jet fighter of West European design to enter service after World War II. The first of three prototypes was test flown on 1 September 1948, powered by a de Havilland Ghost turbojet. All production aircraft were equipped with a Ghost 50 turbojet built under licence in Sweden. The first production model, the J-29A, began to enter service with Day Fighter Wing F14 at Norköping in May 1951, and the aircraft's tubby appearance earned it the nickname of Tunnan (Barrel). Five production versions of the fighter were produced, ending with the J-29F, and the type – supplemented by four squadrons of Hawker Hunters – remained the Swedish Air Force's main first-line equipment until well into the 1960s. The J-29 saw limited active service during the Congo crisis of 1962–63, eleven aircraft being deployed with Fighter Squadron F22 as part of the United Nations peacekeeping force. The J-29 became the first Swedish combat aircraft to be exported, several being delivered to the small Austrian Air Force.

In the autumn of 1946, SAAB began design studies of a new turbojet-powered attack aircraft for the Swedish Air Force, and two years later the Swedish Air Board authorised the construction of a prototype under the designation P1150. This aircraft, now known as the A-32 Lansen (Lance), flew for the first time on 3 November 1952, powered by a Rolls-Royce Avon RA7R turbojet. Three more prototypes were built, and one of these exceeded Mach One in a shallow dive on 25 October 1953. The A-32A attack variant was followed by the J-32B all-weather fighter, which first flew in January 1957. A two-seater, the J-32B was powered by an RM6 (licence-built RA28) turbojet and carried an improved armament, navigation equipment and fire control system. The J-37B, however, was very much an interim aircraft, filling a gap until the advent of a much more potent system, the SAAB J-35 Draken. Designed from the outset to intercept transonic bombers at all altitudes and in all weathers, the Draken (Dragon) was probably, at the time of its service debut, the finest fully integrated air defence system in western Europe. The first of three prototypes of this unique 'double delta' fighter flew for the first time on 25 October 1955, and the initial production version, the J-35A, entered service early in 1960. The major production version of the Draken was the J-35F, which was virtually designed around the Hughes HM-55 Falcon radar-guided air-to-air missile and was fitted with an improved S7B collision-course fire control system, a high capacity datalink system integrating

the aircraft with the STRIL 60 air defence environment, an infrared sensor under the nose and PS-01A search and ranging radar. Total production of the Draken was around 600 aircraft, equipping 17 RSAF squadrons; the type was also exported to Denmark and Finland.

SOVIET SUPERSONICS

In comparison with western combat types that were making their appearance in the early 1950s, Soviet designs appeared crude, lacking the elegance and refinement that were the hallmarks of a successful aircraft. But Soviet designers were learning quickly, and before the end of the decade the Soviet Air Force would have at its disposal some of the most effective military aircraft in the world. The great leap forward came during the so-called Khrushchev decade, from 1955 to 1964. The MiG-17 (NATO code name Fresco), a straightforward development of the MiG-15, was followed by the MiG-19 Farmer, which went into series production in 1955 and was the first Russian fighter with supersonic capability in level flight, making it roughly the equivalent of the F-100 Super Sabre. This in turn was succeeded by the MiG-21 Fishbed, a smaller and lighter aircraft whose delta wing gave it the Russian nickname of Balalaika. One of the most important combat aircraft of the Cold War era, the MiG-21 was a child of the Korean War, where Soviet air combat experience had identified a need for a light, single-seat target defence interceptor with high supersonic manoeuvrability. Two prototypes were

North American F-100D Super Sabre

Type: single-seat fighter
Country of origin: USA
Powerplant: one 17,000lbst
(7711kg) Pratt & Whitney
J57-P-21A turbojet

Performance: maximum speed
864mph (1390km/h)
Weights: empty 21,000lb (9525kg);
maximum take-off 34,832lb
(15,800kg)

Dimensions: wing span 38ft 9in
(11.8m); length 47ft 1in (14.36m);
height 16ft 3in (4.95m)
Armament: four 20mm (0.78in)
cannon

ordered, both appearing early in 1956; one, code-named Faceplate, featured sharply swept wings and was not developed further. The intial production versions (Fishbed-A and -B were built only in limited numbers, being short-range day fighters with a comparatively light armament of two 30mm NR-30 cannon, but the next variant, the MiG-21F Fishbed-C, carried two K-13 Atoll infrared homing AAMs, and had an uprated Tumansky R-11 turbojet as well as improved avionics. The MiG-21F was the first major production version; it entered service in 1960 and was modified and updated over the years that followed. In the early 1970s the MiG-21 was virtually redesigned, re-emerging as the MiG-21B (Fishbed-L) multi-role air superiority fighter and ground attack version. In its several versions the MiG-21 became the most widely used jet fighter in the world, being licence-built in India, Czechoslovakia and China, where it was designated Shenyang F8, and equipping some 25 Soviet-aligned air forces.

FRONTAL FIGHTERS
Pavel Sukhoi, who had earlier fallen from favour with Stalin and been reinstated after the latter's death in 1953, contributed greatly to the Russian air build-up in the late 1950s. From his design bureau came the Su-7 Fitter-A and the Su-9 Fishpot-A, both single-engined, single-seat types. The Su-7, designed for close air support with the

Frontal Aviation, featured 60 degrees of sweep and carried two 30mm (1.18in) cannon in its wing roots; it also carried a relatively heavy load of ordnance, either rockets or bombs, under the wings. The Su-7 remained the Soviet Air Force's standard tactical fighter-bomber throughout the 1960s. Later, the Sukhoi bureau redesigned the Su-7, giving it a more powerful engine, variable-geometry wings and increased fuel tankage. In this guise it became the Su-17/20 Fitter C, which was unique among combat aircraft in being a variable-geometry derivative of a fixed-wing machine. It was an excellent example of a remarkable Russian talent for developing existing designs to their fullest extent. The development of the Fitter-C was a facet of the Russians' practice of constant development, enabling them to keep one basic design of combat aircraft in service for 30 or 40 years and foster long-term standardisation. Also, the use of the same production facilities over a long period of time helped greatly to reduce costs, which is why the USSR was able to offer combat types on the international market at far more competitive rates than the West. Contemporary with the Su-7, the Su-9 Fishpot-A was a single-seat interceptor – to some extent, an Su-7 with a delta wing. It was armed with the first Soviet AAM, the semi-active radar homing Alkali, four of which were carried under the wings. In 1961 a new model, the Su-11 Fishpot-B, was developed from the Su-9,

and was followed into service by the Fishpot-C, which had an uprated engine. The follow-on to this aircraft was the Su-15 Flagon, a twin-engined delta-wing interceptor that first flew in 1965 and was in Soviet Air Force service by 1969. Capable of carrying two AAMs, the Flagon was numerically Russia's most important all-weather interceptor by the mid-1970s.

ALL-WEATHER RUSSIANS
The Flagon was at the end of an all-weather fighter development story that had begun during the Korean War. The communist night fighter component during that conflict comprised the 351st and 298th Night Fighter Regiments, whose piston-engined La-11s were ineffective against the B-29s. The failure of the communist air defences to stem the B-29 night offensive against targets in North Korea did not pass unnoticed in the Soviet Union. Neither did the fact that American reconnaissance aircraft like the RB-29, RB-36 and RB-50 were making frequent night incursions into Soviet air space, radar-mapping Russian airfields and other facilities. These two facts combined to accelerate the development of a viable Soviet night and all weather jet fighter, and there were only two real contenders. The first was the unwieldy Lavochkin La-200B; the second was the Yakovlev Yak-25, and it was this aircraft that was selected for production, although not without a good

deal of political lobbying by the Yakovlev design team. The problem was that Semyon Lavochkin had the backing of Lavrenti Beria, the all-powerful Soviet Chief of Secret Police; but Yakovlev went directly to Josef Stalin, and managed to win him over. In every respect, the Yak-25 was a better aircraft than the La-200B. A mid-wing monoplane with 45 degrees of sweep, it was a tandem two-seater and featured a bicycle undercarriage with outriggers under the wings. It was fitted with an improved version of the Izumrud AI radar under a large plastic radome and was armed with two 30mm cannon mounted under the fuselage. The Yak-25 prototypes had two Mikulin AM-5 engines, but production aircraft had the more powerful AM-5F, the F denoting Forsazh, or reheat. Several prototypes were flying by the summer of 1952 and the aircraft entered service with a Soviet Air Force development unit in 1955, becoming fully operational in the following year. The Yak-25 was allotted the NATO code name Flashlight.

STAND-OFF MISSILES

The Yak-25 was to be the mainstay of the Soviet Air Force's night/all-weather fighter force throughout the 1950s, and in that role it was complemented by the shorter-range MiG-19 Farmer, a night fighter variant of Russia's first truly supersonic jet fighter having been produced. By the late 1950s, however, an extra requirement had been built into specifications for a new generation of Soviet night and all-weather fighters: extended combat radius. No longer was it necessary for American strategic bombers

to penetrate into Soviet air space; they were now armed with stand-off missiles that could be launched from points well outside Soviet territory, and the priority of the IA-PVO, the Soviet Air Force's Air Defence Command, was to destroy SAC's B-52 bombers before they came within launch range. The urgent IA-PVO requirement for an aircraft capable of intercepting Strategic Air Command B-52s before they reached their missile launch points led directly to the development of the Tu-28 long-range, missile-armed all-weather interceptor, first seen by western observers at the Tushino air display of 1961. With a length of 85ft (26m) and a wing span of 65ft (19.8m), the Tu-28, which was given the code name Fiddler, was the largest interceptor to see service anywhere, and western experts noted with interest, after they had gathered more intelligence on the aircraft, that its designation carried the suffix 'P' for Perekhvachnik (interceptor). The interesting point was that this suffix was only applied to the designations of Soviet aircraft which had been adapted to the fighter role, indicating that the Tu-28 had originally been designed as a low-level strike aircraft, possibly in the anti-shipping role. The Tu-28 was estimated to have a combat radius of around 1500 miles (2400km) with maximum fuel, and it was armed with four AA-5 Ash air-to-air missiles on underwing pylons.

AIR SHOW SURPRISES

If the 1961 Tushino air display produced some surprises, so did a similar event at Domodedovo in 1967, when new designs

from the Mikoyan bureau were very much in evidence. One of these was the MiG-23 Flogger, which entered service with the Frontal Aviation in 1971 as a strike aircraft and which by 1973 was being deployed to attack units of the 16th Air Army in Germany. A variable-geometry fighter-bomber with wings sweeping from 23 to 71 degrees, the Flogger was the Soviet Air Force's first true multi-role combat aircraft. Another product of the MiG stable first seen at Domodedovo was a twin-engined, cropped, delta-wing interceptor designated MiG-25 and given the NATO code name Foxbat. The prototype MiG-25 was flown as early as 1964 and was apparently designed to counter the projected North American B-70 bomber, with its Mach 3.0 speed and ceiling of 70,000ft (21,350m). The cancellation of the B-70 left the Foxbat in search of a role; it entered service as an interceptor in 1970, but soon a MiG-25R variant appeared, equipped with cameras and electronic surveillance equipment, and it was in this role that the type found its true value. The experience of the Korean War led to the evolution of a new generation of fighter and attack aircraft for the US Navy. The air war over Korea, in which US naval aviation had played a substantial part, had shown that existing naval types such as the F2H Banshee and F9F Panther were no match for modern land-based fighters like the MiG-15. The US manufacturers, conscious that the war might escalate, tackled the problem with urgency while the conflict was still in progress. The first of the new generation of naval fighters came from

Lockheed TF-104G Starfighter

Type: two-seat fighter/trainer
Country of origin: USA
Powerplant: one 15,600lbst (7076kg) General Electric J79-GE11 turbojet

Performance: maximum speed 1146mph (1845km/h)
Weights: empty 13,995lb (6348kg); max. take-off 29,035lb (13,170kg)
Dimensions: wing span 21ft 9in

(6.36m); length 54ft 8in (16.66m); height 13ft 5in (4.09m)
Armament: one 20mm (0.78in) General Electric M61A1 cannon; two AIM-9 Sidewinder AAMs

North American, designer of the celebrated Sabre. In 1951, the US Navy Bureau of Aeronautics asked North American to 'navalise' two F-86E Sabre airframes for carrier trials, and the first of these aircraft flew on 19 February 1952, designated XFJ-2, and the second aircraft carried an armament of four 20mm (0.78in) cannon in place of the F-86's 0.5in (12.7mm) machine guns. Carrier trials aboard the USS *Midway* were completed in August 1952 and the type entered full production for the US Navy as the FJ-2 Fury. The first unit to receive the FJ-2 was Marine Fighter Squadron VMF-122, in January 1954. The FJ-2 gave way on the production line to the FJ-3, with a Wright J65-W-3 turbojet, and the last variant was the FJ-4, which incorporated so many new design features that it was virtually a new aircraft. The FJ-4 had provision for a wide variety of underwing stores, and a further variant, the FJ-4B, was developed specifically for low-level attack, featuring a good deal of structural strengthening and an altitude bombing system for the delivery of a tactical nuclear weapon. The last of 1115 Furies was delivered in May 1958 and the FJ4B remained in first-line service until September 1962, the last unit to use it being VA-216. In April 1959 an FJ-4B unit, VA-212 (USS *Lexington*) became the first to deploy overseas with Bullpup air-to-surface missiles.

DEMONS AND TIGERS

The second of the new US navy fighters was the McDonnell F3H Demon, which flew for the first time on 7 August 1951, powered by the new Westinghouse XJ40-WE-6 turbojet. This aircraft was subsequently destroyed, but the test programme continued with the second prototype, and the US Navy placed substantial production orders. However, problems with the J40 engine, and the eventual decision to abandon it altogether, caused serious disruption to the whole Demon programme, and production was held up until the Allison J71 turbojet became available. It was with this engine that the Demon became operational with VF-14 in March 1956. The first Demons to be assigned to the fleet were the F3H-2N night and all-weather fighter variant; further variants were the F3H-2M day fighter, armed with Sparrow missiles, and the F3H-2P photo-reconnaissance aircraft. The first Sparrow-armed F3H-2Ms were deployed with the Seventh Fleet in the Pacific late in 1958. Production of the Demon ended in 1959, 119 aircraft being built, and the F2H-3M remained in service until 1961, by which time its designation had changed to F-3B.

To replace the Panther and its swept-wing version, the F9F-8 Cougar, Grumman conceived the F11F Tiger supersonic fighter, which first flew on 30 July 1954. The Tiger's design featured area ruling and other aerodynamic refinements which were then novel, and although the formulae used turned out to be correct, the type experienced some serious technical troubles during early flight testing. These were gradually eliminated, and the F11F-1 Tiger entered service with Navy Squadron VA-156 in March 1937. On 21 September 1956 an F11F-1F Tiger piloted by Grumman test pilot Tom Attridge was involved in an extraordinary incident when it shot itself down during test firings off Long Island, overtaking and colliding with 20mm (0.78in) cannon shells it had fired only seconds earlier. Only 201 Tigers were built, but the type made its mark on aviation history. On 18 April 1958, an F11F-1F broke the world altitude record for the second time in three days, reaching a height of 76,939ft (23,451m).

Another record-breaking US Navy jet fighter of this era was the Douglas F4D Skyray, whose design owed much to the wartime work of Dr Alexander Lippisch, whose delta-wing designs had made an impression on the US Navy's Bureau of Aeronautics. In 1947, the Douglas Aircraft Company was asked to investigate the feasibility of incorporating a delta wing into the design of a short-range naval interceptor capable of climing to 50,000ft (15,240m) in just over three minutes and intercepting bombers travelling at 600mph (965km/h). The result was the XF4D-1 Skyray, which first flew on 23 January 1951. When the first production F4D-1 exceeded Mach One in level flight on 5 June 1954, it seemed probable that the aircraft would soon enter service, but serious problems – including a dangerous high-speed stall at altitude – had to be overcome before the aircraft could be deployed operationally in 1956. Production of the Skyray ended

■ **BELOW: A Saab J-35F Draken demonstrates its ability to take off from a stretch of road. All Swedish combat aircraft have an impressive short-field performance.**

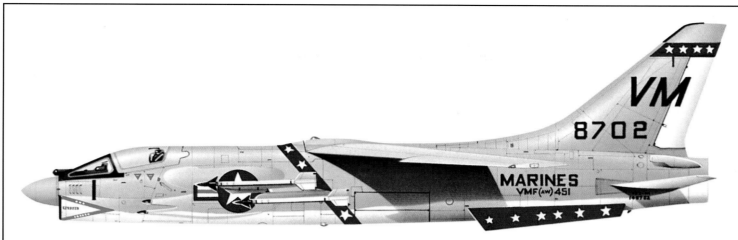

Vought F-8D Crusader

**Type: single-seat carrier-borne
fighter
Country of origin: USA
Powerplant: one 18,000lbst (8165kg)
Pratt & Whitney J57-P-20 turbojet**

**Performance: maximum speed
1227mph (1975km/h)
Weights: empty 19,925lb (9038kg);
max. take-off 34,000lb (15,422kg)
Dimensions: wing span 35ft 2in**

**(10.72m); length 54ft 6in (16.61m);
height 15ft 9in (4.8m)
Armament: four 20mm (0.78in)
Colt Mk 12 cannon; up to four
Sidewinder AAMs**

in 1958 with the 419th aircraft, but the type remained in first-line service until well into the 1960s. During its operational career the Skyray established five new time-to-height records; on one attempt, it reached over 49,000ft (14,935m) in little more than two and a half minutes.

CUTLASS AND CRUSADER
From the design point of view, the oddest aircraft to enter US Navy service, in April 1954, was the Chance Vought F7U Cutlass, which featured a fuselage housing twin engines and a broad, swept wing mounting two tail fins. The prototype XF7U-1 had actually flown some years earlier, in September 1948, but it was underpowered and its performance fell short of Navy requirements. A more powerful version, the F7U-2, was axed by the US defence cuts of 1949–50, but Chance Vought persevered with a much redesigned variant, the F7U-3, and received a development contract in December 1951. The first unit to equip with the Cutlass was VBF-81, and a dozen other carrier-based squadrons used the type. Attack Squadron VA-83, equipped with the F7U-3M Cutlass, became the first US Navy missile-armed squadron to deploy overseas, operating from the USS *Intrepid* as part of the Sixth Fleet in the Mediterranean. By the end of 1958, the Cutlass was being replaced in first-line service by another product of the Chance

Vought stable, the supersonic F8U Crusader. The first carrier-borne fighter capable of supersonic speed in level flight, the Crusader was the winner of a May 1953 US Navy competition for a new day fighter. The prototype XF8U-1 flew on 25 March 1955 and exceeded Mach One on its maiden flight, powered by a Pratt & Whitney J57 engine. The first production F8U-1 flew on 30 September 1955, and completed carrier trials in April 1956. The type was accepted into service as the F8U-1 in the following December, only 21 months after the prototype flew. Production of the F8U-1 (later F-8A) ended in 1958, by which time 218 had been built. The F8U1 was followed in September 1958 by the F8U-1E (F-8B). This version, of which 130 were built, had a larger nose radome and limited all-weather capability. Meanwhile, a reconnaissance version, the F8U-1P (RF-8A), had flown in December 1956. This variant was capable of both day and night reconnaisance and was used extensively for surveillance during the Cuban crisis of 1962 and its aftermath. Of the 144 built, 53 were modernised in 1965-66 and redesignated RF-8G; these were used for fast low-level reconnaissance over Vietnam. The F8U-2 (F-8C) was an improved version of the F-8A with a J57-P-16 turbojet, and flew in December 1967. Externally similar to the F-8A, it carried four Sidewinder AAMs as well as its cannon armament and had an improved fire control system.

It entered service in April 1959 with VF-84, and 187 were built; 87 were later refurbished and designated F-8K. The F8U-2N (F-8D) Crusader, which first flew in February 1960, had an all-weather capability and was powered by a J57-P20 turbojet with reheat, giving it a maximum speed approaching Mach 2.0. Unlike earlier Crusaders, this variant had no HVAR rocket belly pack, but retained its 20mm (0.78in) gun armament and four Sidewinders. Deliveries to the US Navy and Marine Corps were completed in January 1962 after 152 had been built; 89 were later refurbished, given an attack capability and designated F-8H. The last Crusader variant to carry the old US Service nomenclature was the F8U-2NE (F-8E), which was basically similar to the F-8D but with more advanced search and fire control radar equipment. The F-8E was the first Crusader to be developed for the strike role, being fitted with underwing pylons to carry a wide variety of offensive loads. Over 250 F-8Es were built, and 136 were refurbished under the designation F-8J. The F-8E(FN) was a version for the French Navy; 42 were ordered in August 1963 and the last aircraft was delivered in January 1965, this being the final new Crusader to be built.

JETS FOR THE ROYAL NAVY
Despite the British Admiralty's misgivings about the use of jet aircraft in the late 1940s, some forward-thinking

members of the Naval Staff had continued to push hard for the development of carrier-borne jets, and so the idea was not allowed to stagnate entirely. The notion of a swept-wing naval jet fighter was considered to be almost foolhardy, but a straight-wing conventional jet design was treated with much less suspicion. Since both the Meteor and Vampire were deemed to be unsuitable for various reasons, the Admiralty turned to a completely new design: the Vickers-Supermarine E.10/44, which had originally been proposed as a land-based fighter for the RAF. The RAF, however, had decided to adopt the Meteor and Vampire, both of which had a better performance, and so Supermarine offered a naval version to the Admiralty, who wrote Specification E.1/45 around it. The prototype first flew in its naval form on 17 June 1947 and, as the Vickers-Supermarine Attacker, the aircraft went into production for the Royal Navy, entering service in 1951. Sixty Attackers were ordered and served with two Fleet Air Arm squadrons; a further 36 aircraft were supplied to the Pakistan Air Force in 1952–53. The Attacker was followed into Royal Navy Service, in 1953, by the more advanced Hawker Sea Hawk, which started life as the P.1040, a prototype single-seat land-based interceptor. The Admiralty evaluated the design and found it suitable for naval operations, its 'bifurcated trunk' jet exhaust system leaving the rear fuselage free to house a large fuel tank and so provide a wide combat radius. The first prototype Sea Hawk flew on 2 September 1947, and the aircraft entered production as the Sea Hawk F.1, powered by a Rolls-Royce Nene turbojet. As Hawkers were heavily

committed to producing the Hunter day fighter for the RAF, Sea Hawk production was handed over to Armstrong Whitworth Aircraft with the F.2, which had power-boosted ailerons. Later Sea Hawk variants, culminating in the FGA.6, had a strengthened wing to accommodate bombs, rockets or drop tanks. Sea Hawks were issued to Fleet Air Arm squadrons in 1953, and three years later the type saw action with six squadrons during the Suez crisis, carrying out many ground attack operations against Egyptian airfields during the early days of the air campaign. Sea Hawks also served with the Royal Netherlands Navy, the Federal German Naval Air Arm, and the Indian Navy.

VENOMS AND WYVERNS
Two other naval strike fighters, the de Havilland Sea Venom and the Westland Wyvern, also saw action during the 1956 Suez campaign. In 1950, the Royal Navy evaluated the RAF's Venom NF.2 as a potential carrier-borne aircraft, and placed an order for three naval prototypes. The first, designated Sea Venom NF.20, flew on 19 April 1951, and deck trials were carried out on the carrier HMS *Illustrious*. Fifty Mk 20 Sea Venoms were completed and the type became operational in July 1955. The NF.20 was actually preceded by an all-weather fighter variant, the FAW.21, which went into service in May 1955 and equipped four squadrons, three of which carried out cannon attacks on Egyptian airfields in the Suez Canal Zone during the first week of February 1956. Two squadrons were also armed with the Sea Venom FAW.22, which had an uprated de

■ ABOVE: A MiG-19 Farmer pictured in the markings of the Czech Air Force. The MiG-19 was the first Russian aircraft capable of exceeding Mach 1 in level flight.

Havilland Ghost 105 engine. In 1955, 39 Sea Venom FAW.53s were supplied to the Royal Australian Navy, where they equipped four squadrons, and the aircraft was produced under licence in France for issue to the French Naval Air Arm, in whose service it was known as the Aquilon (North Wind). The two units that used it saw extensive service in the ground attack role in Algeria.

The third Fleet Air Arm strike fighter to take part in the Suez campaign was the Westland Wyvern, a unique aircraft in that it was the world's first turboprop-powered combat aircraft and also the only turboprop-powered combat aircraft ever to reach squadron service. Designed to Specification N.11/44, which called for a naval strike fighter capable of operating from both carriers and shore bases, the Wyvern was originally fitted with the Rolls-Royce Eagle piston engine, but the Naval Staff decided to concentrate further development around the Armstrong Siddeley Python turboprop. The first Python-engined aircraft flew on 22 March 1949 and the type was fully operational with No 813 Squadron by September 1953, subsequently equipping three more squadrons. The Wyvern was a very large aircraft, and the Suez operations, in which two were lost, showed it was vulnerable to ground fire, and the type was withdrawn from first-line service by mid-1958. Total Wyvern production was 127 aircraft.

SCIMITAR AND SEA VIXEN

The Supermarine Scimitar was the end product of a lengthy evolutionary process dating back to 1945 and the Supermarine 505, a carrier-based fighter project which was revised several times, its design becoming successively the Types 508, 525 and 529. The design finally crystallised in the Type 544, the first of three prototypes flying on 20 January 1956. The type was ordered into production for the Fleet Air Arm as the Scimitar F.1 and the first production aircraft flew on 11 January 1957, powered by two Rolls-Royce Avon 202 turbojets. The Scimitar became operational with No 803 Squadron in June 1958 and three other squadrons later received the type, an original order for 100 aircraft having been cut back to 76 in the meantime. In 1962 the Scimitar was modified to carry the Bullpup ASM, and its striking power was further extended by provision for four Sidewinder AAMs in addition to its four 30mm (1.18in) cannon. The Scimitar was replaced in FAA service by the Blackburn Buccaneer and was withdrawn from first-line units by the end of 1966.

The Sea Vixen was followed into service by the powerful de Havilland Sea Vixen, an aircraft that had its origin in the DH.110, which had competed with the Gloster Javelin for the RAF's all-weather fighter requirement. The Admiralty's interest in the DH.110 was lukewarm at first, and an order for four naval prototypes was cancelled in 1949, but the project was revived in 1953 and development continued under a new contract. Test flying went ahead with the second prototype DH.110, which had been grounded following the fatal crash of the first prototype at Farnborough in September 1952 and which had undergone some structural modifications in the meantime. Carrier trials were carried out in 1956 with a semi-'navalised' DH.110 pre-production aircraft, and the first fully 'navalised' machine, equipped with folding wings and Rolls-Royce Avon 208 engines, flew on 20 March 1957. Known initially by the designation FAW.20, the aircraft was officially named Sea Vixen later that year and redesignated FAW.1. The first operational squadron to form with the Sea Vixen was No 892, which saw active service during the armed confrontation with Indonesia and against rebel forces in the Radfan in the early 1960s. Two more squadrons subsequently received the Sea Vixen FAW.1. In 1961, two FAW.1s were modified by the installation of additional fuel tanks in forward extensions of the tail booms, and these aircraft served as the prototypes for the FAW.2 variant, which was issued to operational squadrons in 1965. From 1968, the Sea Vixen was progressively phased out as the Fleet Air Arm began to receive the first examples of an aircraft that had already revolutionised the whole spectrum of air combat: the McDonnell F-4 Phantom.

FANTASTIC PHANTOM

One of the most potent and versatile combat aircraft ever built, the McDonnell F-4 Phantom stemmed from a 1954 project for an advanced naval fighter designated F3H-G/H. A mock-up was built, and in October 1954 the US Navy orered two prototypes for evaluation under the designation YAH-1. This aircraft was to have been a single-seater, armed with four 20mm (0.78in) cannon and powered by two Wright J65 turbojets, but when the Navy finalised its requirement in April 1955 the design was changed substantially, the aircraft being fitted with two General Electric J79s, two seats and an armament of four Sparrow AAMs instead of the cannon. The designation was changed to F4H-1, and the XF4H-1 prototype flew for the first time on 27 May 1958. Twenty-three development aircraft were procured, followed by 45 production machines for the US Navy. These were originally designated F4H-1F, but this was later changed to F-4A. The F4B was a slightly improved version with J79-GE-8 engines, and between them the F-4A and F-4B captured many world records over a four-year period. On 25 September 1960, for example, an F4A established a 100km (62 miles) closed-circuit record of 1390mph (2236.5km/h), and in 1962 the F-4B set up eight time-to-height records. Carrier trials were carried out in 1960, and in December that year the first Phantoms were delivered to training squadron VF-121. The first fully operational Phantom squadron, VF-114, commissioned with F-4Bs in October 1961, and in June 1962 the first USMC deliveries were made to VMF(AW)-314.

McDonnell F-4C Phantom II

Type: two-seat all-weather fighter/strike aircraft
Country of origin: USA
Powerplant: two 17,000lbst (7718kg) General Electric J79-GE15 turbojets

Performance: maximum speed 1500mph (2414km/h)
Weights: empty 28,000lb (12,700kg); maximum take-off 58,000lb (26,308kg)
Dimensions: wing span 38ft 5in

(11.7m); length 58ft 3in (17.76m); height 16ft 3in (4.96m)
Armament: four/six AIM-7 Sparrow; four AIM-9 Sidewinder; 20mm (0.78in) M-61 cannon; up to 13,500lb (6219kg) of external ordnance

Total F-4B production was 649 aircraft. Twenty-nine F-4Bs were loaned to the USAF for evaluation in 1962 and proved superior to any Air Force fighter-bomber. A production order was quickly placed for a USAF variant; this was originally designated F-110A, but later changed to F-4C. Deliveries to the USAF began in 1963, 583 aircraft being built. The RF-4B and RF-4C were unarmed reconnaissance variants for the USMC and USAF, while the F-4D was basically an F-4C with improved systems and redesigned radome. The major production version was the F-4E, 913 of which were delivered to the USAF between October 1967 and December 1976. F-4E export orders totalled 558. The RF-4E was the tactical reconnaissance version. The F-4F (175 built) was a version for the Luftwaffe, intended primarily for the air superiority role but retaining multi-role capability, while the F-4G Wild Weasel was the F4E modified for the suppression of enemy defence systems. The successor to the F-4B in USN/USMC service was the F-4J, which possessed greater ground attack capability; the first of 522 production aircraft was delivered in June 1976.

■ **BELOW: Developed originally for the US Navy, the multi-role McDonnell F-4 Phantom was quickly adopted by the US Air Force, and subsequently armed many other air forces.**

FOREIGN PHANTOMS

The first foreign nation to order the Phantom was Great Britain, the British aircraft being powered by Rolls-Royce RB168-25R Spey 201 engines. Versions for the Royal Navy and the RAF were designated F-4K and F-4M respectively. Fifty-two F-4Ks were delivered to the RN in 1968–69 and these were progressively handed over to the RAF with the rundown of the RAF's fixed-wing units, becoming the Phantom FG.1 in RAF service; the FG.1 was used in the air defence role. The RAF's own version, the F-4M Phantom FGR.2, equipped 13 air defence, strike and reconnaissance squadrons; some of the tactical squadrons subsequently disbanded and reformed with the Anglo-French SEPECAT Jaguar strike and reconnaissance aircraft, so that by 1978 all the RAF's F-4M Phantoms, of which 118 were delivered, were assigned to air defence, replacing the Lightning in this role. Other foreign customers for the Phantom included the Imperial Iranian Air Force, which received some 200 F-4Es and 29 RF-4Es; the surviving aircraft, under new management, saw combat during the long-running war between Iran and Iraq in the 1980s. Israel also received over 200 F-4Es between 1969 and 1976, these aircraft seeing considerable action during the Yom Kippur war of 1973. F-4D Phantoms were delivered to the Republic of Korea Air Force as a temporary

measure, pending the arrival of Northrop F-5As. The Japanese Air Self-Defence Force equipped five squadrons with 140 Phantom F-4EJs, most of which were built under licence, and the RAAF leased 24 F-4Es in 1970. The Luftwaffe's F-4Fs, already mentioned, replaced the F-104 Starfighter in the air superiority role and the Fiat G.91 in the ground attack role; the Luftwaffe also received 88 F-4Es in 1971. Smaller numbers of Phantoms were delivered to Spain, Greece, and Turkey, so that by the mid-1970s several key NATO air forces were standardised on the type. By this time, the Phantom had proved its worth many times over in combat, in the hostile environment of Vietnam.

COMBAT AIR PATROLS

On 5 August, 1964, in response to earlier attacks on US warships by North Vietnamese torpedo boats in the Gulf of Tonkin, US strike aircraft from the Seventh Fleet carriers *Ticonderoga* and *Constellation* attacked four torpedo boat bases and oil storage facilities. It was the beginning of America's air war over North Vietnam, and the Phantom was in it from the start, flying combat air patrols to fend off the MiG-17 fighters which the North Vietnamese were known to have deployed. The MiGs did not appear on this occasion, nor did they contest a series of air strikes known as Flaming Dart, launched later in the year against enemy lines of communication. It was not until the

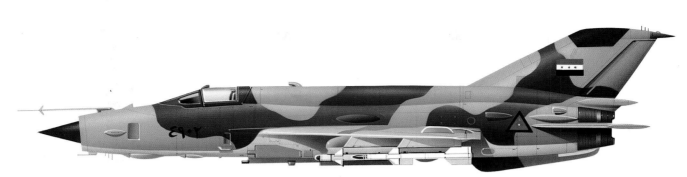

Mikoyan-Gurevich MiG-21PF Fishbed-F

Type: single-seat interceptor
Country of origin: USSR
Powerplant: one 12,676lbst
(5750kg) Tumansky R-11 turbojet
Performance: maximum speed

1243mph (2000km/h)
Weights: empty 17,700lb (8018kg)
maximum take-off 19,500lb
(8833kg)
Dimensions: wing span 23ft 6in

(7.15m); length 44ft 2in (13.46m);
height 14ft 9in (4.50m)
Armament: one 30mm (1.18in)
cannon; two K-13 Atoll AAMs

Americans began to step up the pressure with a bombing offensive called Rolling Thunder, in the early months of 1965, that the first air combats took place. Rolling Thunder began on 2 March 1965, with a strike against an ammunition depot at Xom Bong, 35 miles inside North Vietnam. The strike was led by 44 F-100s from Da Nang, attacking with 2.75in (69.8mm) rockets and 20mm (0.78in) cannon fire. One Super Sabre was lost to ground fire, and a second aircraft was shot down on 3 April during a defence suppression mission in support of F-105s, which were attacking a bridge. The bridge survived, and the mission was repeated on the following day. On this occasion, the strike was bounced by four MiG-17s, which dived straight through the MiGCAP and shot down two of the Thunderchiefs. One F-100 pilot launched a Sidewinder and another engaged a MiG with cannon; both missed. This engagement brought home the message that, powerful though they were, neither the F-100 nor the F-105 was a match for the nimble MiG-17 in combat, their only viable tactic being to use their superior speed to disengage. If attacked by MiG-17s or MiG-21s, which arrived later, the American pilots were briefed to dive to ground level and go supersonic, which neither of the Russian aircraft could do at low level.

PHANTOMS V MIG-17S

Even the mighty Phantom had an inauspicious start in action against the MiG-17. On 9 April 1965, four F-4s from the carrier USS *Ranger* were patrolling near Hainam Island when they were engaged by four MiGs. Having no guns, the Sidewinder pilots used their high speed to get close enough to achieve a lock-on with their Sidewinder AAMs; one of these was seen to explode close to a MiG, which was claimed as probably destroyed, but one Phantom failed to return from the encounter. The first confirmed American victories came on 17 June 1965, when two Phantoms of VF-21, USS *Midway*, destroyed two MiG-17s with their long-range Sparrow AAMs. The USAF's first victories of the Vietnam War came a few weeks later, when two MiG-17s were destroyed over North Vietnam by two F-4C Phantoms of the 45th Tactical Fighter Squadron, recently arrived in the theatre. In November 1965, the Phantom strength in Vietnam was boosted with the arrival of the 12th Tactical Fighter Wing, with F-4Cs, at Da Nang and Bien Hoa. These aircraft were initially used in the MiGCAP role and were committed to ground support operations gradually, employing tactics developed by US Marine Corps F-4 crews earlier in the year. Such tactics now included the evasion of surface-to-air missiles, for Soviet-built SA2 Guideline SAMs were now deployed in North Vietnam in considerable numbers, 56 sites being identified by the end of 1965. The first American aircraft to be shot down over North Vietnam by an SA-2, an F-4C Phantom, had been destroyed on 23 July 1965. The deployment of the Phantom to Vietnam in considerable numbers assured air superiority for the best part of a year, but in September 1966, with the Rolling Thunder campaign in full swing, the North Vietnamese Air Force suddenly began to fight back with renewed vigour, and CAP missions assumed a new priority. The North Vietnamese Air Force had now received some numbers of the MiG-21, armed with Atoll infrared AAMs and operating from five bases in the Hanoi area; at this stage of the war, attacks on objectives close to the North Vietnamese capital were forbidden. The tactics employed by the MiG pilots involved flying low and then zooming up to attack the heavily laden fighter-bombers, mainly F-105 Thunderchiefs, forcing them to jettison their bomb loads as a matter of survival. To counter this, Phantoms armed with Sidewinder AAMs flew at lower altitudes than the F-105s, enabling the crew to sight the MiGs at an early stage in their interception attempt and then use the Phantom's superior speed and acceleration to engage the enemy. These were very much in the nature of hit-and-run tactics, the Phantom pilots avoiding turning combat because of the MiG-21's superior turning ability, but they worked; the Phantom crews had a superb early warning facility in the shape of EC121 electronic surveillance aircraft, which were able to direct the MiGCAP fighters on to their targets in good time. In 1966, American fighters destroyed 23 MiGs for the loss of nine of their own aircraft.

HANOI TARGETS

Early in 1967, Rolling Thunder operations were expanded to include targets in the Hanoi area, which were defended by about 100 MiGs. To inflict

Sukhoi Su-15 'Flagon'

**Type: single-seat interceptor
Country of origin: USSR
Powerplant: two 13,668lbst
(6205kg) Tumanskii R-11F2S-300
turbojets**

**Performance: maximum speed
1386mph (223 km/h) approx
Weights: empty 24,250lb (11,000kg);
maximum take-off 39,680lb
(18,000kg)**

**Dimensions: wing span 28ft 3in
(8.61m); length 70ft (21.33m);
height 16ft 8in (5.1m)
Armament: two R8M AAMS, two
AA-8 'Aphid' AAMs**

maximum destruction on the latter the Americans planned a ruse code-named Operation Bolo, which was designed to bring the MiGs to battle. Thunderchief strike aircraft were used as bait, and they were supported by 56 Phantoms of the 8th and 366th Tactical Fighter Wings as well as by 25 defence-suppression F-105s and EB-66 electronic warfare aircraft. The 8th TFW was led by Colonel Robin Olds, a highly experienced fighter leader with 24 victories to his credit in World War II, when he had flown P-38s and P-51s. In the early post-war years, on exchange to the RAF, Olds had also commanded No 1 Squadron, then equipped with the Meteor F.4. He was therefore a combat pilot of great ability, and it showed. In the air battle that took place on that day, 2 January 1967, Olds and his pilots destroyed seven MiG-21s in 12 minutes for no loss, Olds himself accounting for one of them. Two more MiGs were shot down by Phantoms on 6 January, and following these losses there was a marked decrease in North Vietnamese air activity. The next major enagements took place in April and May; on 24 April, aircraft of the US Navy's Task Force 77 launched their first strikes against fighter bases in North Vietnam with an attack on Kep airfield, 37 miles (60km) northeast of Hanoi. The attack was delivered by A-6 Intruders and A-4 Skyhawks from the USS *Kitty Hawk*. Two MiG-17s were destroyed by escorting F-4B Phantoms of VF-114. On 19 May, the Hanoi Therman Power Plant was hit by Attack Squadron 212, USS *Bon Homme Richard*, with F-8E Crusaders flying escort and flak suppression. Two F-8s and one MiG-17 were shot down during

the attack, and three more MiG-17s were destroyed by F-8s in an air battle southwest of Hanoi. F-8 pilots claimed the destruction of 19 enemy aircraft during the Vietnam War.

NIGHT COMBAT

Neither the MiG-17 nor the MiG-21 were specialised night fighters, but they often operated in that capacity, particularly when the American night bombing campaign against the North intensified during 1972. One US Navy pilot, Captain R.E. Tucker, recalled that:

'During 1972, when Navy A-6s were making a number of single aircraft low-level night strikes all over the area between Haiphong and Hanoi, MiGs were known to launch, making the A-6 drivers nervous (although I personally felt that the MiGs had no night/IFR capability against an A-6 at 300 feet). As a result, we started positioning a single F-4 on MiGCAP along the coastline at night. We figured a single F-4 didn't have to worry about a mid-air with his wingman and had plenty of potential at night against a single MiG. If a MiG launched and headed towards an A-6, the F-4 would vector for the MiG. Invariably MiGs would run for home when the F-4 got to within 25–30 miles of them. Some pilots weren't too overjoyed about the night MiGCAP missions, but I personally felt it was a golden opportunity and my MiG kill proved it. I figured that the MiG had a negligible opportunity to do anyone bodily harm at night with his limited weapons system and Atoll/guns load, whereas the F-4 had a good solid head-on or tail shot against any MiG he could find and get close enough to shoot at.'

Tucker, then a Lieutenant-Commander, was flying an F-4 Phantom of VF-103, operating from the USS *Saratoga*, when he destroyed a MiG-21 on the night of 10/11 August 1972. The Phantom was armed with two AIM-7E Sparrows and two AIM-9D Sidewinders. Tucker was refuelling from a KA-6D tanker when he heard the fighter controller vector another Phantom on to a MiG. He immediately broke contact and joined the other F-4 in the search, the controller advising him that the enemy aircraft was at 8000ft (2438m), 140 degrees at 12 miles (19.3km) range. Tucker descended to 8000ft and his RIO, Lt (JG) Bruce Edens, got a radar contact at once. Lighting his afterburners, Tucker accelerated to 650 knots and closed to within five miles of the MiG, at which point Edens advised the pilot that he had lost radar contact. Realising that the MiG pilot had probably descended, Tucker went down to 3500ft (1067m); Edens announced that he had regained contact and that the MiG was seven or eight miles ahead. Tucker jettisoned his centreline fuel tanks and accelerated to 750 knots, overtaking the MiG from directly astern. At a range of about two miles the pilot launched two Sparrows, the second one leaving the under-fuselage rack just as the first warhead detonated. 'There was a large fireball,' Tucker reported, 'and the second missile impacted in the same spot. I came right slighty to avoid any debris. The target on our radar appeared to stop in mid-air and within a second or two the radar broke lock. The MiG-21 pilot did not survive. If he ejected after the first missile, the second missile must have done him in.

We couldn't see any debris in the dark...The kill was confirmed about three days later.'

ISRAEL'S AIR WARS

On 5 June 1967, while America remained embroiled in Vietnam, Israeli combat aircraft carried out heavy dawn attacks on Egyptian airfields in Sinai and the Suez Canal Zone in what was the first of a series of pre-emptive strikes designed to neutralise the power of Egypt and her allies. Airfields in Jordan, Syria and Iraq were also attacked. By the end of the day the Israeli Air Force had flown about 1000 sorties for the loss of 20 aircraft, all but one to ground fire. Arab losses totalled 308 aircraft, of which 240 were Egyptian; 30 were destroyed in air combat. In these first strikes of what was to become known as the Six-Day War, the Mirage III reigned supreme, its prowess lending more impetus to an already healthy export drive by its manufacturer, Dassault. Ground operations in Sinai, on the Golan Heights and the West Bank of the Jordan were supported by Fouga Magister light attack aircraft, Dassault Ouragans, Mystère IVAs and Super Mystère B.2s. By the time a UN ceasefire was imposed on 10 June, the Arab air forces had lost 353 aircraft, about 43 per cent of their effective strength, and the Israeli Air Force, 31 aircraft, just over ten per cent of its effective strength. The Israelis, therefore, had achieved overwhelming air superiority in the most efficient way, by destroying a high proportion of the enemy's air force on the ground. The Germans had attempted to

achieve a similar result towards the end of World War II, when they launched Operation Bodenplatte (Baseplate), a major attack on Allied airfields in northwest Europe, on 1 January 1945 in support of their flagging offensive in the Ardennes. Like the Israelis, the Germans had achieved complete surprise and had destroyed some 300 Allied aircraft on the ground, but they had lost around one-third of the attacking force, mostly destroyed by friendly fire because of faulty communications. The Israeli attack, very carefully planned and brilliantly executed, left nothing to chance, and so succeeded. A primary threat to the attacking aircraft – the SA-2 Guideline surface-to-air missile, which had recently been deployed in Egypt – was quickly eliminated, the Israelis having assimilated the American experience of this weapon in Vietnam.

YOM KIPPUR

In the wake of the Six-Day War the Israeli Air Force received two new types of combat aircraft, the Phantom and the A-4 Skyhawk attack aircraft, both of which had performed very successfully in Vietnam. The IAF's Phantoms first went into action in 1969 in a series of air strikes against Egyptian artillery positions on the west bank of the Suez Canal. The strike squadrons then set about the systematic destruction of Egyptian missile and radar sites in the Canal Zone, concentrating on installations spread along an 18-mile-wide defence perimeter between the Canal and Cairo, and on strategic roads

in the same area. The Russians augmented the Egyptian air defences, supplying several more squadrons of MiG-21s, and air combat between the opposing sides intensified. On 30 July 1970, a section of four Phantoms was attacked by 16 MiG-21s over the Gulf of Suez, but the Egyptian (or Soviet) pilots failed to see the Mirage top cover, and in the battle that followed the Mirages and Phantoms shot down five MiGs for no loss. In another action, on 23 September 1973, Mirages and Phantoms engaged Syrian MiG-21s and shot down 13 for the loss of one Mirage. For the Israelis, however, the sternest test was still to come. On 6 October, 1973, the Jewish Day of Atonement (Yom Kippur), Egypt launched a surprise attack with some 70,000 troops, supported by 400 tanks, against Israeli positions across the Suez Canal. At the same time, Syrian forces attacked the Golan Heights. In support of the Egyptian attack, an estimated 250 MiG-21s and Sukhoi Su-7 fighter-bombers struck at Israeli air bases, radar and missile sites in the Sinai. The Israelis counter-attacked strongly, using all available air power, but the IAF now had to contend with a formidable arsenal of air defence weaponry. As well as fixed SA-2 and SA-3 missile sites, mobile SA-6 SAM systems and ZSU-23/24 tracked AAA systems – each with four radar-controlled 23mm (0.9in) guns – were brought into play. The IAF's Phantoms were used mainly in the defence suppression role and suffered heavy losses, mainly because the relatively flat terrain offered no cover for aicraft carrying out low-level

Dassault Mirage IIICJ

Type: single-seat fighter/strike aircraft
Country of origin: France
Powerplant: one 14,110lbst (6400kg) SNECMA Atar 9B turbojet
Performance: maximum speed

1336mph (2230km/h)
Weights: empty 15,540lb (7050kg); maximum take-off 27,760lb (13,500kg)
Dimensions: wing span 27ft (8.22m); length 48ft 6in (14.77m);

height 13ft 11in (4.25m)
Armament: two 30mm (1.18in) DEFA cannon; 3000lb (1360kg) of external ordnance

■LEFT: A McDonnell Douglas F-15C Eagle during in-flight refuelling. The F-15, with its array of air-to-air missiles, brought a new dimension to the science of air fighting.

with missiles at beyond visual range. The United States Air Force and various aircraft companies in the USA began discussions on the feasibility of just such an aircraft and its associated systems to replace the F-4 Phantom in 1965, and four years later it was announced that McDonnell Douglas had been selected as prime airframe contractor for the new aircraft, then designated FX; as the F-15A Eagle, it flew for the first time on 27 July 1972, and first deliveries of operational aircraft were made to the USAF in 1975. Simply stated, the F-15 Eagle was designed to outperform, outfly and outfight any opponent it might encounter in the foreseeable future, in engagements extending from beyond visual range (BVR) right down to close-in turning combat. Irrespective of starting conditions, most air combats come down to around or below 1.2M and often fall to subsonic speeds, so manoeuvrability must be optimised for these conditions. The pilot who enters combat with most aircraft energy, either in the form of height or speed, will have the advantage in manoeuvrability, but if the combat continues this advantage is soon lost, superiority passing to the aircraft with most latent energy: in simple terms, this means the aircraft with the most excess thrust, a measure of the aircraft's ability to accelerate and climb. In a sustained turn, when a pilot is endeavouring to get into the best position for a gun attack, the maximum rate of turn and the minimum turn radius are achieved when the drag generated in the turn is equalised by the available thrust. The maximum rate of turn depends either on the available lift or on the maximum g forces the airframe can stand. However, it is difficult to sustain a maximum rate turn without losing height. Everything depends on the thrust/drag and lift/weight ratios, key factors which must be taken into account in the design of an agile air superiority fighter's wing. In this respect, the F-15's wing is a remarkable piece of aerodynamic engineering.

EAGLE INTERCEPTOR

The F-15C – the main interceptor version – has a wing loading of only 54lb per square foot (25kg/0.09m^2) and this,

attacks. Israeli pilots adopted new tactics which involved diving their aircraft steeply on the SAM sites, which kept their aircraft outside the low-angle missile launch trajectory; unfortunately this brought them within range of the AAA, which in fact accounted for the majority of the Israeli losses, which were high. In the first week of the conflict the IAF lost over 80 aircraft, mostly victims of SAMs and AAA, and 38 more were lost in the second week. Having outfought the Syrians, the Israelis turned the full weight of their counter-offensive against the Egyptians, pushing forces across the Suez Canal and encircling the Egyptian Tenth Army before a ceasefire was arranged by the UN on 24 October. In all, the Israeli Air Force lost 118 aircraft, the Egyptians 113 and the Syrians 149. The Iraqi Air Force, assisting the Syrians, lost 21. For once,

Arabs and Israelis had fought each other to a standstill.

AIR SUPERIORITY FIGHTER

During the air war over Vietnam, the Americans had quickly learned one important lesson: that speed and sophistication were no substitutes for manoeuvrability, and an all-missile armament was no substitute for guns. Aircraft like the F-4 Phantom, designed for combat at supersonic speeds and for multiple roles, found themselves fighting nimble MiG-17s and MiG-21s in turning combats at 500kt (926 km/h) or less, and they had to be retrofitted with 20mm (0.78in) cannon for this close-in work. What was required was a dedicated air superiority fighter, a highly manoeuvrable aircraft capable not only of engaging an opponent in close combat and winning, but also of engaging him together with its two Pratt & Whitney F-100 advanced technology turbofans, gives it an extraordinary turning ability and the combat thrust-to-weight ratio (1.3:1) necessary to retain the initiative in a fight. The high thrust-to-weight ratio permits a scramble time of only six seconds, using 600ft (183m) of runway, and a maximum speed of more than 2.5M gives the pilot the margin he needs if he has to break off an engagement. Primary armament of the F-15 is the AIM-7F Sparrow radar-guided AAM, with a range of up to 35 miles (56km). The Eagle carries four of these, backed up by four AIM-9L Sidewinders for shorter-range interceptions and a General Electric 20mm M61 rotating-barrel cannon for close-in combat. The gun is mounted in the starboard wing root and is fed by a fuselage-mounted drum containing 940 rounds. The aircraft's Hughes AN/APG-70 pulse-Doppler air-to-air radar provides a good look-down capability and can be used in a variety of modes; it can pick up targets at around 100nm (180km) range and, in the raid assessment mode, can resolve close formations into individual targets, giving the F-15 pilot an important tactical advantage. When the radar detects a target in the basic search mode the pilot directs the AN/APG-70 to lock on and track by putting a bracket over the radar return, using a selector mounted on the control column. The locked-on radar will then show attack information such as target closing speed, range, bearing, altitude separation and parameters governing the F-15's weapons release. When the target enters the kill envelope of the weapon selected, the pilot decides whether to attack using his head-down, virtual situation display, which

gives a synthetic picture of the tactical situation, or go for a visual attack using his head-up display (HUD).

COMBAT-PROVEN

The concept of the F-15 as an air superiority fighter was first proven in the summer of 1982, when the Israeli Air Force, which was then re-arming with the American aircraft, embarked on a period of intensive action in support of the invasion of southern Lebanon. Israeli and Syrian combat aircraft had been involved in a series of skirmishes over Lebanese territory since 1979 and, in the course of these, F-15s encountered MiG-25s for the first time. Since the F-15 had been brought into service to counter the MiG-25 in the first place, the results of these actions, which were firmly in the F-15's favour, attracted a lot of attention. The Israelis reported that the Foxbat was fast at high altitude but that its manoeuvrability was poor, as was the visibility from the cockpit. At medium and low altitudes the heavy MiG-25's speed fell away markedly and its handling qualities were sluggish. The MiG-23 Flogger, according to the Israelis, was a much better proposition, but the Syrian tactics left much to be desired. The vast majority of the Israeli kills were in the Bekaa Valley, less than a minute from the Syrian border. As the Israeli pilots were forbidden to cross into Syria, it meant they only had about two minutes in which to engage and destroy their opponents as the latter made swift forays into the Bekaa. History was to repeat itself; during the 1991 Gulf War, F-15s claimed no fewer than 30 of the 39 Iraqi aircraft destroyed in air combat. In every case, the Iraqi pilots failed

completely to get the best out of their aircraft, even though some of the latter were MiG-29s, which in theory were a match for the F-15.

FIGHTING FALCON

Another US combat aircraft that performed with distinction in the Gulf War was the Lockheed Martin F-16 Fighting Falcon. The F-16, designed and built by General Dynamics, had its origin in a USAF requirement of 1972 for a lightweight fighter and first flew in February 1974. In service with many air arms other than the USAF, it carries an advanced GEC-Marconi HUDWACS (HUD and Weapon Aiming Computer System) in which target designation cues are shown on the head-up display as well as flight symbols. The HUDWAC computer is used to direct the weapons to the target, as designated on the HUD. The F-16 HUDWAC shows horizontal and vertical speed, altitude, heading, climb and roll bars and range-to-go information for flight reference. There are five ground attack modes and four air combat modes. In air combat, the 'snapshoot' mode lets the pilot aim at crossing targets by drawing a continuously computed impact line (CCIL) on the HUD. The lead-computing off sight (LCOS) mode follows a designated target; the dogfight mode combines snapshoot and LCOS; and there is also an air-to-air missile mode. The F-16's built-in armament is a General Electric M61A1 multi-barrel cannon mounted in

■BELOW: Air-to-air shot of a Lockheed Martin F-16C Fighting Falcon of the 422nd Test and Evaluation Squadron, Nellis AFB, on a training mission near Las Vegas.

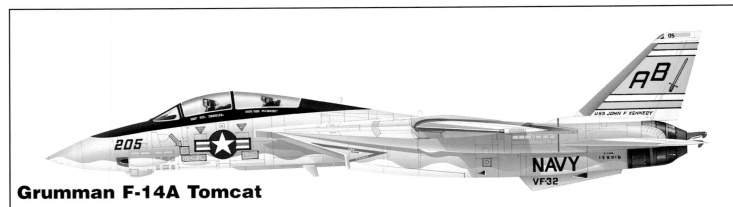

Grumman F-14A Tomcat

Type: two-seat carrier fighter
Country of origin: USA
Powerplant: two 20,900lbst
(9480kg) Pratt & Whitney TF30-P-412A turbofans
Performance: maximum speed

1564mph (2517km/h)
Weights: empty 40,104lb
(18,191kg); maximum take-off
74,349lb (33,724kg)
Dimensions: wing span 64ft 1in
(19.55m); length 62ft 8in (19.10m);

height 16ft (4.88m)
Armament: one 20mm (0.78in)
M61A1 Vulcan rotary cannon:
combination of AIM-54 Phoenix
AAMs, AIM-7 Sparrow AAMs, and
AIM-9 Sidewinder AAMs

the port side wing and fuselage fairing, with provision for 515 rounds of ammunition. The aircraft has a combat radius of up to 866nm (1604km), depending on the mission profile. There is a mounting for an AIM-9L Sidewinder at each wing-tip, an under-fuselage centreline hardpoint, and six underwing hardpoints for various stores. All the hardpoints are stressed for manoeuvres up to 9g, enabling the F-16 to dogfight while still carrying weaponry. The Fighting Falcon is powered by either a 29,588lb (13,421kg) thrust General Electric F-110-GE-129 or 29,100lb (13,200kg) thrust Pratt & Whitney afterburning turbofan and can lift many combinations of air-to-surface weapons. A typical stores load might include the two wing-tip-mounted Sidewinders, with four more on the outer underwing stations; a podded GPU-5/A 30mm (1.18in) cannon on the centreline; drop tanks on the inboard underwing and fuselage stations; a Pave Penny laser spot tracker pod along the starboard side of the nacelle; and bombs, ASMs and flare pods on the four inner underwing stations. The aircraft can carry advanced beyond-visual-range missiles such as Sparrow and Sky Flash, Maverick ASMs, HARM and Shrike anti-radar missiles, and a weapons dispenser carrying various types of sub-munition including runway denial bombs, shaped-charge bomblets, anti-tank and area denial mines.

GRUMMAN'S BIG CAT

Sharing the combat air patrol task with the F-15 Eagle in the Gulf War was the

US Navy's Grumman F-14 Tomcat, a formidable interceptor designed from the outset to establish complete air superiority in the vicinity of a carrier task force and also to attack tactical objectives as a secondary role. Selected in January 1969 as the winner of a US Navy contest for a carrier-borne fighter (VFX) to replace the Phantom, the prototype F14A flew for the first time on 21 December 1970 and was followed by 11 development aircraft. The variable-geometry fighter completed carrier trials in the summer of 1972 and deliveries to the US Navy began in October that year, the Tomcat forming the interceptor element of a carrier air wing. At the heart of the Tomcat's offensive capability is the Hughes AN/AWG-9 weapons control system, which enables the two-man crew to detect airborne targets at ranges of up to 170nm (315km), depending on their size, and cruise missiles at 65nm (120km). The system can track 24 targets and initiate attacks on six of them at the same time, at a variety of altitudes and ranges. The Tomcat's built-in armament consists of one General Electric M61A1 Vulcan 20mm gun mounted in the port side of the forward fuselage, with 675 rounds. Main missile armament comprises four Sparrow AAMs partially recessed under the fuselage, or four Phoenix AAMs mounted below the fuselage. In addition, four Sidewinder AAMs, or two Sidewinders plus two Phoenix or two Sparrow AAMs, can be carried on underwing pylons. The Tomcat can carry a mixture of ordnance up to a maximum

of 14,500lb (6577kg), and is fitted with a variety of ECM equipment. A task force's Tomcats are normally required to fly three kinds of mission: Barrier Combat Air Patrol, Task Force CAP and Target CAP. Barrier CAP involves putting up a defensive screen at a considerable distance from the task force under the direction of a command and control aircraft. Since fighters flying Barrier CAP are likely to encounter the greatest number of incoming enemy aircraft, Tomcats usually carry their full armament of six Phoenix AAMs. These weapons, which carry a 132lb (60kg) warhead, reach a speed of more than Mach 5 and have a range of over 125 miles (200km), which makes them highly suitable for long-range interception of aircraft flying at all levels and also sea-skimming missiles. Hostile aircraft that survive the attentions of the Tomcats on Barrier CAP are engaged by fighters of the Task Force CAP, which operate within sight of the ships and which are armed with a mixture of Phoenix, Sparrow and Sidewinder AAMs. If targets still show signs of breaking through and all defensive AAMs are expended, the Tomcats can continue the engagement with their Vulcan cannon at close range. The Tomcat's two Pratt & Whitney TF30-P414 turbofans give it a maximum low-level speed of 910mph (Mach 1.2) and a high-level speed of 1544mph, or Mach 2.34.

LONG-RANGE TORNADO

The Royal Air Force also deployed a long-range interceptor to the Gulf. This was the Tornado F.3, developed from the Panavia Tornado GR.1 strike aircraft specifically to intercept Soviet bombers at long range, preferably before they could launch stand-off missiles against targets in the British Isles. The variable-geometry Tornado F.3, which could not match aircraft like the MiG-29 in close combat, was restricted to defensive border patrols during the Gulf War. The intercept radar selected for the Tornado ADV (Air Defence Variant), as the aircraft was originally known, was the Marconi (later GEC Marconi) Avionics AI24 Foxhunter, development of which began in 1974. The essential requirement was that detection ranges should in no way be limited to target altitude. Look-down capability against low-level targets was the most demanding case, particularly when the interceptor itself was at low altitude. Severe and sophisticated electronic countermeasures also had to be overcome. In its definitive form, the Tornado ADV carried four Sky Flash and four Sidewinder AAMS, as well as a built-in Mauser 27mm (1.06in) gun. Three Tornado ADV prototypes were built. All were powered by the Turbo-Union RB199 Mk103 turbofan, which was also to power the initial production batch of Tornado F2s for the RAF. These aircraft also featured manually controlled wing sweep, which would be automatic on

■BELOW: Designed for long-range fleet defence, the Grumman F14 Tomcat was – and still is – one of the most viable and effective combat aircraft in the world.

later production aircraft. Early in 1982, to demonstrate that the ADV could fulfil its CAP requirements in all respects, a development aircraft flew a CAP of two hours twenty minutes over the North Sea, involving a flight of 325nm (602km) to the CAP area and a similar return flight. The aircraft was climbed out of Warton, Lancashire, and cruised at high altitude over the North Sea, then descended to medium altitude to take up a CAP racetrack pattern. On arriving back at base the aircraft loitered in the local area for 15 minutes at low level before landing with more than five per cent internal fuel remaining after a total flight time of four hours thirteen minutes. Trials proved that, despite serious problems with the AI radar, there was nothing wrong with the aircraft and its other systems, and orders for the RAF stood at 165, to be delivered in three batches. Pilots of 'A' Squadron of the Aeroplane and Armament Experimental Establishment (A&AEE) at Boscombe Down, who evaluated it, were very enthusiastic about all aspects except the radar, which failed to meet its specification in no fewer than 52 areas. The problems with the Foxhunter were still far from resolved when the first Tornado F2s were delivered to No 229 Operational Conversion Unit (OCU) at RAF Coningsby, in Lincolnshire, in November 1984. The first 18 aircraft were all powered by Mk103 engines; aircraft after that had the more powerful Mk104, which combined a 360mm (14.2in) reheat extension with a Lucas Aerospace digital electronic engine

control unit (DECU). These later aircraft, designated Tornado F3 – the definitive production version of the design – also featured the full armament of four Sky Flash and four AIM-9Ls, auto wing sweep, and automanoeuvre devices with the slats and flaps deploying as a function of angle of attack and wing sweep. It was not until 1986 that the first modified AI24 Foxhunter radars were delivered for installation in the OCU aircraft, the necessary modifications having cost an additional £250 million. The first squadron, No 29, formed at RAF Coningsby in May 1987 and was declared operational at the end of November. The aircraft eventually armed seven squadrons in addition to No 229 OCU (which became No 56 Reserve Squadron on 1 July 1992).

HORNET'S STING

While the F-14 replaced the Phantom in the naval air superiority role, the aircraft that replaced it in the tactical role (with both the USN and USMC) was the McDonnell Douglas F-18 Hornet. First flown on 18 November 1978, the prototype Hornet was followed by 11 development aircraft. The first production versions were the fighter/attack F-18A and the two-seat F-18B operational trainer; subsequent variants are the F-18C and F-18D, which have provision for AIM-120 AAMs and Maverick infrared missiles, as well as an airborne self-protection jamming system. The aircraft also serves with the Canadian Armed Forces as the CF-188. For the intercept role the Hornet carries four fuselage-

mounted Sparrow AAMs, supplemented by a built-in M61A1 cannon, and for the strike role it has a fuselage-mounted forward-looking infrared and laser spot tracker/strike camera pods. The equipment necessary for the two different tasks can be changed in about an hour. As the Hornet is a single-seater, much thought was given to cockpit systems designed to reduce the pilot's workload. His primary instrument is the head-up display (HUD), which forms an integral part of the Kaiser multi-purpose cockpit display. The HUD provides the pilot with attack steering information once the Hughes AN/APG-65 tracking radar has locked onto and designated a target. More radar symbology, forward-looking infrared (FLIR) and weapon seeker images, stores management, radar warning and engine condition data can be called up on two CRT displays, while the pilot can make keyboard imputs governing communications, navigation, IFF and autopilot on a console immediately below the HUD, removing any necessity to look down in the cockpit. Thanks to progressive refinements in the course of its development the Hornet has exceptional handling qualities. It is fitted with a digital fly-by-wire control system, leading- and trailing-edge flaps are computer-programmed for optimum lift and drag in both manoeuvring and cruise configurations, while ailerons and flaps are also deflected differentially for roll. This means that when the pilot initiates a roll with a sideways movement of the stick, all these computerised factors are brought into play to give the aircraft a rate of roll in excess of 220 degrees per

second. The flight computers also enable the pilot to retain full control at angles of attack of up to 60 degrees by automatically cancelling aileron deflection, retracting the trailing-edge flaps and selecting the leading-edge flaps fully down. The Hornet's two General Electric F404-GE-400 turbofan engines provide enough power to get a fully laden aircraft into the air without the use of reheat, to take it up to more than 40,000ft (12,192m) in about eight minutes and to enable the pilot to perform sustained 5g combat manoeuvres at medium altitude – again, all without reheat, although when the afterburners are cut in during combat manoeuvres the results are spectacular. The Hornet's maximum speed is Mach 1.8, its operational ceiling is 50,300ft (15,331m) and it carries a maximum warload of 18,300lb (8300kg).

THE VERSATILE HARRIER

One of the most versatile and potent weapon systems that took part in the air onslaught against the Iraqi army of occupation in Kuwait was the United States Marine Corps' AV-8B Harrier II, the V/STOL (Vertical/Short Take Off and Landing) aircraft developed jointly by British Aerospace and McDonnell Douglas. The Harrier II traces its lineage back to 1957, when Hawker Siddeley Aircraft Ltd launched the concept of the P.1127 V/STOL aircraft. The P.1127 was designed around the Bristol BE.53 vectored-thrust engine, the forerunner of the Rolls-Royce Pegasus. In this revolutionary turbofan, air from the fan and the low-pressure compressor is

diverted to the front pair of vectoring nozzles, while the remaining engine thrust is directed through the rear pair of rotating nozzles. A development of the P.1127, the Kestrel, was evaluated in 1965 by pilots of the RAF, US Air Force, US Navy, US Army, and the Federal German Luftwaffe. The aircraft was selected by the RAF and, named Harrier GR.1, entered service on 1 April 1969. This, the world's first operational V/STOL aircraft, was followed by the GR.1A and GR.3, the latter having a nose-mounted laser rangefinder and an uprated Pegasus Mk 103 engine. In 1966, six Kestrels were sent to the USA for tri-service trials on land and sea under the designation XV-6A, and in 1969 the US Marine Corps received approval to buy the first of 102 aircraft, with the designation AV-8A. American funding had played a key role in the development of the Harrier, and it was Vietnam, a land war requiring timely, fixed-wing close air support, that finally influenced the purchase decision. However, although the AV-8A Harrier was conceptually correct, the Marines needed an aircraft with more capacity. As a result, the AV-8B Harrier II programme was launched. Design leadership of the advanced Harrier rested with McDonnell Douglas, but it soon developed into a joint effort between that company and British Aerospace, and it was to become the biggest Anglo-American collaborative aircraft programme ever. In RAF service, the Harrier II is designated GR.5 or GR.7, the latter having a night attack capability.

SEA HARRIER COMBAT

A decade before the Marine Corps Harriers took part in the Gulf War, the Harrier – or rather its naval version, the Sea Harrier – had distinguished itself in action over the stormy waters of the South Atlantic, when Britain launched a naval task force to recapture the Falkland Islands from Argentina in 1982. Four Fleet Air Arm squadrons totalling 28 Sea Harrier FRS.1s were deployed on the carriers *Hermes* and *Invincible*, and from the start their primary task was fleet air defence, with ground attack a secondary role pending the arrival of the

■LEFT: The Panavia Tornado ADV was intended as a long-range interceptor to defend the integrity of United Kingdom air space against attacks from the direction of Norway.

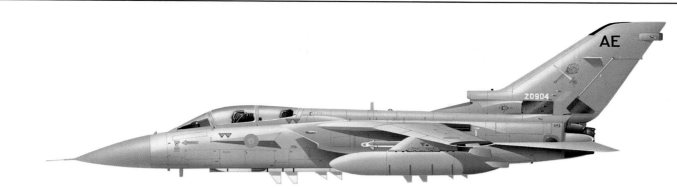

Panavia Tornado ADV

Type: all-weather interceptor
Country of origin: Germany, Italy, UK
Powerplant: two 16,520lbst
(7493kg) Turbo-Union RB-199-34R
Mk 104 turbofans
Performance: maximum speed

1452mph (2337km/h)
Weights: empty 31,970lb
(14,501kg); maximum take-off
61,700lb (27,987kg)
Dimensions: wing span 45ft 8in
(13.92m) spread and 28ft 2in

(8.6m) swept; length 61ft 3in
(18.68m); height 19ft 6in (5.95m)
Armament: two 27mm (1.06in)
Mauser cannon; mix of Sky Flash
medium-range and AIM-9L
Sidewinder short-range AAMs

RAF's ground attack GR.3s. Combat air patrols were carried out in increasing numbers each day as the British task force came closer to the Falklands. CAPs were flown at between 60 and 80 miles (96km and 129km) from the British ships, and during the approach to the Total Exclusion Zone, which the UK Government had set up for 200 miles (322km) around the islands, a good deal of night flying took place. When the action began, the combination of Sea Harrier and AIM-9L Sidewinder proved a deadly one. The 28 Sea Harriers deployed with the task force destroyed 20 Argentine aircraft, ranging from A-4 Skyhawks to ground attack Pucaras, and probably destroyed three more, which was no mean achievement under the vile operating conditions of the South Atlantic winter, and given the fact that the aircraft's Blue Fox air intercept radar had limited capabilities. Aircraft were steered towards incoming raiders by radar air defence ships; pilots then mostly had to rely on their eyesight to locate the attackers, which were almost always at low level. The Sea Harriers overcame problems of distance, too. At times, their two aircraft carriers were positioned up to 250 miles (400km) east of the Falklands, which meant that for every two Harriers on CAP, another pair would be returning to their ship, and a third pair on the way out. Three CAP stations were normally maintained, so that with 18 aircraft needed to patrol those areas, full CAP was only achieved because of the Sea Harrier's excellent

serviceability record, which was a remarkable 95 per cent. At the height of the campaign, on 21 May 1982, Sea Harriers were being launched on CAPs at the rate of a pair every 20 minutes. No Sea Harrier was lost in air-to-air action. The Royal Navy subsequently converted its 31 Sea Harriers to FA.2 standard, with the Blue Vixen pulse-doppler radar and more advanced weaponry.

RUSSIAN AIR SUPERIORITY

Just as the F-15 was developed to counter the MiG-25 Foxbat and the MiG-23 Flogger, both of which were unveiled in the late 1960s, the MiG-29 Fulcrum and another Russian fighter, the Sukhoi Su-27 Flanker, were designed in response to the F-15 and its naval counterpart, the Grumman F-14 Tomcat. Both Russian aircraft share a similar configuration, combining a wing swept at 40 degrees with highly swept wing root extensions, underslung engines with wedge intakes, and twin fins. The combination of modest wing sweep with highly swept root extensions, designed to enhance manoeuvrability, is also used on the Lockheed Martin F-16 Fighting Falcon and the McDonnell Douglas F-18 Hornet.

The MiG-29, the first of the new Russian air superiority fighters to enter service, is powered by two Klimov/Sarkisov RD-33 two-spool low bypass turbofan engines which, at the aircraft's normal take-off weight of 15 tons, give a thrust-weight ratio of 1.1. Design emphasis from the start was on very high manoeuvrability and the ability

to destroy targets at distances of between 660ft (200m) and 32nm (60km). Forty per cent of the MiG-29's lift is provided by its lift-generating centre fuselage and the aircraft is able to achieve angles of attack at least 70 per cent higher than earlier fighters. The aircraft has an RP-29 pulse-Doppler radar capable of detecting targets at around 62 miles (100km) against a background of ground clutter. Fire control and mission computers link the radar with a laser rangefinder and infrared search/track sensor, in conjunction with a helmet-mounted target designator. The radar can track 10 targets simultaneously, and the system allows the MiG-29 to approach and engage targets without emitting detectable radar or radio signals. The Fulcrum's primary armament is the AA-10A Alamo, the equivalent of the F-15's AIM-7 Sparrow, with the AA-8 Aphid infrared AAM as the close-range weapon. A 30mm (1.18in) gun, with 150 rounds, is fitted in the port wing root leading edge extension.

The larger, longer-range Sukhoi Su-27, like the F-15, is a dual-role aircraft; in addition to its primary air superiority task it was designed to escort Su-24 Fencer strike aircraft on deep penetration missions. (USAF F-15s escorted strike aircraft during the Gulf War, as well as fulfilling their primary counter-air task.) The Su-27 also has a lift-generating fuselage and is capable of quite extraordinary angles of attack. Powered by two Lyulka AL-31F turbofans, the Su-27 first flew on 20 May 1977 and

entered service with the Soviet Air Force in 1984. It can carry up to 10 AAMs, usually a mix of medium- and extended-range AA-10 Alamos and short-range AA-8 Aphids or AA11 Archers. The Su-27's combat agility may be greatly enhanced by fitting moveable exhaust nozzles that angle the thrust up, down or sideways. Known as multi-axis thrust vectoring (MATV), it is a more flexible version of the vectoring in forward flight (VIFF) technique used by the British Aerospace Harrier. (VIFF is a combat technique, developed by the US Marine Corps, in which the Harrier's jet nozzles are used to enhance manoeuvrability.) If an aircraft features MATV – as does the Sukhoi Su-37, another highly agile Russian counter-air fighter which made its first flight in this configuration in April 1996 – the system is computer-controlled, the pilot having no direct control over the angle of thrust during a combat. Multi-axis thrust vectoring can produce manoeuvres like one known as the J-turn, in which the nose of the aircraft rises quickly until it is pointing vertically upwards. The aircraft continues to travel horizontally, but loses speed. The pilot then flicks the aircraft to left or right through 180 degrees, as the nose

comes down towards the vertical, the aircraft picks up speed and the pilot returns to level flight, heading back the way he came. Pilots of the V/STOL Harrier use a somewhat similar technique in combat manoeuvre called a 'flop'; the pilot selects 30 degrees of nozzle and augments it with full back stick, which gives a pitching movement of about forty degrees per second – in effect, a very tight loop in which the Harrier seems to revolve round its own axis. In combat, the 'flop' is used to change quickly from nose-up to nose-down. Using VIFF, the Harrier can pull up to 122 degrees angle of attack. Some designers believe, however, that the quest for extra manoeuvrability is unnecessary, and that future combats will be fought with short-range fire-and-forget missiles like ASRAAM (Agile Short-Range Air-to-Air Missile). With such weapons, and a helmet-mounted sight, all a pilot needs to do is look at the opposing aircraft, fire, and let the missile complete its work of destruction.

ULTRA-MODERN MIG
Just as the MiG-29 and the Su-27/37 were developed to take on the air superiority role, the MiG-31, a greatly

■ABOVE: The Soviet Union's answer to the F-15 Eagle in the air superiority role was the MiG-29 Fulcrum, which is capable of some highly impressive combat manoeuvres.

developed version of the MiG-25 that received the NATO reporting name of Foxhound, was developed to replace the Su-15 as a long-range all-weather interceptor. Initiated to counter the threat to the former Soviet Union from B-52s and B-1s carrying air-launched cruise missiles, the MiG-31 is a two-seat, all-weather, all-altitude interceptor designed to be be guided automatically to its targets and to engage them under ground control. It is equipped with an electronically scanned phased-array fire control radar (known as Flash Dance to NATO) which has a search range of 108nm (200km) and can track 10 targets, engaging four simultaneously. In a typical mission profile, an interception would be made by a flight of four aircraft, the leader being linked to the AK-RLDN ground radar guidance network and the other three linked to the leader by APD-518 digital datalink. This arrangement permits a line abreast radar sweep covering a zone some 485nm (898km) wide. The MiG-31 carries four AA-9 Amos semi-active radar homing long-range AAMs on ejector pylons under the fuselage, plus two AA-6 Acrid medium-range infrared AAMs and four AA-8 Aphid short-range infrared AAMs on underwing pylons. One variant of the MiG-31, the MiG-31D, is a dedicated anti-satellite aircraft.

EUROFIGHTER

Europe's answer to modern, highly sophisticated Russian combat aircraft is Eurofighter, developed jointly by Britain, Germany, Italy and Spain. To prove the necessary technology for the project, a contract was awarded in May 1983 to British Aerospace for the development of an agile demonstrator aircraft – not a prototype – under the heading Experimental Aircraft Programme, or EAP. This flew for the first time on 8 August 1986, only three years after the programme was conceived. Powered by two Rolls-Royce RB199 Mk104D engines, it was the most advanced aircraft ever produced in Britain. A single-seat delta-canard aircraft, its design emphasis was on air combat performance, which in practice means a combination of high turn rates and high specific excess power – the measure of a fighter's ability to regain speed or altitude after a manoeuvre. The EAP demonstrator was, in fact, a superb blueprint for the fighter that was originally intended to form much of NATO's front line and project the Alliance's air forces into the 21st

century, providing the means to counter any foreseeable air threat. The task of Eurofighter is to fight effectively throughout the combat spectrum, from engagements beyond visual range down to close-in combat. The technologies that enable it to do this are so advanced, and in some cases so unique, that the role of the EAP aircraft was vital to the Eurofighter project as a whole. In the air defence role, as soon as a hostile aircraft is detected beyond visual range, Eurofighter must accelerate from its combat air patrol (CAP) loiter as quickly as possible in order to give its medium-range, fire-and-forget missiles maximum launch energy, fire as soon as it is within range, and then manoeuvre hard without losing energy to force incoming enemy missiles into making violent course corrections near the end of their flight, reducing their chances of scoring hits. This phase of the engagement, therefore, requires high acceleration and good supersonic manoeuvrability. The next phase – close-in combat – requires maximum usable lift and a high thrust-to-weight ratio, so that energy lost in turns can be quickly regained. In this respect Eurofighter uses all-aspect short-range weaponry, the engagement starting with fast head-on attacks and then breaking down into a turning fight, with pilots manoeuvring hard to acquire good firing positions quickly. The weapons chosen for Eurofighter are the Hughes AIM-120 AMRAAM as the primary weapon, with the AIM-132 ASRAAM as

the secondary. The aircraft also has a built-in gun armament. A major asset is the pilot's head-mounted sight, avoiding the need to pull tight turns to achieve missile lock-on and consequently reducing the risk of g-induced loss of consciousness (G-loc).

ADVANCED SYSTEM

One of the most advanced and ambitious Eurofighter systems is the Defensive Avionics Sub-System (DASS), which was designed to cope with the multiple and mass threats that would have been a major feature of a war on NATO's central front. The system combines and correlates outputs from Eurofighter's radar warning receiver, laser detectors and other sensors and then automatically triggers the best combination of active and passive defences while warning the pilot of the threat priority. To engage targets, particularly in the vital beyond-visual-range battle, the aircraft is equipped with the Euroradar ECR90 multimode pulse-Doppler radar. This is a development of GEC Ferranti's Blue Vixen radar, which is fitted in the British Aerospace Sea Harrier FRS2. The ECR90 is designed to minimise pilot workload; radar tracks are presented constantly, analysed, allocated priority or deleted by

■ BELOW: A British Aerospace Sea Harrier FRS.1 being readied for take-off during the Falklands War of 1982. The Harrier was a key element in the recapture of the islands.

track-management software. A third generation coherent radar, the ECR90 benefits from a considerable increase in processing power and has all-aspect detection capability in look-up and look-down modes; it also has covert features to reduce the risk of detection by enemy radar warning receivers. Its full capability is classified, but it is thought to be able to engage at least ten targets simultaneously.

Eurofighter is powered by two EJ200 high-performance turbofan engines developing 13,500lbst (60kN) dry and 20,000lbst (90kN) with reheat. The first two Eurofighter prototypes flew in 1994, followed by several more. The original customer requirement was 250 each for the UK and Germany, 165 for Italy and 100 for Spain. The latter country announced a firm requirement for 87 in January 1994, while Germany and Italy revised their respective needs to 180 and 121, the German order to include at least 40 examples of the fighter-bomber version. The UK's order was 232, with options on a further 65. Deliveries to the air forces of all four countries were scheduled to begin in 2001. Although Eurofighter is optimised for the air superiority role, a comprehensive air-to-surface attack capability is incorporated in the basic design. Eurofighter is able to carry out close air support, counter-air, interdiction and anti-ship operations; it will also have a reconnaissance capability. Typically, the aircraft has a lo-lo combat radius of 350nm (648km) and a hi-lo-hi combat radius of 750nm

(1395km). Eurofighter has a maximum speed of 2.0M, depending on altitude.

FRANCE'S SQUALL

France, originally a member of the European consortium that was set up to develop Eurofighter, decided to withdraw at an early stage and develop her own agile combat aircraft for the 21st century. The result was the Dassault Rafale (Squall). As with Eurofighter, a technology demonstrator was built; known as Rafale-A, this flew for the first time on 4 July 1986. Powered by two SNECMA M88-2 augmented turbofans, each rated at 19,950lbst thrust dry and 16,400lbst thrust with reheat, Rafale is a single-seat aircraft with a compound sweep delta wing, all-moving canard, single fin and semi-vented intakes. It incorporates digital fly-by-wire, relaxed stability and electronic cockpit with voice command. Wide use of composites and aluminium-lithium have resulted in a seven to eight per cent weight saving.

In the strike role, Rafale can carry one Aerospatiale ASMP stand-off nuclear bomb; in the interception role, armament is up to eight AAMs with either IR or active homing; and in the air-to-ground role, a typical load is sixteen 500lb (227kg) bombs, two AAMs and two external fuel tanks. The aircraft is compatible with the full NATO arsenal of air-air and air-ground weaponry. Built-in armament comprises one 30mm (1.18in) DEFA cannon in the side of the starboard engine duct. The aircraft has a maximum level speed of 2.0M at altitude and

■ABOVE: France's Dassault Rafale will provide the French Air Force and Navy with a formidable strike capability well into the 21st century, and is the subject of a major sales drive.

864mph (1390km/h) at low level. France, which plans to have 140 Rafales in air force service by 2015 (the naval version, Rafale M, will equip France's aircraft carriers) sees the aircraft as vital to the defence of her territory, particularly in view of rising hostility towards Europe by the governments of some Arab nations on the other side of the Mediterranean. Low-level penetration combat radius with twelve 250kg (550lb) bombs, four AAMs and three external fuel tanks is 570nm (1055km).

DEADLY RAPTOR

Without doubt, the most exciting combat aircraft of the early 21st century is the Lockheed Martin F-22 Raptor. A far different aircraft from either Eurofighter or Rafale, the F-22's development history reflects the many problems, both technological and financial, that can beset an advanced system of this kind. In the late 1970s, the USAF identified a requirement for 750 examples of an Advanced Tactical Fighter (ATF) to replace the F-15 Eagle. The goal was to produce a tactical aircraft that would remain viable for at least the first quarter of the 21st century; an aircraft that would have a range 50–100 per cent greater than that of the F-15, be capable of short take-off and landing on damaged airfields, and be able to engage multiple targets at once, beyond visual range. It must incorporate stealth technology and supercruise (supersonic cruise without afterburning) and, operated by a single pilot, it must be able to survive in an environment filled with people, both in the air and on the ground, whose sole purpose is to destroy it. To test the concepts that would eventually be combined in the ATF, the USAF initiated a series of parallel research programmes. The first was the YF-16 control-configured vehicle (CCV) which flew in 1976–77 and demonstrated the decoupled control of aircraft flight path and attitude; in other words the machine could skid sideways, turn without banking, climb or descend without changing its attitude, and point its nose left or right or up or down without changing its flight path.

Other test vehicles involved in the ATF programme included the Grumman X-29, which flew for the first time in December 1984 and which was designed to investigate forward-sweep technology, and an F-111 fitted with a mission adaptive wing (MAW) – in other words, a wing capable of reconfiguring itself automatically to mission requirements. Flight testing of all these experimental aircraft came under the umbrella of the USAF's Advanced Fighter Technology Integration (AFTI) programme. In September 1983, while the AFTI programme was well under way, the USAF awarded ATF concept definition study contracts to six American aerospace companies, and of these, two – Lockheed and Northrop – were selected to build demonstrator prototypes of their respective proposals. Each produced two

prototypes, the Lockheed YF-22 and Northrop YF-23, and all four aircraft flew in 1990. Two different powerplants, the Pratt & Whitney YF119 and the General Electric YF120, were evaluated, and in April 1991 it was announced that the F-22 and F119 formed the winning combination. The F119 advanced technology engine, two of which power the F-22, develops 35,000lbst (155kN) and is fitted with two-dimensional convergent/divergent exhaust nozzles with thust vectoring for enhanced performance and manoeuvrability.

STEALTH FEATURES

The F-22 combines many stealth features. Its air-to-air weapons, for example, are stored internally; three internal bays house Sidewinders, four AIM-120As or six AMRAAMs. Following an assessment of the aircraft's combat role in 1993, it was decided to add a ground attack capability, and the internal weapons bay can also accommodate 1000lb (454kg) GBU-32 precision-guided missiles. The F-22 is designed for a high sortie rate, with a turn-round time of less than 20 minutes, and its avionics are highly integrated to provide rapid reaction in air combat, much of its survivability depending on the pilot's ability to locate a target very early and kill it with a first shot.

The F-22 was designed to meet a specific threat, which at that time was presented by large numbers of highly agile Soviet combat aircraft, its task being to engage them in their own airspace with beyond-visual-range weaponry. That threat was very real: the USAF's last fighter, the F-16, had entered service in 1979, and in the

decade that followed the Russians introduced no fewer than five fighter/attack types. The Su-24 Fencer, with its all-weather, low altitude penetration capability, greatly enhanced Soviet ability to carry out deep strikes into NATO territory; the Su-25 Frogfoot ground attack aircraft quickly proved itself to be an excellent close-support fighter in Afghanistan; the MiG-29 Fulcrum and the Su-27 Flanker were a match for NATO aircraft in the air superiority role, as well as having a substantial ground attack capability; and the MiG-31 Foxhound, developed to counter US bombers armed with cruise missiles, brought a new dimension to the Soviet air defence system. The Russians clearly had the ability to develop an aircraft in the F-22 class, and there were serious concerns that they would do it first. Then came the break-up of the Soviet Union, with its attendant economic problems, and it soon became clear that the Russians, instead of developing new combat aircraft, were applying new technology to existing designs in order to make them viable into the next century. The trend was exemplified in the Sukhoi Su-37, a single-seat fighter and ground attack aircraft developed from the Su-27/35 and incorporating three-dimensional vectoring nozzles to give it super-agility. The Su-37 can, for example, pitch up rapidly beyond the vertical, perform a tight 360-degree somersault within its own length, and pull out to resume level flight with no height loss. The surprising fact is that the Russian money-saving exercise appears to have worked, and has produced a generation of jet fighters capable of performing much of the F-22's mission at a fraction of the cost. Some of them will be available on the world export market in the 21st century, probably at cut prices, creating a dangerous imbalance. They will be available to nations which hitherto could only afford small, relatively cheap multi-role aircraft, of which the British Aerospace Hawk, in its several variants, is a good example. The Hawk serves with several air arms worldwide and, as the T-45 Goshawk, is also used in the training role by the US Navy.

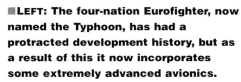

■LEFT: The four-nation Eurofighter, now named the Typhoon, has had a protracted development history, but as a result of this it now incorporates some extremely advanced avionics.

IDEAL MIX

For any air force, an ideal mix would be a majority of high-performance subsonic V/STOL aircraft, covered by a minority of supersonic interceptors. Many current combat aircraft are supersonic, multi-role and have a very short take-off capability; none of them, however, can recover vertically, which would be essential for true invulnerability to anti-airfield counter-attacks. Configurations for supersonic V/STOL designs have varied over the years, and it is worth remembering that the prototype of a supersonic V/STOL strike aircraft, the Hawker Siddeley P.1154, was well advanced in construction when the project was cancelled in 1965. (The French went a step further; in February 1965, Dassault flew a supersonic V/STOL fighter prototype, the Mirage III-V, which reached Mach 2.04. The project was abandoned after the aircraft was destroyed in November 1966.) The cancellation of the P.1154 led directly to the development of the P.1127 (RAF), which first flew 18 months later and which was the progenitor of today's substantial Harrier family. Although the P.1154 was cancelled, a later similar supersonic configuration was studied in 1973 for the US Navy. Designated AV-16S, this project was the

product of a joint programme between Hawker Siddley Aviation and McDonnell Douglas, and stemmed from a US Navy requirement for a supersonic deck-launched aircraft capable of VTOL intercept missions as well as long-radius subsonic strike against surface targets. The AV-16S engine was to have been a large-diameter Rolls-Royce Pegasus 15 with PCB (Plenum Chamber Burning, a new type of exhaust boost system). Performance was initially aimed at a 1.7M capability, with a 1.9M potential. The wing design was larger than that of the P.1154 and the main undercarriage units were moved to pods on the wing trailing edge, although the design was still recognisable as a Harrier derivative. However, the programme never moved beyond the Phase One study stage due to the predicted development costs versus the available budgets in the US Navy. Even a complementary subsonic project – the AV-16A – was seen as needing almost $1bn for research, development and testing. There was little chance at that time that the USN could be persuaded to spend that kind of money on a weapons system just for the Marine Corps. However, the loss of the AV-16 programme led to the development, in 1975–76, of the Harrier II, an aircraft that will continue to

ABOVE: The Lockheed Martin F-22 Raptor incorporates many 'stealth' features. It will be complemented, in the future, by advanced projects such as the Joint Strike Fighter (JSF).

provide a viable strike system in the 21st century.

PROHIBITIVE COST

It was once suggested that, by the middle of the next century, the entire gross national product of a country like the USA would not be sufficient to develop a new combat aircraft, but that was before computer technology absorbed much of the strain of research and development. The world's major defence research agencies are, through computer simulation, currently studying the designs of agile aircraft for the year 2050, a generation beyond the F-22, Eurofighter and Rafale. Such aircraft will be able to manoeuvre closely around one another in situations where missiles will be of little use, and the gun will be all-important. The pilot who has the ability to out-manoeuvre the other in close-in combat, and the means of delivering a killing blow, will win. In the future, use may be made of Remotely Piloted Vehicles (RPVs) in air combat. Meanwhile the agile combat aircraft, and fighter pilot, will rule tomorrow's skies.

Index